Racial Politics in Post-Revolutionary Cuba

Using interviews, as well as survey and archival research, this book analyzes race relations under the Castro regime and places the Cuban revolution in a comparative and international framework. In doing so, Sawyer challenges other scholarly arguments either that the regime has eliminated racial inequality or that it has been profoundly racist.

By providing a balanced view of race relations, this book shows how static racial ideology has remained since the revolution and how Cuba has not become a racial democracy, but has done more than any other society to eliminate racial inequality. In fact, the current implementation of market reforms, especially tourism, has exacerbated these inequalities. Despite these shortcomings, the regime remains popular among blacks because they perceive their alternatives of the United States and the Miami exile community to be far worse.

Mark Q. Sawyer currently holds appointments as an associate professor with the Department of Political Science and with the Bunche Institute for African American Studies at UCLA. He is currently on leave until 2005 as a postdoctoral Fellow in the Robert Wood Johnson Foundation Scholars in Health Policy Program at the University of California at Berkeley and will be a visiting professor at the Harvard University Department of African American Studies. In 1999, he received his Ph.D. in political science from the University of Chicago. He joined the faculty at UCLA in 1999 and has taught undergraduate and graduate courses on the politics of the African diaspora, urban politics, African American political thought, and a general education cluster in interracial dynamics. Professor Sawyer has published articles in journals that include *The Journal of Political Psychology*, *Perspectives on Politics*, and *SOULS*.

"Anyone who eats a yam..." Havana community mural art. Courtesy of the author.

Racial Politics in Post-Revolutionary Cuba

MARK Q. SAWYER

University of California, Los Angeles

CAMBRIDGE
UNIVERSITY PRESS

CAMBRIDGE UNIVERSITY PRESS
Cambridge, New York, Melbourne, Madrid, Cape Town, Singapore,
São Paulo, Delhi, Dubai, Tokyo

Cambridge University Press
32 Avenue of the Americas, New York, NY 10013-2473, USA

www.cambridge.org
Information on this title: www.cambridge.org/9780521612678

First published 2006

A catalog record for this publication is available from the British Library

Library of Congress Cataloging in Publication data

Sawyer, Mark Q., 1972–
Racial politics in post-revolutionary Cuba / Mark Q. Sawyer.
  p.   cm.
Includes bibliographical references and index.
ISBN 0-521-84807-5 (hardback) – ISBN 0-521-61267-5 (pbk.)
1. Race discrimination – Cuba – History – 20th century.   2. Cuba – Race relations –
Political aspects.   3. Cuba – Politics and government – 1959–   I. Title.
F1789.A1S29   2005
305.8′0097291′09045–dc22   2005008113

ISBN 978-0-521-84807-7 Hardback
ISBN 978-0-521-61267-8 Paperback

Transferred to digital printing 2010

For my parents, Ernest and Theresa Sawyer, with love

Contents

Figures and Tables

Figures

Tables

Acknowledgments

There are too many people to name who have made invaluable contributions to this project. It has truly been a collective effort. First, I thank the Cuban people who aided me in my research in every way imaginable. This book seeks only to convey the beauty and spirit of the island and its people. I have done my best to keep faith with them and their story.

I also thank the various organizations that supported my research work on this project. This project was supported in various ways by the Mellon Dissertation year fellowship at the University of Chicago; the Center for the Study of Race, Politics, and Culture Travel Grant; the University of Chicago Office of Minority Student Affairs; the UCLA Institute for American Cultures Faculty Grant; the UC Senate Faculty Grant; the Rockefeller African Diaspora Fellowship Grant at the University of Texas at Austin; the UCLA Multi-Disciplinary Seed Grant; and the Robert Wood Johnson Scholars in Health Policy Program. While they did not provide any resources, I also offer special thanks to the organization Pastors for Peace, which along with Dean Alison Boden of the Rockefeller Memorial Chapel facilitated my first trip to Cuba. I also thank the National Conference of Black Political Scientists and the Race and Democracy in the Americas Project for providing venues to present and further develop this book.

There are a series of people who have been both pioneers in the discipline and critical to my own development as a scholar. They are Dianne Pinderhughes, Michael Dawson, Michael Hanchard, Marvin A. Lewis, and Carlos Moore. Without them I would never have made it to this point. I am constantly inspired and awed by their commitment to excellent scholarship and the development of young scholars like me. I can never thank them enough for all they have done. In addition, I thank the other members of my dissertation committee, William Sewell and Susan Stokes, for their steadfast help and support.

I also received substantial support from friends and colleagues. These include Robert L. James Jr., Sarita Gregory, Taeku Lee, Mathew Hill, and Zoltan Hajnal, whom I met at University of Chicago. Distinguished scholars like Charles Tilly and Doug McAdam aided in the formulation of parts of this project during their Summer Institute at the Center for Advanced Study in the Behavioral Sciences in Palo Alto.

At UCLA, a number of friends and colleagues have contributed to this project in different ways. I thank Laura Gomez and Edward Telles for reading early versions of the manuscript. I also must thank Edmund Keller, Franklin Gilliam, Darnell Hunt, Vice Chancellor Claudia Mitchell-Kernan, Mike Lofchie, Victor Wolfenstein, and Joel Aberbach for their support and mentorship. I especially want to thank Raymond Rocco for his friendship. Life at UCLA would not have been the same without him, and I look forward to his forthcoming book. James Sidanius has also been a friend, colleague, and co-author who made a large portion of this possible. I cannot begin to explain how much I have learned from him about scholarship. Hector Perla has also been a wonderful friend whom it has been a pleasure to watch grow into a top-flight scholar.

I also have a number of friends both inside and outside academia who directly aided and supported me in my project. Jerry Minton has been an invaluable force in my life over the course of this project. Christopher Parker has grown to be one of my closest colleagues and friends as we have both struggled to find our niche in the academy. My friend and co-author John Guidry has been an important touchstone whose wisdom and spirit always set me on the right path. My close friend James Vreeland contributed critical advice to the final draft of the book. I also must thank Dominique Apollon for his help in reading drafts of the manuscript.

At UCLA I have been fortunate to work with excellent graduate students. Sarah Blue was an indispensable part of collecting survey data. Also, Yesilernis Peña provided such excellent work as a research assistant that almost no part of this book is untouched by her influence.

I also acknowledge at least some of my undergraduates who helped in various ways with the project. They include Erica Sosa, Marco Durazo, Francisco Lacayo, John Dobard, Veronica Salinas, Renata Faiman, Christina Vargas, Blanca Martinez, Laura Hernandez, Michelle Leah Velazquez, Tianna Paschel, and Frances Azizi.

Further, I thank Lewis Bateman, my acquisitions editor at Cambridge University Press. His faith in me and this project was critical and will never be forgotten. I also thank the anonymous reviewers who helped make this a much better book. In addition, I thank Rhonda Wheatley and Ruth Homrighaus (www.ruthlessediting.com), who both edited versions of the manuscript at different stages. I also thank photographer Kenneth McGough (www.photomaya.com) for use of his photo entitled *Santeria* for the cover.

Finally, I thank my family. My brother Michael Sawyer has always been a role model and inspiration for me. His wife, Mishaune, and two children, Ashley and Ellis (aka "Butch"), have also been wonderful to me. My grandmother Ruth Kocher and aunt Joyce Kocher have also been powerful forces in my life. I also must thank my boxer, Kalil. He has lived through every phase of this project and always reminded me that the simple pleasures are sometimes the best. I also have to thank my life partner, Celia O. Lacayo. She has consistently exceeded the call of duty in terms of loving me and supporting my work. I could not have done this without her. And to my parents, Ernest and Theresa Sawyer, I owe all of my accomplishments and who I am. This book is dedicated to them. I love you all!

Introduction

In 1997, I stepped off a Cubana Airlines plane in Havana, having to that point experienced the mystery of modern Cuba only as a prospective researcher and tourist. There were several other Americans on the flight. We stood in a queue waiting to enter the country. When I arrived at the Customs check, the officer took my passport and motioned me to a side room. Two black Cuban guards moved to my sides and escorted me into an area with a small metal table and a chair.

In the room, they first patted me down and then asked me to sit. My ear had not yet attuned to Cuban Spanish, so my responses were quite slow. First, they asked me where I was from. I responded, "The United States" and showed them my papers. Unsatisfied, they asked, "Where are you really from?" I became annoyed and thought I should get more specific. "Chicago," I replied. They did not seem satisfied and countered, "But where were you born?" By this time, I was deeply confused and unclear as to how to respond. I replied, "Chicago."

They looked at each other and seemed to agree on the next question: "Where are your parents from – where were they born?" I responded, "Chicago and Alabama, the United States." At this point, they seemed confused. One took a second look, and said with relief, "So you're not Cuban?" I responded, "No." The other then asked, "Not your family? But you look Cuban." Confused, I just shook my head and sat there. They looked at each other, laughed, waved me out of the room, and helped me through Customs with my bags after asking some friendly personal questions.

At first, I was quite flabbergasted by the event. How could I be mistaken for Cuban? I had never in my life been told I looked American, so what did it mean to "look Cuban"? Also, how did race mark me for differential treatment and scrutiny? The irony was that, in the Customs officials' eyes, my blackness made me "Cuban" and marked me as a possible native or exile returning home, yet at the same time it made me subject to increased scrutiny and perhaps the presumption of criminality or even terrorism. The legal scholar and critical race theorist Devon Carbado notes in an article on his emigration from Great Britain to the United States that only through an encounter with racist members of the Los Angeles Police Department did he become "American." Carbado writes: "I became American long before I acquired citizenship. Unlike citizenship, black racial naturalization was always available to me, even as I tried to make myself unavailable for that particular Americanization process" (2002, 946). Just as Carbado was introduced to the problematics of race within the United States, I was introduced to the experience of race in Cuba. My racial identity marked me as Cuban and "other" simultaneously; it meant I was both part of the Cuban nation and singled out for special scrutiny.

Racialized experiences are common throughout the diaspora, but much is at stake in exploring these experiences within Cuba. The Cuban Revolution has been widely hailed for having solved the race problem domestically and internationally through socialism and for supporting antiracist and anticolonial struggles worldwide. The view from the ground in Cuba, however, indicates that the race situation on the island nation is much more complex. Before the revolution, blacks faced substantial discrimination in all walks of Cuban life. Cuba's was a highly unequal society based upon race that at times experimented with Jim Crow–style policies. More frequently, however, it was a society in which blacks held formal citizenship status but lived under highly unequal terms. Discrimination was practiced in important organs of civil society like schools, unions, professional organizations, and private clubs. The Cuban Revolution's policies greatly transformed Cuba's racial, political, social, and economic legacy. The Cuban Revolution eliminated racial exclusion in those areas of civil society where it was practiced and transformed many of the material conditions of blacks in positive ways. Blacks benefited from higher literacy rates created by better access to education. Furthermore, blacks took advantage of better income distribution, new opportunities in professions, and an expanded health system that greatly increased life expectancy (de la Fuente 1995).

Yet, to some degree, the same contradictory situation of black inclusion and inequality that could be seen in the post-independence period has also characterized the revolution. In Cuba today, Afro-Cubans are embraced as "authentic" Cubans and the primary supporters of the regime at the same time that they are constructed as "socially dangerous" (de la Fuente 2001). Following brief periods of improvement and longer periods of stagnation, and partly as a result of the collapse of the Soviet Union and the ongoing influence of pre-existing racial disparities, racial inequality is again growing in Cuba. Job discrimination against Afro-Cubans in the tourist sector and their unequal access to dollars through remittances from the United States exacerbate the problem. Daily life in Cuba is filled with contradictions: While the large number of black police officers signals the unprecedented ways in which blacks have been integrated into Cuban society since the revolution, for example, the ways in which these officers tend to single out blacks for harassment and scrutiny indicate that racial stereotypes and inequality are alive and well.

This book seeks to unlock such contradictions, to better understand how racial inequality has persisted in Cuba despite substantial efforts by the government to create equality and even stronger efforts to convince Cubans and the international community that the nation has solved its race problem. Admittedly, this is quite a thorny area in which to tread. For a variety of reasons, racial equality has become a central part of the Cuban Revolution's international and domestic reputation. The ongoing experiment that is the Cuban Revolution has been as much about race as it has been about attempts to institute socialism and develop both Cuban nationalism and Third World internationalism. Thus, there is much at stake in this analysis.

It is an understatement to suggest that racial issues in Cuba are complex. The regime has done more than the government of any other nation, perhaps, to address the problem of racial inequality, yet it has taken some missteps. This book will examine the approach of the Cuban Revolution to pursuing color-blind, class-based means of solving racial problems, and it will explore the limits of that approach. But as far as race relations are concerned, the revolution cannot be examined as a clear point of demarcation in Cuba's history. The legacy and acknowledgment of racial mixture, as well as denials of the existence of racism, are key pre-revolutionary constructs that have influenced race relations on the island after the revolution. These constructs were themselves shaped by Cuba's colonial legacy of slavery and the unequal inclusion of blacks in the nation at the moment of independence. Critical events and developments in Cuban racial history, like racial violence against blacks who organized an independent black political party at the turn of the twentieth century, helped to structure race relations within the context of the revolution.

I argue that racial inequality has persisted in post-revolutionary Cuba as a result of ideological and structural factors, some of which existed prior to the revolution and others of which were products of, or exacerbated by, events following the revolution. The ideology of Latin American exceptionalism – which denied the existence of racism and suppressed black agency – was a significant factor in preventing more comprehensive racial reforms before and after the revolution. Furthermore, the unequal education of blacks in the pre-revolutionary era, as well as their location in poorer neighborhoods and regions and their participation in the sugar sector of the economy, had a substantial impact on relative racial inequality after the revolution. During the revolution, the ideology of Marxism combined with the ideology of Latin American exceptionalism to limit reforms so that class-based solutions, rather than potentially more effective race-specific measures, were proposed to eliminate the problem of blacks' relative inequality.

Yet behind such specific causes of racial inequality in Cuba has been the influence of broader structural changes in Cuban politics and society; the specific story of the Cuban Revolution is important, but it also may contain lessons about racial politics in general. The Cuban Revolution raised questions about the effects of recognizing multiracial categories and the benefits and limits of color-blind policies in eliminating racial hierarchy that are still in the process of being answered. The revolution allows us to examine the interaction between race and class in a socialist state attempting to produce a classless society and to assess the similarities and differences between the effects of liberal and Marxist ideologies on racial politics. This approach enables us to witness the simultaneous acknowledgment and denial of racial problems in Cuba that is a hallmark of color-blind state discourse. We are also able to analyze the variable terms of racialized inclusion that are at work throughout the modern nations of the Americas. With the advance of capitalism and the devolution of the state in the Cuban economy, furthermore, Cuba may now be on a convergent path with societies like those of the United States and Brazil in terms of race. Looking at the cultural, political, and international legacy of the Cuban Revolution, then, can yield insights for those concerned about racial politics in the United States and elsewhere in the world.

This book explores the evolution of Cuban ideology and policies concerning race in order to examine, first, whether there is in fact racial hierarchy in Cuba today. If it does exist, why has it persisted through more than forty years of socialist government? The book's central argument is that racial politics within Cuba have followed patterns of opening and retrenchment that have been driven by the need of the state to mobilize blacks to support state projects and to protect the state from hostile forces. Once the state's projects have been completed or the threats against it neutralized, it has consolidated around new racial orders. Within this process, racial ideology has played a critical role in setting the boundaries for improvement on racial issues and providing justifications for retrenchment. The mechanisms of racial change and of the consolidation of racial orders are not unique to Cuba. In understanding them, we can come to understand racial politics more generally and to arrive at conclusions that allow for further comparison.

The approach of this book, therefore, is explicitly transnational – transnational both in the sense that international factors drive racial politics and in the sense that racialization is frequently thought of and experienced in transnational and comparative terms. Racialized experiences have common threads that transcend national boundaries in a way that has been consciously recognized by leaders, activists, and everyday people. International politics are, in this sense, a powerful factor in "domestic" racial politics. I argue explicitly that Cuba, the United States, and Africa have played critical roles in one anothers' racial histories. As a consequence, we must focus on transnational flows of people and ideology in order to understand completely the historical evolution of racial politics on the island. Specifically, we must examine the Cold War interaction among nations and its impact on racial politics.

   Chapter 1 proposes a theory to explain why racial hierarchy is so persistent, and racial progress so sporadic, in Cuba. The "race cycles theory" outlines the relationship among racial progress, mechanisms like state crisis, and the influence of racial ideology. I argue in Chapter 1 that Cuban racial ideology is characterized by what I call "inclusionary discrimination." While mechanisms like state crises create openings for racial progress, the ideology of inclusionary discrimination encourages the ongoing marginalization of Afro-Cubans in Cuban social, economic, and political life. The race cycles theory and the idea of inclusionary discrimination improve upon existing models of racial politics by introducing a dynamic model of racialization.

   Chapter 2 uses the model developed in Chapter 1 to look at racial politics in pre-revolutionary Cuba. It argues that the Cuban War of Independence represented a significant opening for Afro-Cubans, who pressed for freedom and equality in the context of the struggle for independence. Following independence, racist beliefs surfaced that justified racist attacks on independent black organizations as white elites sought to consolidate their power around a new racial order that made blacks junior partners in the new nation. Cuban elites developed a myth of racial democracy – and a fear of black insurgency – that justified racial violence and denied the existence of racial inequality. This closure represented a form of state consolidation.

   The pattern of opening and closure appeared again during the Cuban Revolution, which followed similar ideological scripts. Examining the Cuban Revolution, Chapter 3 shows that the initial change in regime generated great reforms and a comparative embrace of blacks. Following the crisis created by the change of regime, however, Castro's government consolidated its power by curtailing the freedoms of organizations in general and those of black organizations in particular. The regime also blended a version of the old myth of racial democracy with the new idea that socialism had eliminated Cuban racial inequality. While blacks have not reached parity with whites under Castro's regime, they have nevertheless benefited greatly from redistributive efforts and from the economic growth created by socialism and aided by Soviet subsidies.

   The third chapter also examines how progress toward racial equality was made when Cuba committed thousands of troops to supporting the MPLA in Angola against UNITA and the South African government.

The Cuban mobilization opened up new discussions on the island about race and created both greater black representation in positions of power and a new acceptance of black culture. Following the victory in Angola, a new crisis emerged. The looming collapse of the Soviet Union and the increasingly threatening stance of the Reagan administration created, because of the need to mobilize support for the regime, further openings for racial advance. For the first time, the Castro regime suggested the possibility of instituting affirmative action policies. However, the ensuing economic collapse was so great that it thwarted these mobilization efforts. The economic retraction caused by the fall of the Soviet Union made it impossible to expand opportunities for blacks. The regime created a new hybrid socialist/capitalist economy, and the new order again asserted the myth of racial democracy.

Chapter 4 takes a historical step backward and examines the interaction between 1960s and 1970s Black Nationalists from the United States and the Castro regime. The chapter sheds light on the contradictions between Cuba's domestic racial policy, which attacked black organizations and black autonomy, and its international policy, which supported organizations like the Black Panther Party. In doing so, this chapter provides a clear example of the limits of the Castro regime's racial politics as experienced by activists from the United States. Their experiences illuminate the contradictions of inclusionary discrimination as well as the transnational and comparative nature of black politics. The chapter shows how the experiences of U.S.-based activists and leaders in Cuba helped foment an ideological divide between U.S.-based cultural nationalists, who saw race as the primary source of black oppression and rejected socialism, and U.S.-based revolutionary nationalists, who saw socialism as essential to solving racial problems and who were, in consequence, much less critical of the Castro regime's approach to race in Cuba.

Chapter 5 looks at race in contemporary Cuba. Drawing on in-depth interviews, it shows that racial discrimination is still perceived as a problem by Afro-Cubans. The chapter also demonstrates that the new capitalist economic order is creating significant inequalities based upon race: Whites have greater access to remittances from abroad and employment in the new, lucrative tourist industry, while blacks are frequently forced into criminal or black market activities in order to survive. In conjunction with subscribing to myths of racial democracy, many Cuban whites hold that black disadvantage in the new economy is due to their inherent inferiority. The professed gains of the revolution have become a justification for inequality.

Chapter 6 uses public opinion surveys I conducted in Havana in 2000 and 2001 to test the existence of racial hierarchy, the salience of race in daily life, and the effect of race on political attitudes in Cuba. The chapter challenges notions that race is not salient in Cuba and shows that race profoundly structures attitudes about Cuban racial issues, politics, and economics. Race is also a determinant of several key measures of life chances; blacks are at the bottom of a stair-step racial hierarchy in Cuba, and whites are at the top. I argue that despite persistent inequality, Afro-Cubans generally support the current regime because of both its past successes and their pessimism about leadership alternatives like the Miami exile community.

Chapter 7 examines the racial politics of the Miami exile community and suggests that the conservative leadership of the community has been at best insensitive with regard to racial issues. The chapter looks at a number of historical incidents and examines survey data that compares Cuban racial attitudes with those of other major groups of Latinos in the United States. I argue that the exile community's general tendency to conflate the struggle for racial equality with communist sympathies and its racial insensitivity have made it hopelessly out of step with the citizens of Cuba, who have become increasingly darker since the revolution.

Finally, the Conclusion examines how well the empirical case of Cuba fits the race cycles theory and the idea of inclusionary discrimination described in Chapter 1. It summarizes the issues discussed throughout the book and considers the future of Cuba and its revolution. The Conclusion also looks at the implications of what I have demonstrated about the Cuban experiment for racial politics and policy in the United States and beyond.

Race Cycles, Racial Hierarchy, and Inclusionary Discrimination

A Dynamic Approach

This book has two agendas: (1) to use the case of Cuba to examine why racial politics change and what limits the amount of improvement for subordinate racial groups and (2) to analyze racial politics in modern Cuba empirically in the context of theories that have been used to explain racial politics in Cuba specifically and in Latin America generally. It is tempting to believe that a single underlying narrative can be found to explain racial politics in post-revolutionary Cuba. The central argument of this book, however, is that at the level of both state and individual, there are often contradictory forces at work with regard to racial politics. Mechanisms of racial change have a strange duality, as they can simultaneously create greater racial equality and reinforce ideas that maintain racial hierarchy. One such mechanism is the myth of color-blindness, which has become a dominant discourse of modern nation states, including Brazil, Cuba, and later the United States (Guinier and Torres 2002).

The contradictory forces at work in racial politics have been expressed in Cuba through its history, state policy, culture, and racial ideology, and in the everyday experiences of Cubans. There has been no linear improvement in racial politics, but an iterative process of opening and closure that has been limited by racial ideology. This book explores all of these elements and their individual, varied effects on racial politics in postrevolutionary Cuba. I look first at broad historical elements and then at the day-to-day situation on the island. In this way, I try to bridge the gap between the study of broad structural changes and ideologies and the study of micro-level behavior and experience. I argue that a grasp of both domestic and international politics is essential to understanding racial politics in any country, and that Cuba is no exception.

The theoretical perspective I employ to accomplish these tasks is the "race cycles" perspective. This perspective takes a decidedly non-linear approach to understanding racial politics. Below, I describe the race cycles approach and how it might apply to Cuba. Later in this chapter, I contrast the race cycles approach with the linear ways in which Cuban racial politics has been studied thus far. I also evaluate postmodern perspectives on race that have sought to reinvent myths of racial democracy, or color-blindness, by questioning the salience of racial categories. Finally, I demonstrate that Cuban racial ideology reflects a pattern of "inclusionary discrimination" that explains the uneven inclusion and inequality that has been a part of Cuban politics since before the revolution.

My approach synthesizes a few important and powerful streams of social science literature. It borrows liberally from the work of Anthony Marx, who has focused on nation building and its relationship to the development of racial politics. Marx's model, however, provides little guidance for understanding the development of racial politics beyond the moment of nation building. For this, I turn to a fusion of William Sewell's insights on historical events as transformations of structure with McAdam, Tarrow, and Tilly's ideas about contentious politics. These perspectives, when combined with Marx and with Omi and Winant's work on racial formation, provide a pathway to understanding how race is a structure that itself experiences transformation and interacts with other structures and historical events in a systematic fashion. We are able to relate "racial formation" on the one hand to state formation and change on the other. The race cycles model also allows us to understand how racial ideology and the agency of subordinated individuals transform racial politics. Thus, I attempt with the race cycles model to fuse a discussion of ideology, structure, events, and agency into a single perspective, whereas others have tended to address them one at a time or not to explicitly discuss their relationship to the development of racial politics.

Race Cycles

The race cycles model attempts to build on the growing literature on race, World War II, and the Cold War. Books like Klinkner and Smith's *The Unsteady March* highlight how gains for blacks in the United States were driven by openings created by war mobilizations (1999). The historians Ada Ferrer, Aline Helg, and Alejandro de la Fuente have developed similar perspectives pointing to the transformations in Cuban racial politics brought about by the wars of independence, the revolution, and other key moments in Cuban history. While these books provide important critical perspectives, they do not offer a general model that can be used to understand these transformations across time and space. In this chapter, I propose a model – with an eye to building principles for other cases – that draws upon recent scholarship and offers a general and comparative framework with which to explain transformations in racial politics in Cuba.

The race cycles perspective proposed in this chapter has five central points. First, racial politics is driven by mechanisms such as state crisis, regime change, racial ideology, transnational politics, and endogenous shocks to the system, or critical events. Second, mechanisms like state crisis, transnational politics, and critical events lead to transformations in racial politics. These transformations are followed by the process of state consolidation, which relies on racial ideology to limit and ultimately halt any gains made as a result of the mechanism.[1] Third, because of conflicting state priorities, each mechanism provides opportunities for gains for subordinate racial groups, but it also places limitations on the magnitude and duration of these gains. The mechanisms

---

[1] I use the terms "mechanisms" and "processes" in the way that Doug McAdam, Sidney Tarrow, and Charles Tilly use them in their book *Dynamics of Contention* (2001). In the book, "mechanisms" are defined as "a delimited class of events that alter relations among specified sets of elements in identical or closely similar ways over a variety of situations" (24). An extension of this process is "regular sequences of such mechanisms that produce similar (generally more complex and contingent) transformations of those elements" (24). There are three kinds of mechanisms described in *Dynamics of Contention*, and this book focuses on all three of them: environmental mechanisms, cognitive mechanisms, and relational mechanisms. While only broader comparative analysis can reveal whether these mechanisms operate in an identical way in a variety of situations, without such language we are unable to describe in any systematic way the patterns of transformations in racial politics. Thus, the language serves to provide some general descriptions of critical variables that drive racial change, but it serves this function metaphorically rather than directly.

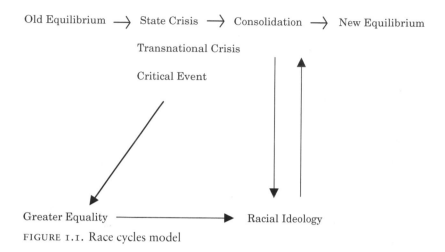

FIGURE 1.1. Race cycles model

that drive the change trend toward an equilibrium position of stagnation in the racial situation. Fourth, gains in racial politics are directly related, in a positive fashion, to the magnitude of the state crisis, but the duration of the gains is inversely related to the degree of the crisis. Finally, following a significant shock and subsequent consolidation, a new equilibrium is created that is different from the previous one. As a consequence, racial ideology and policies are altered (see Figure 1.1).

Race cycles are sporadic, and they do not necessarily cause racial politics to improve in a linear fashion. William Sewell provides theoretical guidance to bolster this point of view. When writing about transformations of structures (racial politics can be considered a structure), Sewell notes: "When changes do take place, they are rarely smooth and linear in character; instead, changes tend to be clustered into relatively intense bursts. Even the accumulation of incremental changes often results in a build-up of pressures and a dramatic crisis of existing practices rather than a gradual transition from one state of affairs to another" (1996, 843). I argue that intense bursts such as Sewell describes occur in the context of, or are driven by, mechanisms like state crisis, transnational politics, and critical events. The following sections discuss these three mechanisms, the process of state consolidation that follows them, and the role of racial ideology as an interlocutor between them.

State Crisis

State crises in the form of foreign wars, civil wars, regime change, and so on are critical moments for racial politics (Helg 1995; Plummer 1996; Layton 1998; Klinkner and Smith 1999; Dudziak 2000). State crisis is one of several "environmental mechanisms," a category described by McAdam, Tarrow, and Tilly as "externally generated influences on conditions affecting social life" (2001, 25). A state crisis is any situation in which the state or regime, or the sovereignty of the state or nation, is in jeopardy. While moments of state crisis tend to pose great danger for all groups within society, they also open up critical political opportunities (McAdam 1999; Kryder 2000; Dudziak 2000; Layton 1998). Such crises expand the need for the state to incorporate the support of more social groups in order to consolidate its power and achieve objectives, including its very survival (Becker 1971). During periods of state crisis, subordinate groups' demands for rights, power, and social or political advancement are most likely to be heard.

The context of state crisis, however, also places profound limitations on potential gains. Wars (civil and otherwise) and government changes mean that many of the rules of the game of politics are suspended or changed. While subordinate groups may be able to make added demands during periods of state crisis, the call to "close ranks" that opens opportunities for outsiders can also limit both the range of issues that subordinate groups might pursue and their means to pursue them (Plummer 1996; Dudziak 2000; Kryder 2000; Parker 2005). The asymmetry in power that exists in this bargaining process means that minority groups may push, but also that they are at great risk if they choose to defy the state openly. The high degree of uncertainty that accompanies state crisis, then, creates opportunities while also often foreclosing more radical options. The Cold War enabled African Americans to fight for rights, for example, but it also required them to purge communists from black organizations (Plummer 1996; Layton 1998). Disadvantaged groups are aware in periods of state crisis that the environment of uncertainty means that things are as likely to become much worse as they are to improve.

Minority groups are also often in particular danger during violent times. When the state is threatened, race can become a convenient, though blunt, standard for determining friends and enemies. The events of World War II in the United States again offer an excellent case in point. While the war expanded opportunities for African Americans, the vulnerability of Japanese Americans suggests that war presented both great opportunity and great danger for minority groups. Similarly, during the bloody civil wars in Central America, indigenous peoples faced violence and repression despite the fact that few indigenous peasants were actively involved in the conflicts. As Said, Goldberg, and others note, race can become a proxy for judging good versus evil, modern versus primitive, capitalist versus communist, and so forth. During times of crisis, subordinate racial groups often become scapegoats and are used to help mobilize and eliminate dissident elements (Said 1979; Goldberg 1993). In Cuban history, I argue, three moments represent significant state crises that expanded opportunities for black Cubans: the Cuban wars of independence from Spain, the Cuban Revolution, and the war in Angola. These crises all involved the need to mobilize blacks behind state projects, and they all created significant opportunities in other areas of social, political, and economic life for blacks.

Transnational Politics

Other types of events, however, can have powerful effects on racial politics, stretching the scope of racial politics beyond national boundaries. The Cuban state has used race as a means of accumulating international prestige and building support for the Cuban nationalist project worldwide. International forces are a powerful but undertheorized mechanism for change in racial politics. They can serve as environmental mechanisms that create new environments and change conditions affecting social life; they can also serve as "relational mechanisms." MacAdam, Tarrow, and Tilly defined relational mechanisms as those that "alter connections among people, groups, and personal networks" (2001, 26). This study addresses relational mechanisms in a transnational context, but the basic definition remains the same. Connections among people alter the landscape, as well as opportunities for contestation and social change. Several writers have studied how both World War II and the Cold War set the stage for the civil rights movement in the United States (Plummer 1996; Layton 1998; Klinkner and Smith 1999; Dudziak 2000; Kryder 2000; McAdam 1999). World War II made it necessary for the federal government to mobilize blacks in order to win the war, and the Cold War made it necessary to reform racial problems in the United States because of the growing ideological battle in the South and the specter of Soviet propaganda on racial issues. The Cold War, then, is an example that invites the exploration of transnational politics as a mechanism for transformation in racial politics.

Diplomatic conflicts can open opportunities for minority groups. The process of mobilization and the call to close ranks against a common ideological enemy open new opportunities for making claims against the state. Ethnic minorities can manipulate the needs of the state to mobilize public opinion in order to bargain for greater reforms. The state's need to respond to the real or imagined threat of minority defection forces it to adopt reforms. The development of cross-national alliances can also play an important role in internal racial politics. Cross-national alliances are often the products of international conflicts or potential conflicts. Providing resources that previously did not exist, alliances can offer greater economic opportunities to the parties involved, and they can increase the symbolic importance of internal constituencies. There is substantial evidence, for example, to prove that the ideological battle over the so-called Third World made U.S. blacks important symbolically in ways that had previously not been the case: Embarrassment over the treatment of U.S. blacks produced a symbolic imperative to improve conditions in order to win a propaganda battle with the Soviet Union (Plummer 1996; Layton 1998; Dudziak 2000). Black activists used their position in this propaganda battle to promote the cause of civil rights, bolstering their claim in reference to the Soviet Union and the atrocities of the Nazis. Similarly, the need for better bilateral relationships with Mexico, China, and Korea opened opportunities for naturalization to the nationals of these countries residing within the United States and temporarily changed the terms of their racialization (Chung 2002; Menchaca 2002). Allying with other nations, moreover, may cause greater resources to flow to a variety of internal constituencies, and in some cases to racialized groups. New trading partners, subsidies, and other benefits of alliances can be positive for both dominant and subordinate groups.

Cuba's alliance with the Soviet Union provided critical resources for the Cuban government, allowing for economic growth and programs of redistribution to occur simultaneously. The alliance made resources available for blacks to advance toward equality and improve their standard of living under the rubric of Cuban socialism and nationalism. Cuba also played an important and critical role in the black struggle for freedom in the United States. Cuba's discursive and material support of revolutionary nationalist movements like the Black Panthers and other Black Power organizations embarrassed the United States in the context of the Cold War and helped to encourage reform within the United States.

Critical Events

The state, however, is not the only agent of change in race relations. Critical events are environmental mechanisms that shape racial politics outside of the contexts of state crisis and transnational politics, changing the landscape of contention. Critical events capture the state's and the public's attention but do not threaten the very survival of the state or the regime. They may also concatenate with other mechanisms like state crisis and transnational politics. They can unfold literally overnight or at a glacial pace. It is difficult to define "critical events" in a satisfactory manner, yet they are an important variable. William Sewell's definition of "historical events" is helpful here; while Sewell admits that even his definition leaves open ambiguities, it is the best analytical tool we have to understand the nature of events as causal variables for social change. Sewell defines three key components of historical events: "(1) a ramified sequence of occurrences that (2) is recognized as notable by contemporaries, and that (3) results in a durable transformation of structures" (1996, 844). Racial politics are one such structure that can be transformed by critical events.

The deindustrialization of American cities is one example of a critical event that unfolded over an extended period of time, while the currency crisis that set off ethnic violence in Asia in 1999 is a critical event that happened literally overnight. These critical events were both economic transformations. Changes in race relations are sometimes an unintended consequence of broader economic restructuring that both offers opportunities and presents limitations for ethnic minorities. As modes of production shift, shifts in family relationships, migration, and how people consume and utilize their leisure time are not uncommon. Some types of restructuring, such as the transition to an industrial economy, can open opportunities, while other types, like the move from a Fordist to a post-Fordist economy, can harm opportunities for minorities because they involve a contraction of possibilities rather than an expansion. Similarly, a severe and deep economic crisis can foment racial animosity and harm minorities because it creates greater competition for scarce resources. Thus, economic decline limits resources and harms minority interests. Economic crises in general, then, have the opposite effect of other kinds of crises.

There are also other types of critical events, such as social movements or events that have broad symbolic import. Taeku Lee's work on the violence surrounding the Selma, Alabama, march in 1965 indicates that it was a social movement that took on broad symbolic significance; it interacted with other incidents of contestation and symbolic politics to shift attitudes about U.S. civil rights policies (2002). The murder of Martin Luther King Jr. and the subsequent rebellion in 1968 deeply transformed U.S. racial politics. The Rodney King beating and rebellion, too, took on both national and international significance (Hunt 1997; de la Fuente 2001). These critical events were watched in Cuba, China, and Africa and had ripple effects on all parts of the United States. Similarly important critical events include, for example, the protests in Soweto, South Africa, and the Emmitt Till lynching, which was covered extensively in Cuba.[2] Many critical events are protests, and frequently they are contentious interactions – like Bloody Sunday in Ireland – that bring issues of minority justice to the forefront. It is also possible for state institutions to generate critical events that are not simply responses to pressure to reform, but that themselves open new possibilities for contestation and agency. The 1954 Supreme Court decision in *Brown v. Board of Education*, for example, fueled substantial debate on racial issues and led to ugly incidents in which the federal government had to enforce federal law. Again, these incidents were not just structural reforms; they took on a broader symbolic significance and created openings that social movement activists attempted to exploit. Protests and important symbolic incidents usually happen, however, when contestation over a potential state consolidation heightens protest movement activity, and these incidents are usually more effective in the context of a state crisis or of significant transnational political developments.

It is critical to note, finally, that these kinds of events and their influence on racial politics are deeply affected by regime type. During critical

---

[2] It is worth noting that one of the most famous Cuban poems on race and anti-colonialism, written by the black Cuban poet Nicolas Guillen, is entitled "Elegy to Emmitt Till." The events surrounding Till's murder by a white mob for whistling at a white woman captured the imagination and shocked the consciousness of blacks not only in the United States but also in Cuba and elsewhere.

events, uncertainty creates opportunities – and also danger – for out-
groups. Challenges to the existing racial regime are more likely in places
where there is greater freedom to express dissent within civil society.
Thus, regimes that allow more freedom of the press and of expression
are more susceptible to demand protest activity that extends cycles of
change in race relations. In the case of Cuba, we will see that the exten-
sive power of the state has generally prevented demand protest activity.
Racial ideology and negative stereotypes can also work during critical
events to limit possibilities for minorities by creating hegemonic nar-
ratives that disarm, dismiss, or attack agents of disadvantaged groups.
There is a duality to critical events and a strong tendency toward equilibrium in race relations contained within the need to find comfort in
the midst of uncertainty.

State Consolidation

Racial politics are often an arena in which broader anxieties about
the direction of society are played out, and state consolidation – the
mechanism that follows state crisis – tends to return racial politics to
a state of normalcy, or equilibrium. Following a crisis, states have a
strong desire to consolidate their power and hegemony. State consolidation produces a contraction effect that halts many of the gains made
by marginalized groups during the crisis period; the more threatening
these gains are to state cohesion, the more swift and violent the state
consolidation will be. The need to build consensus, eliminate dissent,
and produce certainty and assurance among actors generally means
that the progress of marginalized racial and ethnic groups is slow, if
it does not cease altogether, during periods of state consolidation. The
needs of the emergent state or regime take precedence over all else in
a manner that tends to produce a new equilibrium. As the new order
emerges from the more chaotic situation that preceded it, the state has
a strong incentive to declare the race problem "solved." As Goldberg
notes, the modern state uses race as a primary means of establishing its
rationality, and in many cases the rationality of the state is articulated
in terms of its avowals of "color-blindness," regardless of whether or
not racial problems have actually been solved (2002).

States that are more authoritarian in nature are also more effective
at consolidation. Their ability to intervene with active and direct coercion aids the consolidation process, while states that must use forces

of persuasion rather than direct coercion consolidate more slowly. I reject a clear categorical divide, however, between authoritarian and nonauthoritarian regimes. Civil rights protesters in the United States, for instance, faced what was indistinguishable from an authoritarian regime in their clashes with local authorities in the South and in the indifference of federal officials. But states of all varieties use whatever means are available to them, including ideological, symbolic, and coercive policies, to return to normal.

Because the chaos that drove the state to reach out to subordinates in the crisis period no longer exists during the period of consolidation, and because improvements from the previous period are major accomplishments, the new regime attempts to use ideology and symbols to justify its actions. State consolidation frequently dovetails with the old racist ideology; the state's declaration that the problem of racial inequality has been solved provides fuel for racist explanations of continuing subordinate group disadvantage. That is, ongoing inequality is frequently blamed on the victims of racial marginalization, and a set of legitimizing myths about racial inequality grows out of the state's misrepresentation that the race problem has been solved. If substantial improvements are made in the crisis phase, they become a set of justifications for why the state no longer needs to engage in such "risky" and potentially "divisive" activity. In this mode, racial problems that were previously used to mobilize support come to be seen as potential barriers to unity. This is also the point at which demand protest activity and the potential for racial violence are often high (Morris 1986): Populations mobilized and emboldened by previous, though limited, success do not give up easily; they will sometimes seek to extend their gains despite the state's attempt to stop them. Protest marches, clashes with the state, and similar events may extend the process of improvement if they capture the public imagination and force the state to reconsider its decision to stave off further improvements. Agents seek to challenge consolidation, then, by acting as catalysts for various types of critical events.

Consolidation periods are often very long. They may span decades as the residual effects from the crisis continue and the backlash persists. I argue that the more violent and serious the crisis, the more violent and abrupt the consolidation phase. In some cases, there may be transitional phases between crisis and consolidation. Reconstruction in the United States was in many ways a transitional phase. Reconstruction was a period during which the acute phase of the crisis – the war – was over, but a new and stable social order had not yet taken form. In fact, as McAdam, Tarrow, and Tilly note, we cannot pinpoint clear beginnings and endings to periods of consolidation: "We see such episodes not as linear sequences of contention in which the same actors go through the repeated motions of expressing pre-established claims in lock-step, but as iterative sites of interaction in which different streams of mobilization and demobilization intersect, identities evolve, and new forms of action are invented, honed, and rejected as actors interact with one another and with opponents and third parties" (2001, 30). While this argument applies specifically to consolidation, it also explains the ongoing and overlapping nature of race cycles more generally as they appear in history.

Using the case of Reconstruction, we can think of the product of state consolidation as a new equilibrium in race relations in the same way that McAdam, Tarrow, and Tilly suggest. Anthony Marx (1998) describes how a stable regime arose following the Civil War only when white supremacy gained currency in the United States and served to "bind up the nation's wounds."[3] The example of Reconstruction demonstrates the dynamics and power of state consolidation. The epidemic of racial violence that followed the withdrawal of support for African American rights by the North showed how abrupt and violent consolidation can be. The North's priority – to find a way to bring white Southerners back into a broader consensus – sacrificed many of the gains made during the Civil War and Reconstruction for African Americans. Reconstruction also shows the often-fuzzy nature of the transition from crisis to consolidation.

---

[3] While Anthony Marx's model of the interaction of race and nation building grounds the differentiation between societies like those of South Africa, Brazil, and the United States in an initial moment of nation building, it does not account for subsequent changes and transformations in racial politics. With the race cycles model, I attempt to build on Marx's model, noting the importance of his argument but extending the lessons learned to other cases. As will be discussed in Chapter 2, moreover, Cuba introduces an interesting complication into his model. Marx argues that divisions among white elites drove segregationist policies in South Africa and the United States. The mixed response in Cuba, however, where a significant division among white elites resulted in the coexistence of formal racial inclusion with elements of U.S.-style Jim Crow, speaks to the necessity for a different model to explain how ideology and the circumstances of black mobilization for Cuban independence contributed to this alternative outcome.

State consolidation in Cuba occurred after the wars for independence ended in a violent massacre of blacks (Helg 1995). The period after the Bay of Pigs was a second period of consolidation and retrenchment during which the Castro regime maintained silence on the race issue and cracked down on black organizations. The war in Angola and, later, the economic problems of the 1990s also created openings that were followed by attempts to consolidate and deny the existence of racial issues. Latin American exceptionalism and, later, Marxist exceptionalism, which I discuss later in this chapter, both at various points served to justify the repression of blacks and to limit policies aimed at helping blacks.

Racial Ideology

The state is not the only agent of movement toward equilibrium; non-state actors play a powerful role, both ideologically and practically. Racist "common sense," which fosters stagnation, is perpetuated by the mass public. Racial ideology is an interlocutor between the radical process of state crisis and the conservative force of state consolidation. In the race cycles model, it serves as a mechanism of stagnation. In terms of McAdam, Tarrow, and Tilly's work, it is one of the "cognitive mechanisms" that "operate though alterations of individual and collective perception; words like recognize, understand, reinterpret, and classify characterize such mechanisms" (2001, 26). Racial ideology most often shifts during state crisis. Groups can make new demands, and the expansion of the state means that racist logics and discourses must be altered to fit the new moment. Old hypocrisies and contradictions are exposed during these periods of heightened tension, and opportunities to create new understandings can be driven by elites and by the mass public (Lee 2002). It is important to note, moreover, that racial ideology can change and develop elements that enhance egalitarianism in this process.

In the Western hemisphere, racial ideologies have frequently contained a healthy dose of both racist justifications for oppression and legitimizing myths for inequality. Despite regime changes, changes in state organization, and challenges to states, racial ideology – and racist ideology in particular – often proves to be highly adaptable to suit new circumstances and to fit neatly among a variety of state ideologies. (I draw a distinction between "racial" and "racist" ideology because there are always multiple racial ideologies at work at any given moment that may have both racist and nonracist elements.) Scholars like Charles Mills, Michael Dawson, Larry Bobo, James Sidanius, David Theo Goldberg, and George Lispitz have all demonstrated how racist ideology adapts to liberalism, Marxism, and transitions in economic regimes (Mills 1997; Sidanius et al. 1997). Several authors have shown how racist ideology, which some thought would disappear with industrialization, survived and in many cases thrived in the new context (Greenberg 1980; Holt 2000). Racist ideology can be grafted onto what appears to be antiracist or egalitarian discourse.

Racial ideology in the New World since the importation of slaves has most often been racist ideology, but other racial ideologies are frequently in operation, some of which contain egalitarian strains. Omi and Winant refer to these differing racial policies as competing racial projects (1994). Later in this chapter, I explore both the ideology of racial democracy in Latin America and Marxist ideology, and I consider the complexities that they present with regard to race. Both have significant egalitarian elements as well as elements that are compatible with racist ideology. It is the compatibility of racist ideology with other ideologies that makes racial hierarchy so persistent.

Tom Holt notes in his work on race and the twenty-first century that there is always a dialogue about race between the past and the present. Holt explains the durability of certain kinds of racist discourses: "We recognize that a new historical construct is never entirely new and the old is never entirely supplanted by the new. Rather the new is grafted onto the old. Thus, racism too, is never entirely new. Shards and fragments of its past incarnations are embedded in the new. Or, if we switch metaphors to an archeological image, the new is sedimented onto the old, which occasionally seeps or bursts through" (2000, 20). Hence, racial discourse is repeated inexactly. The texture and contours change to fit the moment, but much of the discourse remains familiar.

The ability of racism to transpose itself onto new structures and processes, both at the individual and structural level, is critical to the race cycles model. Racist ideology interacts with mechanisms like state crisis and consolidation rather than operating separately. There is a clear bridge among events, structures, individual attitudes, and hegemonic discourses. This connection is facilitated by the adaptability of racist discourses. The anthropologist Ann Stoler notes: "The force of racisms is not found in the alleged fixity of visual knowledge, nor on

essentialism itself, but on the *malleability* of the criteria of psychological dispositions and moral sensibilities that the visual could neither
definitely secure nor explain. . . . I am more interested in exploring the
ways in which racisms take on the form of other things, wrap themselves around heated issues, descend upon political pulse points, appear
as reasoned judgments, beyond sentiment, as they penetrate impas-
sioned bodies" (1997, 200). The wrapping and penetration described
by Stoler delineates the bridge between the racial content of structures
and events within the polity. The bridge connects racist ideas to even
antiracist activities and nonracial events and processes in a manner that
maintains racial hierarchy. This connection is established by means of
"legitimizing myths," or hegemonic explanations of racial politics that
seek to normalize racial hierarchy and shift blame for its existence away
from an analysis of oppression by dominants and toward the actions
or inadequacies of subordinates (Sidanius et al. 1997). These myths
mask the structures and attitudes that work to maintain inequality.
Ultimately, racial ideology works with the process of state consolidation following a state crisis to produce stagnation.

A key event in the reconfiguration of racial ideology following a
period of improvement is the development of what the sociologist
Lawrence Bobo calls "laissez faire racism" (2000). According to Bobo,
a new form of racism developed to defend whites' dominant position
within the changed economic context, in which blacks became participants in the broader national economy that is based on free market capitalism (2000). *Laissez-faire* racism therefore consists of (1) the
ongoing negative stereotyping of blacks and (2) the placing of responsibility for the socioeconomic racial gap on blacks themselves. Thus Bobo
argues that blacks' primary shortcoming is no longer some inherent
inferiority but their cultural resistance to the work ethic (2000). While
Bobo links his analysis to a particular period in U.S. history and a
transformation in American racial attitudes, the process he describes is
strikingly similar to the "new racism" described in Paul Gilroy's work
on Great Britain (1987). The general story these two scholars tell is
not only about the adaptability of justifications for racial hierarchy
but also about how transformations in the racial order, and in economic and social organization, *themselves* create new justifications for
racial inequality. I contend that *laissez-faire* racism develops in part
out of both perceptions of state policy and actual gains made by racial
minorities. Dominants tend to emphasize reforms undertaken during

the crisis period and use them as a justification to do nothing further, to argue that any remaining gap for blacks must be a result of their own shortcomings; there is a strong tendency among both state and nonstate actors to suggest that the race problem has been solved. As a result, there is little justification for continued reforms, and any challenge to structures of inequality that might have been highlighted during the crisis period transforms into the attribution of blame for inequality to the subordinate group. While the term *"laissez-faire"* is often tied to a particularly capitalist set of assumptions about the operation of the marketplace, my analysis of Cuban racial politics will show that the response of *laissez-faire* racism can be particularly sharp even in a Marxist context. In Cuba, the prevalence of the belief in racial democracy and in Marxist ideology encourages the belief that inequality is a result of the individual incapacities of blacks. These beliefs can act both as impulses to egalitarianism and as ideologies that deny the existence of racism.

The shift in ideology has powerful implications for the mobilization of out-groups. Structures of inequality are no longer powerful and useful symbols that subordinates can rally themselves and allies against. The power of a clear recognition of the problem and of state support is lost, and minority groups must work internally and externally to shift public attention to other, often less obvious sources of inequality. Given the commitment to the now useless symbols, however, this process is quite difficult, and it makes mass mobilization more challenging. The symbolic and real issues that connected members of the group seem diminished, and a shared sense of "linked fate" and group identity wanes. In Cuba after the revolution, the emphasis on Marxism and racial democracy limited Afro-Cubans' sense of a linked fate and worked, along with state repression, to prevent black mobilization.

Racial Ideology and the Case of Cuba

Now we must look at the critical part of the model: racial ideology as it pertains to the study of Cuba. Racial ideology in Cuba has revolved around two central questions: (1) Is race salient in determining life chances? and (2) What is the role for blacks in the Cuban nation? Several theories on these questions have been presented by both political actors and scholars. An examination of the academic discourse about racial ideology reflects both elite opinion and popular ideas.

There are three major theories about racial politics in Cuba: Latin American exceptionalism (also known as "Iberian exceptionalism" and, in one of its forms, "racial democracy"), Marxist exceptionalism, and Black Nationalism. Below, I explore each, discuss their shortcomings and the way they shape racial politics on the island and beyond, and, finally, suggest a fourth alternative, the idea of "inclusionary discrimination," that synthesizes parts of the three perspectives but largely grows out of the historical and empirical case. The synthetic perspective I advance argues that the patterns of racial inclusion and exclusion both exist at the same time. These patterns are created by the circumstances under which blacks were incorporated into the Cuban nation and by the peculiarities of Cuban racial ideology.

The theories I discuss in this chapter are used as analytical tools, yet at the same time they serve as discursive boundaries that help to structure the meaning of race in Cuba. This process can best be understood by viewing race itself not as a given but as a product of social, political, and economic interactions. Here, I explicitly take a racial formation perspective as described by Omi and Winant – that racial divisions are not natural but form out of a collision of social, economic, and political factors. While it is well delineated in the social science literature that race is not a biological construct, it is not altogether clear what race is. It is tempting to suggest that race is a figment of the public imagination that is less real than constructs like class (Fields 1982).[4] Even if it is, however, it has real social, political, and economic consequences.

The tendency to discount the reality of race is heightened by those who combine a constructivist view of race with the ambiguity of racial

---

[4] Barbara Fields, in her article "Ideology and Race in American History," argues that class is a more "real" concept than race. She explains: "Class and race are concepts of a different order; they do not occupy the same analytical space, and thus cannot constitute explanatory alternatives to each other. At its core, class refers to a material circumstance: the inequality of human beings from the standpoint of social power. The reality of class can assert itself independently of people's consciousness. Race, on the other hand, is a purely ideological notion. Once ideology is stripped away, nothing remains except an abstraction which, while meaningful to a statistician, could scarcely have inspired all the mischief that race has caused during its malevolent historical career." I tend to disagree with Fields. The meaning of various measures of class and how we construct categories are equally ideological. Individuals who make between $20,000 per year and $300,000 per year, for example, all consider themselves to be "middle class." Furthermore, individuals' experiences of class are limited by the constructs that are available for understanding class. Race, similarly, involves both lived experience and constructed concepts that have become very real over time.

categorization in Latin America to conclude that race – and by consequence racial categorization – is not salient in Latin America (Loveman 1999; de la Fuente 2001; Bailey 2002). Scholars in this camp deny that race should be used as an analytical or political category (Loveman 1999). We need not end our journey at this point, however. It is possible to understand race as a product of patterned interactions while simultaneously acknowledging the ambiguity and the agency of the concrete object those interactions constitute. Race, despite having no biological significance, can still structure interactions and life chances.

Nancy Stepan (1991) provides a framework that effectively states what race is not and equally effectively builds a useful definition of race for the purpose of social scientific inquiry. Stepan establishes the definition by interrogating the discourses that have created race and how those discourses are enforced and renegotiated over time:

Scientists' many disputes over racial classifications, and the inability to find a classification that would satisfy once and for all the requirement for authoritative ways to divide the human species into fixed types, are powerful indicators that racial categories are not representations of preexisting biological groups transparently understood but distinctions based on complex political-scientific and other kinds of conventions and discriminatory practices. Racial distinctions are not timeless but have constantly been renegotiated and experienced in different ways in different historical periods. We should think, then, of the races that constituted the objects of the movement of race improvement as "artifactual" aspects of human sciences. I take this term to refer to an object of knowledge that is constructed as biological and social "fact" grounded in what is taken to be empirical nature. At the same time, the term indicates that we do not experience human variation or human difference "as it really is, out there in nature," but by and through a system of representations which in essence creates the objects of difference. (13)

Stepan's flexible definition allows us to think of race as a construct that is constantly renegotiated. Central to that negotiation is how the practice of discrimination is either supported or tolerated by the state. Stepan defines an essential function for the state: helping to form the substance of what is commonly understood as race through its mediation of discriminatory practices. Therefore, we can examine each theory about race and politics in Cuba in terms of what role it ascribes to the state in forming race, what the substance of the formation is, and, finally, whether the theory adopts a static or a dynamic view of race. We also must understand, of course, how these racial ideologies interact with critical events and the concerns of the state. Any theory we apply must explain the dynamic changes in the racial order and the persistence of racial inequality despite broad transformations in political economy that theorists believed would relegate race to the dustbin of history.

Thinking in terms of a flexible racial hierarchy and using the concept of what I call "inclusionary discrimination" fulfill these requirements. The concept of a hierarchy allows us to think of racism not as a dichotomous variable but rather as a continuum that changes over time. Thinking in terms of a continuum, furthermore, allows us to avoid the rigid categorization notable in much of the research on race and to explain the dynamic and contradictory changes that occur in any given era. We are able to explore racial hierarchy in the context of ambiguous racial categories and patterns of inclusion and exclusion. We can also understand racial ideology as something that states and other actors can draw upon to suit different purposes at different times. The concept of inclusionary discrimination allows for the idea of racial and ethnic inclusion to exist alongside discriminatory practices. Inclusionary discrimination recognizes that in most cases it is not a question of whether race determines inclusion or exclusion: Race determines the *terms* of inclusion.

In order to understand racial hierarchy and its persistence, it is critical to transcend the tendency to define race in linear and static terms. We must not only acknowledge the episodic nature of the historical events that transform racial politics; we must also understand how these events transform the content of race. It is the flexibility of race, connected with the types of events in which racial politics are formed, that allows race to transpose itself into new sociopolitical structures even in the face of revolutionary social and cultural dynamics. The modularity of racial inequality creates inclusionary discrimination – a vast middle ground in which improvements can occur, but the central hierarchy endures. The idea of a vast middle ground extends to the more complex actions taken in the interest of the state that are a key feature of post-segregation racial politics. By retheorizing the state in nonmonolithic terms, we can explain the persistence of racial hierarchy by exploring the state's competing interests involving race and how these interests work in conjunction with historical events and competing threads of racial ideology.

Western philosophy and concepts of national identity, when not explicitly racist, are silent on racial issues, and they lend credence to the strategies of preserving or building national unity by quickly declaring the problem solved or avoiding the issue of race altogether. Enlightenment discourses and constructions of objectivity, science, nations, democracy, justice, citizenship, and other core concepts cannot be separated from the unequal terms upon which racialized subjects in general, and people of African descent in particular, were included in the project of the construction of modern nation-states. The pretense of "universalism" in Western philosophy, including liberalism and Marxism, seeks at once to naturalize this unequal inclusion and to obscure the practice and ideologies of slavery, racism, violence, and exploitation that have driven the project itself (Gilroy 1987; Hanchard 1994; Mills 1997). These "universal" ideologies provide the legitimizing myths that justify racial hierarchy and deny the histories of racialization that created it. They also connect race and racism, and our assessments of them, to global historical processes that interact with local circumstances and provide for constant comparison across national boundaries. Thus, I will demonstrate that it is important to examine transnational forces and identities and transcend national boundaries in order to explain the persistence of racial hierarchy. More specifically, I argue that racial politics involves inherent comparison to politics elsewhere that conditions responses to racial issues.

Each of the three major schools of thought on race in Cuba has been defined by means of analysis of race in the Cuban situation and by means of the politics of the groups that have supported the model. Thus, we cannot think of the models in isolation; we must examine how they have interacted to form a powerful discursive context that has shaped the "commonsense" understanding of race in Cuba for various discourse communities. These ideas are drawn upon in times of crisis and consolidation, and they form the terrain upon which Cuban racial politics is shaped. They overlap and interact with one another and form a hybrid, hegemonic racial ideal. While analyzing them separately and together can explain much, each separate model fails to explain the vast improvements and stagnation in race relations that have characterized the Cuban Revolution.

Latin American Exceptionalism

It is often said that racial politics in Latin America is somehow "different" from racial politics in the United States. While this position is widely held in scholarly and popular discourse, the more extreme position that Latin American countries are "racial democracies" remains popularly current but has come under assault from scholars in a wide range of fields in recent years. A discourse of difference, however, frequently suggests that racial politics is "better" in Latin America or serves as a caution against developing comparative models of racial politics and racialization. Because of its ongoing impact on racial politics and on the more nuanced scholarly positions that are its progeny, then, it is important to address the argument for Latin American exceptionalism.

The most important feature of arguments for Latin American exceptionalism is that Latin America more closely approximates a racial democracy than does the United States (Freyre 1951; Degler 1971; Harris 1974; Wright 1990; Hanchard 1994). The theory proposes that the history of intermarriage and race mixing in countries like Mexico, Brazil, Colombia, Puerto Rico, and Cuba has created much more fluid societies in which race is a less salient category (Degler 1971; Kronus and Solaun 1973; Wright 1990; Lewis 1992; Hanchard 1994, 1995). The historian Hugh Thomas theorizes a specifically Iberian approach to race that has allowed for more miscegenation and thus a more fluid racial system: "Since race is so much a problem of noticeable physical attributes, the predominantly sallow-skinned Spaniards, with their strong draughts of Moorish and Jewish blood, probably blended more easily, at least with mulattos, than did the pink beige Anglo-Saxons, Celts, Germans and Slavs who constitute the majority in the US" (1998, 1123). Similar arguments have been made about Brazil and Colombia by social scientists like Degler (1971). In these societies, class is often thought to be a much more salient category than race.

The nation that is considered to be the most shining example of a racial democracy is Brazil. Social, political, and economic inequalities in Brazil are often thought to be better explained in terms of class than race. Brazil and the United States are cast at opposite ends of the spectrum, with the United States pursuing segregationist politics in which race is far more salient than class and Brazil representing a racial democracy with deep and lasting class inequality (Degler 1971;

Hanchard 1995; Thomas 1998). Thomas echoes this sentiment in his book *Cuba* when he argues, "It would be correct to assume, no doubt, that as in 1900, racial distinction in the country was still the superficial visible symbol of a distinction which in reality was based on ownership of property" (1120). The Latin American exceptionalist viewpoint implicitly treats racism as a dichotomous variable that either exists or does not. Therefore, any evidence of race mixing or incomplete segregation is taken to be evidence that racism does not exist – as, in fact, a causal explanation for the absence of racism.

The argument for Latin American exceptionalism in Cuba often hangs upon the prevalence of miscegenation and the lack of institutionalized segregation in the post-emancipation period. A Cuban exile stated, for example, "Before Castro, Cuba was entirely bereft of interracial antagonisms" (Montenegro 1993). In both Cuba and Brazil, many popular religious symbols and symbols of beauty and culture contain images of black or mulatto bodies (Hanchard 1995). Proponents of the Latin American exceptionalist school argue that race in Cuba is fundamentally different from race in the United States; this comparison has always been essential. They assert that incidents of racism and discrimination were all but eliminated before the revolution and that there is no reason to believe this process did not continue afterward.

The Latin American exceptionalist account of race in Latin America ranges between two poles. The moderate position can be characterized by authors like Dominguez, who have argued that there was less discrimination in Cuba than in the United States but that the problem existed and has improved in a linear fashion since the revolution. Dominguez maintains that integration was occurring before the revolution and that the revolution helped this process along by means of education and housing policies. He asserts of the period after the revolution, "On balance, there was probably an increase in national integration in Cuba and a reduction in, though not the total elimination of, discrimination against blacks" (1978, 485).

The more extreme view is prevalent among some Cuban exiles. They argue that Castro's discussion of racism is merely the invention of an issue to endear him to the blacks in the country (Montenegro 1993). Montenegro makes an assertion that is a common among exceptionalists of the second type – that talking about race creates the problem where it previously did not exist: "SPEAKING of races always leads to racism. In Cuba there never was a Martin Luther King Jr. because there were no segregated coffee shops, or rest rooms either. For want of a program of betterments for the entire population, Castro has maximized the racial problem in order to pretend that at least the blacks have been redeemed and have regained their lost dignity. He is the most racist ruler that Cuba has endured" (1993). Latin American exceptionalists of this group see the regime as having moved Cuba away from a previously egalitarian position. While their point of view is extreme, even many political moderates in the exile community would argue that race was not a central an issue before the revolution and that it is not now. In contrast, I will argue that the absence of race in exile dialogue often serves to hide racial prejudice or deflect it with discussions of anticommunism. The exile dialogue proposes a "raceless" – but by default white, European-based – Cuban identity in opposition to what exiles see as a divisive recognition of Afro-Cuban identity and experience. The exile community has been noted for being disproportionately white and for its conflicts with African Americans and Haitians (M. C. Garcia 1996; Croucher 1997). I will demonstrate that its racial attitudes in fact limit its credibility on the island as the major political alternative to the Castro regime, partly because the exile community is perceived as seeking to turn back the clock on racial progress in Cuba.

Effective critiques of the Latin American exceptionalist model have been developed. Toward the end of his classic work, Degler (1971) argues that in the post–civil rights era there is greater similarity between the United States and Brazil and, in consequence, less distance between what was thought to be the Latin American model and the U.S. model. Degler argues: "Perhaps the time has now come to recognize that today comparison of race relations in the two countries is not always favorable to Brazil. For one thing, as we have seen in this book, Brazil is not devoid of color prejudice or discrimination. For another, since World War II, race relations and attitudes in the United States have strikingly altered" (268).

Others have used the formerly shining example of Brazil to demonstrate that race mixture does not mean that discrimination cannot and does not exist. Scholars and black activists have shifted the debate about the existence of racial democracy to discuss the implications of the "myth of racial democracy." Hanchard (1994) argues that miscegenation does not prevent discrimination against blacks. He accomplishes this by demonstrating that there is a discourse about both "whitening" and "passing" in Brazil and that family social mobility is achieved by becoming whiter through intermarriage, a move that involves a denigration of blackness and the placing of positive value upon whiteness. Hanchard writes: "The equation of blackness with sloth, deceit, hypersexuality, and waste of all kinds is confirmed by the relative infrequency in which the terms preto or negro (black) are used in daily life. Brazilians reluctantly use these terms to describe friends this way, for fear of insulting them. One person's mulatto is another's negro; yet negro remains a racial category many people do not want ascribed to them" (1995, 181). Both Hanchard and Marx (1998) argue that mulattos in Brazil are not much better off than their black counterparts. A recent book by the sociologist Edward Telles uses public opinion data from Brazil about affirmative action to show that racial politics is not so exceptional in Brazil (2004). Even earlier, Hoetink argued in his 1967 book *Caribbean Race Relations: A Study of Two Variants* that North American scholars frequently tended to conflate mulattos with blacks. When they concluded that mulattos had some level of social mobility, they then incorrectly assumed that blacks shared that mobility.

Peter Wade, in *Race and Ethnicity in Latin America* (1997), discusses how miscegenation and multiple categories have been mishandled by politicians and social scientists and suggests an alternative approach that I will explore at length. "One of the problems" with recent analyses, he argues, "was that increasingly, observers wanted to emphasize that racism did exist in Brazil and elsewhere and highlighting the flexibility of these categories seemed to work against this trend." Wade concludes, "The point in my view is to reach an understanding of how both flexibility and racism co-exist" (68). Miscegenation in the Latin American model does not mean a lack of discrimination, nor does it necessarily improve the life chances of mulattos.[5]

---

[5] The literature on Brazil attempts to explain the lack of black social movements in the country (Degler 1971; Skidmore 1993; Hanchard 1994; Marx 1998). Several works attempt to explain why, despite obvious discrimination, blacks do not identify as blacks in Brazil and have largely failed to form a social movement based on race. Marx argues that this is primarily a result of the peculiar history of racial formation in Brazil. The absence of *de jure* segregation has meant that blacks do not have the basis or rallying

A similar literature has developed specifically on Cuba. Historical works by Aline Helg (1995), Vera Kutzinski (1993), Robin Moore (1997), Alejandro de la Fuente (2001), Tomas Robaina (1990), and Ada Ferrer (1999) all track the historical struggle of Afro-Cubans within the context of the Cuban nation. More contemporary works of social science by Nadine Fernandez (1996), Lourdes Casal (1989), Jorge Domingez (1978), Laurence Glasco (1998), and Alejandro de la Fuente (2001) also focus on inequality in Cuba over the course of the Cuban revolution and in recent years. All of these works interact with the growing literature on racism in Latin America to debunk the myth of Latin American exceptionalism, but they disagree about whether race relations in Latin America were more cordial than in the United States and about whether it is possible theoretically to see the United States and Latin America as similar.

In fact, a new group of scholars – whom we can think of as neo-exceptionalists – recognizes that some level of racial prejudice exists in Latin America but suggests that it is nonsystematic, fluid, and, more to the point, a poor moral or practical basis for social science inquiry or political organization (Loveman 1999; Bailey 2002). These scholars emphasize that the myth of racial democracy creates widespread sentiment against racial prejudice. Thus, they conclude, studying race reifies racial categories and supports racial organizations instead of emphasizing the openness of the societies. De la Fuente places this construction in value terms: "But just as social realities are 'not so pretty,' the Latin American paradigms of racially mixed, integrated nations are not so ugly. The rhetorical exaltation of racial inclusiveness has made racially defined exclusion considerably more difficult, creating in the process significant opportunities for appropriation and manipulation of dominant racial ideologies by those below while limiting the political options of elites" (2001, 8). De la Fuente suggests implicitly that race relations are "better" in Latin America and that black organization is not needed as it was in the United States. This line of argument is consonant with Bourdieu and Wacquant's critique of Hanchard's work, which argues that Hanchard imposes a North

point for racial organization they have found in the United States and South Africa. Hanchard, however, argues that in Brazil in particular, and also more generally, racial categorizations always involve ambivalent racial identities and the ability to produce hegemonic discourses that deny the problem of race.

American frame on Brazil's much more fluid and nonracial politics (1999). Bourdieu and Wacquant maintain, furthermore, that U.S.-based scholars are imposing a North American conception of racial inequality and social organization onto Latin America that is inappropriate because of Latin America's legacy of race mixture. They specifically attack black organizations and affirmative action politics as signs of U.S. imperial thinking.

Bourdieu and Wacquant, however, lapse into the pitfalls of the old Latin American exceptionalism. They fail to take seriously Wade's admonition that flexibility and racism can coexist, and they dismiss black activism and demands for racial equality, which have frequently been violently repressed in Latin America, as a series of disconnected aberrations. They also deny the connections between grassroots politics and the ways in which blacks have consistently drawn from one another's experiences across the diaspora. Their view marginalizes the racialized experiences of blacks and obscures experimentation with Jim Crow and other racist practices in Latin America. It also silences forms of black agency that have challenged the hegemonic denial of racism and racist practices. Bourdieu and Wacquant's argument is related to Latin American scholars' fears about racial organization in Latin America and to concerns on the U.S. side about black organization and the role of whites on the American left in the post–civil rights era. In the 1960s, Hoetink discussed North American scholars' attempt to find a racial paradise in order to resolve problems in the United States: "The North American seems to have a psychic need to hold up to himself the mirror of a society which 'proves' that the relations between Negro and whites can be different. It is a mirror that disguises shortcomings and by its ideal image intensifies the observer's own feelings of guilt. . . . Similarly there is a general tendency in the Latin Caribbean to take over the North American tendency to polarize, not from the feelings of guilt about the racial situation in the United States, but from a feeling of dislike for that country which stems from wholly different causes" (1967, 54).

Thus, reflections on race relations in Latin America and the United States have always been about interactions between the societies as much as they have been about even-handed assessments of racial politics in Latin America. In the case of the post–civil rights era, the mirror of Latin American race relations does not intensify the guilt but provides absolution. For U.S.-based neo-exceptionalists, the model demonstrates the fluidity of race generally and provides a means of arguing against the need for racial organizations, affirmative action, and reparations. For Latin American scholars who subscribe to the neo-exceptionalist view, their belief in some modified form of racial democracy is an expression of nationalism and a commentary on what they see as the need for a retreat from the identity politics of the post–civil rights era United States. Positively contrasting Latin American with U.S. racial politics becomes a means of challenging U.S. hegemony and dominance. For scholars from both places, however, color-blindness becomes the solution to race problems, and a lack of action in the United States in the post–civil rights era is justified by the Latin American example. It is for this reason that I take an explicitly transnational and comparative approach that includes consideration of the effects of color-blind policies as a central part of the analysis.

One can discuss qualitative differences in racial politics, furthermore, without necessarily making judgments of preference. Works by Telles (2004), Wade (1997), and others show that such judgments have often been incorrect when they have used formal segregation (or the lack thereof) and miscegenation as measures of the existence of racism. A growing literature points out that neither of these variables clearly determines the level of racial inequality across social, economic, and political dimensions in any given society. Miscegenation and segregation are considered in a problematic fashion to be both measures of inequality and causes of inequality simultaneously, without serious consideration being given to the nature of racial relationships or to what factors drive the level of racial inequality at any given moment. In order to solve the problem, we must look closely at historical and contemporary circumstances. The race cycles model, when applied to Cuba, provides a comparative general framework that allows us to address the limitations of Latin American exceptionalism.

Proponents of the Latin American exceptionalist model suggest that race has played a relatively minor role in Cuban history. In Chapters 2 and 3, however, I argue that discrimination, racial violence, and racial politics played central roles in Cuban history, in particular in the political struggle for independence. While addressing the limitations of the Latin American exceptionalist model, nevertheless, it is important to note that it has helped to frame debates about race and influenced other schools of thought on the issue (Segal 1995). Castro subscribed to the exceptionalist model of race relations before evolving toward a Marxist point of view later in his career as a revolutionary; the some-times reductionist policies and beliefs about race that characterize the Marxist Castro regime are, perhaps, overdetermined by vestiges of the exceptionalist way of thinking. The exceptionalist view also helped to cast the United States as an enemy of the Cuban Revolution, not only because of its open hostility and imperialist designs on the island but also for its racial politics, which was seen to be in sharp contrast to that in Cuba.

Marxist School

The Marxist school of thought on race relations in Cuba is the most institutionally powerful, though not widely supported by contempo-rary scholars of the racial politics of Cuba. It is based upon a Cuban reading of the Marxist tradition inflected by elements of Cuban cultural history, including the Latin American exceptionalist school of thought and pragmatic policy concerns like the Cold War. It argues that the Cuban Revolution and socialism have wiped away the basis for con-tinued discrimination (C. Moore 1991; Serviat 1993; McGarrity and Cardenas 1995). The Marxist model predicts a linear improvement in race relations based upon the ability of socialism to eliminate the economic basis of racism. Racism, in this approach, is understood to depend upon the existence of class: Once the inputs of economic equal-ity are adjusted, the model predicts, racism will no longer exist. The Marxist view is expressed by Pedro Serviat in his classic work *The Black Problem and Its Definitive Solution* (1993). Serviat argues elo-quently: "Because the ruling classes had vested interests in maintain-ing racial discrimination as a mechanism of competition and division between the black and white worker, and thereby profited more, it is precisely through the expropriation of these classes that the main eco-nomic factor propping up racial or sexual discrimination is eliminated" (90). Serviat, Castro, and others have often accused the United States of importing racism during the period of U.S. influence on the island (Elliot and Dymally 1986; Serviat 1993; Moore 1995; Fuertes 1998).[6]

---

[6] The idea that racism was "imported" from the United States rests on both an anti-colonial mentality and the idea of Latin American exceptionalism. The United States is

They argue that continued racism is incompatible with a socialist system.[7] In the context of Marxist confidence about race relations, the concerns of Afro-Cubans have faded to the background of revolutionary discourse, and the concerns of Chinese Cubans have been made almost invisible. This tendency reflects an interesting irony – that the persistence of racial problems in Cuba is perhaps directly related to the early interest the regime took in "solving" the problems and staking its domestic and international reputation on having done so. The need to declare an early victory over the race question overwhelmed concerns about racial inequality itself.

Cornel West identifies three analytical frameworks within which race relations have been considered in the Marxist tradition (1988). He delineates the three in terms of U.S. history, but they are equally useful when considering Cuba. "The first conception," West argues, "subsumes Afro-American oppression under the general rubric of working-class exploitation. This viewpoint is logocentric in that it elides and eludes the specificity of Afro-American oppression outside of the workplace; it is reductionist in that it explains away rather than explains this specificity" (18). While it may be tempting, considering Serviat's comment, to place the Cuban regime's views in this first category, I argue that Cuban Marxism has more closely mirrored West's second conception of race in the Marxist tradition – one that recognizes the specificity of race but sees the solution in primarily economic terms. West explained: "The second conception of Afro-American oppression in the Marxist tradition acknowledges the specificity of Afro-American oppression beyond general working-class exploitation, yet it defines this specificity in economistic terms. This conception is anti-reductionist in character yet economistic in content. This viewpoint holds that African people in the United States of America are subjected to general working-class exploitation owing to racial-discrimination

seen as having been the cause of racial antagonism as a colonial power in a society that was fundamentally different from that of the United States. I prefer to take a middle road with regard to this issue. In Chapter 2, I will demonstrate that racism in Cuba resulted from a mixture of internal processes and U.S. influence.

7 This does not mean the racial attitudes have been completely wiped away. Supporters of this point of view argue that it is impossible to change completely the hearts and minds of individuals but that it is possible to change the institutions that support racial prejudice. In this study, however, I hope to show that the regime has had successes and failures in both areas.

at the workplace" (19). We can apply this logic to the case of Cuba to explain the Castro regime's commitment to both workplace access (eliminating formal discrimination in hiring, unions, and access to education) and ending segregation in social spheres (shutting down private clubs, professional organizations, and schools that were sites of discrimination).

The regime has had a tendency to conflate formal racial segregation with racism itself, ignoring the myriad other potential problems that race poses. The regime and Cubans more generally note that personal racism is still a problem in Cuba but argue that it is not "institutional," meaning that because there are no legal or formal barriers, racist attitudes have no real impact on the society as whole. This argument defines the needed transformation in racial attitudes as an issue of individual consciousness rather than as a problem to be taken on by the state. In this formulation, the state's work was completed with the implementation of socialism, which is expected to help change consciousness or to render racist attitudes ineffective. There is no continued analysis of the separate life of race or of the possibility that individual and unexpressed racist attitudes affect social outcomes. Afro-Cubans are blamed for their deficiencies and for not taking advantage of the new freedoms and opportunities the revolution has provided.

A group of Cuban scholars attempting to revive concern for racial issues has been forced to operate within the constraints of the Marxist paradigm. Their work has outlined the ways in which racial prejudice is reproduced in the family and other organs of civil society by means of stereotypes, but they have built their analyses on the assumption that the revolution has made institutions free of discrimination (Hernández 1998; Peralta 1998; Ramos 1998; Pérez 1999, *América Negra*). It is my intent not to attack Cuban scholars working under these constraints but rather to demonstrate that even when there is renewed interest in race, the analysis of racial inequality is limited to nonstate spheres and to the realm of attitudes and stereotypes.

Castro has adopted a generally paternalistic tone toward Afro-Cuba, positing racial equality as a gift granted by the revolution rather than a goal to be attained through a process of constant vigilance and empowerment (C. Moore 1991). Despite the positive moves the regime has made toward eliminating racism in the workplace and social segregation, it has failed to engage Afro-Cuba in debate about how its particular concerns and needs could be met in the context of the revolution.[8] While there is recognition of some racist attitudes and episodic discrimination in Cuba, there is little exploration of how these factors affect Afro-Cuban life chances or conceptions of a unified Cuban nation. When attempting to define the nation, the Castro regime has often denied the specificity of the Afro-Cuban and Sino-Cuban experiences and ignored their implications for the construction of a unified national identity.

Black Nationalism

The Black Nationalist school of thought has been the most poignant, though marginal, source of critique of the Castro regime's record on race relations. The Black Nationalist point of view has argued that Cuban society was fundamentally racist before the revolution and that it remains so today. The theory is most prominent among a group of black middle-class intellectuals and activists who became frustrated with their inability to integrate into the revolutionary regime. Black Nationalists see race – to the exclusion of other categories like class – as the primary force in the history of the development of the Americas (Dawson 2001). In their eyes, the Cuban regime failed to promote Afro-Cuban leadership and culture.

There has been a tendency to think of Black Nationalism solely within the context of U.S. race relations, but the basic ideological components of Black Nationalism followed from negritude in the 1920s and the black consciousness movements in the 1960s, and it is problematic to place their origins or expressions entirely within the United States. Both the negritude and black consciousness movements, while finding strong expression within the United States, were international in nature and were based upon personal networks and conscious

---

[8] While I focus on the Afro-Cuban community, I do not want to ignore the existence of the Chinese community, particularly in Havana. The revolution's policy toward the Chinese market culture, however, essentially obliterated their community. The Chinese have for the most part intermarried with Afro-Cubans, and little remains of El Barrio Chino (Chinatown) in Havana. There have been recent promising attempts to revive the culture and history of the Chinese in Cuba that are a part of the warming relationship between the People's Republic of China and Cuban officials. Of late, El Barrio Chino, like many aspects of Afro-Cuban culture, has become a prime tourist attraction.

attempts to form a conception of blackness that transcended national boundaries and considered Africa and the diaspora to share a common, interconnected set of struggles (Gilroy 1994). That is not to say that there have not been distinct movements in different countries, but rather to emphasize that these movements draw from a common discursive and symbolic toolbox and look to one another for ideas, inspiration, and symbols. In the case of Cuba, Carlos Moore is the most prominent Black Nationalist voice. His book *Castro, the Blacks and Africa* (1991) documents, in his opinion, how the regime has systematically attacked black leadership on the island, suppressed black culture, and failed to eradicate discrimination. The book is one of the most revealing accounts of the impact of the revolution on Afro-Cubans and is largely told through the eyes and experiences of its author. Moore writes: "Cuban society was profoundly racist prior to 1959 and remained steadfastly so after. All of the basic racist assumptions which cut across class lines continued to govern the everyday life of blacks and whites, despite the Revolution or on account of it, since under its protective cover most of the old and new racial attitudes and assumptions are perpetuated by Cubans of all walks of life in their daily lives" (1995, 210).

According to the Black Nationalists, then, little has changed in Cuba, and the current regime has used a rhetoric of racial egalitarianism but has not matched it with action. Much of the nationalists' criticism is directed at Fidel Castro, whom Moore attacks: "One of the most important things to Castro in his quest for power was to reassure Cuba's upper and middle classes that he shared their cultural and ideological prejudices" (1991, 7). Castro did this, Moore argues, before he announced his Marxist intention and began to address issues of race directly in the early days of the revolution. Black activists like Carlos Moore, Walterio Carbonell (1961), and Juan Bentacourt (1961) initially supported the Castro regime and hoped it would be a positive change from the previous regime (Rout 1976). Their hopes were dashed, however, as Castro – in their opinion – gave a few prominent blacks positions but failed to consistently engage their demands for greater power and leadership.

Moore concludes that Castro, like other leaders, merely used the language of racial equality and reconciliation to hide his own racist and paternalistic beliefs and to avoid dealing with the issue of black self-determination. In this sense, Castro's image of himself as a *caudillo* (leader) fit with black passivism and a tradition of white paternalism. Moore writes: "Politically, this situation translates itself in the de facto belief that whites have the right to rule and blacks have the duty to obey. Socially, whites also arrogate the prerogative of assigning blacks 'a place' in society: neither separate and equal, nor together and equal" (210). In Moore's words, the attitude of whites in the current regime is, "You people had it rough before the Revolution but you're living it up now. So what more do you want?" (211). Black Nationalists feel that the regime has continued to rob blacks of opportunities for greater power and self-determination.

Beyond these claims, the Black Nationalists have often charged the regime with racism. They argue that little progress has been made in economic and political spheres for blacks. Black Nationalists see race as a dichotomous variable; to them, the existence of any racial inequality is proof that little has changed. They suggest that the regime has used relationships with black activists in the United States and Africa to hide its racism at home. They cite continued inequality in housing, education, income, and employment between whites and blacks as examples of the racist nature of the regime. They also attack the regime's efforts to eliminate black opposition and its frequently negative view of black culture. Moore argues: "Since 1959 Cuba has been experiencing a process aimed at the imposition of a new supposedly 'non-racial' outlook. The major problem is that the revolutionary regime has endeavored to arrive at a common 'non-racial' and 'universal' outlook by attempting to stamp out the black one." Moore lists as evidence "assaults on the Afro-Cuban religions; abolition of the Afro-Cuban mutual aid Sociedad de Color: persecution of the secret male brotherhood, or Sociedad Abakua; [an] unofficial offensive against Afro-Cuban language patterns"; and "attempts to discredit the African religious outlook as 'primitive,' 'irrational' and 'superstitious'" (218). Moore concludes: "The 'new' outlook proposed to all Cubans as 'non-racial' and 'universalist' was in fact distinctly European. Marxism, imposed as the 'national' ideology, was the most accomplished version of the Western rationalist tradition. And the promoted opera and ballet forms had no more 'proletarian' qualities than Marxism itself (an ideological whim of the alienated, atheistic, intellectual petit-bourgeoisie of the Old Continent)" (219).

The Black Nationalists' reading of racial politics in Cuba is a very static perspective. According to Black Nationalists, attempts to incorporate blacks are only bad-faith efforts to confuse the black populace, and the black population is the victim of both coercion and false consciousness in its continued support of the regime. The Black Nationalist model, like the Latin American and Marxist models, is perhaps too static and linear to capture the complex reality of race in Cuba, but it provides an important critique upon which to build a more nuanced perspective. While Black Nationalists illuminate many ongoing problems and the blindness of the regime to issues of race, they fail to address theoretically the complexity of effecting improvement in conditions for Afro-Cuba – the power of racial inequality and the extreme difficulty for any regime of accomplishing the daunting task of undoing more than 300 years of history. The Black Nationalist point of view also fails to take into account the ideological, strategic, and material constraints that are a result of Cuba's geopolitical position; it discounts the role that a powerful enemy like the United States has played in placing constraints on the regime. In the context of the improvements in health, employment, education, and participation in government that have been effected under the current regime, the Black Nationalists' wholesale critique is unconvincing. The concept of a transhistorical racism, furthermore, fails to account for changes in the fabric of Cuban race relations, including changes in the material conditions of Afro-Cubans and in the texture of racial discourse. Although unequal, the incorporation of blacks into the common national identity and culture has been a critical part of the revolution and has had decidedly positive effects.

Racial Hierarchy: Charting the Vast Middle Ground

As I have already noted, a growing literature unearths the frequently denied existence of racial hierarchy and racism in Latin America in general and in Cuba in particular. This literature illuminates how each of the three major modes of thought falls short of adequately explaining racial politics in post-revolutionary Cuba. So how do we understand racism in a society that has fluid racial boundaries and no overt racial segregation, but nevertheless maintains other forms of formal and informal "racial regulation"?[9] The race cycles model, combined with the concept of inclusionary discrimination, represents an interesting antidote to the limitations of other perspectives and develops a language to capture the nuances of racial ideology in societies with inequality but no formal segregation. Together, these two concepts allow us to better understand the uneven and often contradictory influences on Cuban racial politics and how they have produced moments of transformation, but more often stagnation.

The sociologist Edward Telles notes: "Contemporary analysts of Brazilian race relations seem to have discarded the possibility that race mixture and exclusion can coexist. If white Brazilians are so racist, then why would they mix with nonwhites? Current scholars emphasize exclusion; past scholars emphasized race mixture. These two generations of scholars accepted either racial exclusion or inclusion as truth while ignoring or discrediting the other. Rather than considering the possibility that both racial inclusion and exclusion may coexist, the current generation of scholars has treated that possibility as the confusion of reality with popular beliefs" (2004, 14). Telles's comment calls us to embrace the contingency of race itself as a construct and the fact that the relationships between the state, citizens, and race are frequently fuzzy, uncertain, and contradictory. The race cycles approach allows us to explain how dialogues of inclusion can exist at the same time as overtly racist practices and ideologies. It also enables us to see how racial improvement can exist at the same time as reassertions of racist dialogues and practices. This is not to say that we can never develop a unified understanding of racial politics but rather that what we arrive at must account for the existence of simultaneous and frequently contradictory forces and limitations. Again, what we are after is not to understand inclusion or exclusion in a dichotomous sense but to comprehend the unequal terms of inclusion and the ideological and structural circumstances that condition them. This project calls for a view of race as a product of ambiguity and malleability.

---

[9] By "racial regulation," I mean a set of circumstances, norms, and rules, both formal and informal, that reinforce and maintain the existing racial order.

2

Freedom and Discrimination

Uneven Inequality and Inclusion in Pre-Revolutionary Cuba

In order to understand racial politics in post-revolutionary Cuba, we must first understand the set of concerns, interests, fears, anxieties, and problems that surrounded the intertwined processes of the emancipation of people of African descent from the institution of slavery, the struggle for an independent Cuba, and the development of concepts of Cuban citizenship. The bloody transition to independence from Spain and the development of a Cuban nation created a crisis that Afro-Cubans took advantage of by fighting for their freedom. They won emancipation and a measure of formal equality. Later, however, the state consolidated under a Creole elite, using extreme violence to deter Afro-Cubans from pushing for greater equality. While some of the revolutionary gains were lost in this period of consolidation, others were institutionalized. Racial exclusion morphed into a form of discrimination: Cuba maintained a public veneer of racial democracy while Afro-Cubans were denied access to important private organizations, schools, and professional organizations. The pattern of informal discrimination and formal inclusion became an essential part of the trajectory of Cuban racial politics.

Early on in the struggle for independence, the white elites' competing objectives of enlisting the help of blacks in the fight against Spanish colonialism and preventing them from dominating the island influenced both domestic and international discourse about Cuban independence (Dominguez 1978; McGarrity and Cardenas 1995; Helg 1995;

Ferrer 1999; Pérez 1999). Later, after the defeat of Spain, the question of what character Cuba would have as a nation became a major dilemma in Cuban life. Cuban elites were concerned about preserving their relationship with the United States and Spain and were loath to emphasize and embrace a Creole identity that would have drawn heavily on the culture of former slaves and immigrants from Haiti and Jamaica (Dominguez 1978; McGarrity and Cardenas 1995; Pérez 1999). Thus, black immigration and political parties were officially banned. In some parts of the country, Cuban elites even experimented with U.S.-style Jim Crow segregation. The national debate, it is important to note, was never about whether to include blacks in or exclude them from the Cuban nation but rather about the terms on which they would be included.

In response, blacks in Cuba sought to make claims to citizenship and equality while insulating themselves from potential racial violence. Their task included figuring out to what degree they could draw on the Pan-Africanist ideas of black leaders in the United States, the Caribbean, South America, and Africa. Attempting to assert their identity, they forged transnational alliances among artists and intellectuals. Afro-Cubans have always been powerful agents of political, economic, and social change on the island; this agency is often cited as evidence of a color-blind Cuban national identity. But a close look at the historical record reveals that Afro-Cubans' political, economic, and social involvement has been motivated by their quest for citizenship and racial justice, and that same historical period demonstrates that many white elites sought to thwart Afro-Cubans' participation, identity formation, and assertion of claims in profound and often violent ways.

The history of race in Cuba prior to the revolution debunks the myth that race was somehow less salient in Cuba than elsewhere in the world and helps us to understand the interaction between race and the development of the Cuban nation. This chapter discusses the impact of three moments of state crisis on racial politics in Cuba during the period leading up to the revolution in 1959: the Ten Years' War (1868–77), La Guerra Chiquita (1879), and the War of Independence (1895). It will also analyze the origins and influence of the massacre of 1912, a moment of state consolidation, and its relationship to the development of Pan-Africanism in Cuba.

Race and Politics Before the Revolution

In the past century, Cuban politics has frequently been preoccupied with the "race question" (Sarduy and Stubbs 1993). The race question can best be defined as the attempt, usually by whites of various political affiliations, to ascribe the role that Cubans of African descent and their culture will play in a Cuban nation. In these discussions, whites have considered whether any restrictions should be placed on the citizenship rights of Afro-Cubans (Helg 1995, 1990; McGarrity and Cardenas 1995; Ferrer 1999; Pérez 1999). These debates, however, have not occurred without significant input from the Afro-Cuban population. Blacks have discussed the prudence of seeking self-determination or subsuming racial identity and claims to racial justice in movements based on class consciousness and communist or nationalist ideals (Serviat 1985; Robaina 1990; C. Moore 1991).

The race question has been complicated by the willingness of Cubans of African descent to participate in struggles for national liberation. Aline Helg explains: "A second characteristic that makes Cuba particularly interesting in the context of the hemisphere is its high level of voluntary military participation by blacks in nationalist wars. The association of Cuba's independence struggle first with abolition and later with social reform gave Afro-Cubans a rare opportunity to fight for their own cause" (1995, 4). Afro-Cubans' military mobilization, however, did not always prevent the victory of the forces that sought to limit their citizenship rights (Jimenez 1993; Sarduy and Stubbs 1993; Serviat 1993).

Blacks used the long struggle for independence to advance the cause of emancipation. In the meantime, white elites on all sides of the national issue became concerned about what would become of free blacks and how they would be classified. Anthony Marx demonstrates that the issue of race played a central role in the process of nation building in the United States, Brazil, and South Africa; in each country, race influenced coalition building and conflicts among white elites (1998). Marx argues that divisions among white elites in South Africa and the United States at the moment of nation building led to the creation of racially exclusionary systems. Though it experimented with segregation after independence, Cuba settled on a flexible system of racial categorization that was more similar to that of Brazil than to

those of the United States and South Africa. This happened despite
the fact that in Cuba there was a strong division among white elites,
much as there was in the United States and South Africa (Helg 1995).
Thus, Cuba defies Marx's model of race and nation building. In Cuba,
the role of blacks in fighting for Cuban independence and the development of Cuban racial ideology were as important as the conflicts
among whites in shaping Cuba's racial legacy. The race cycles model
allows us to extend Marx's analysis by discussing state consolidation,
its relationship to the events that preceded it, and their influence on the
texture and character of Cuban racial politics.

The race question became central during the first fight against
Spanish colonialism, the failed Guerra de los Diez Años (Ten Years'
War, 1868–77). Blacks took up the cause of fighting against Spain
in order to free their enslaved brethren and to ensure their rights in
a new Cuban nation (Helg 1995; Ferrer 1999; Pérez 1999). Their
participation led to a gradual emancipation that concluded after the
war with the absolute abolition of slavery by the Spanish crown in
1886. Afro-Cubans also played major roles in the later wars for Cuban
independence – La Guerra Chiquita (the Small War, 1879) and what we
now call the Spanish-American War (1895–98) (Helg 1995; McGarrity
and Cardenas 1995; Ferrer 1999; Pérez 1999). Blacks constituted
more than 70 percent of the armies that fought these wars, but their
participation was greeted with substantial ambivalence (Helg 1995;
Ferrer 1999). White elites used the Afro-Cuban soldiers and leaders
to advance their cause against Spain, but they were very concerned
about the impact of militant freedmen on Cuban society (Helg 1995;
McGarrity and Cardenas 1995; Ferrer 1999; Pérez 1999).

The "black problem" was intertwined with the call for Cuban independence. General Antonio Maceo, an Afro-Cuban, fought with José
Martí for Cuban independence from Spain. Maceo's comrades and
enemies alike, however, feared him for his popularity and his potential to arouse discontent and to overthrow white domination in the
future. The Cuban agrarian elite that opposed Spanish rule felt that
Cuba was "better Spanish than African" (Jimenez 1993, 40). L. Pérez
notes of this critical juncture: "The image of savage spirits loomed
large in the Creole imagination throughout the nineteenth century,
always in the form of slave uprisings and race war. The dismantling
of slave structures occurred concurrently with the assembling of the

minions of nationality and the two developments were not unrelated. The subtext of nation had, in fact, become very much a narrative about race relations, and increasingly it was impossible to contemplate discarding colonial structure without first putting to rest the specter of race conflict that had long united defenders of Spanish rule and divided supporters of Cuban independence" (1999, 90). Many who supported Cuban nationalism were more concerned with maintaining the racial order than they were with securing freedom from Spain.

This ordering of priorities can be seen in the comments of José Martí, the intellectual and spiritual leader of Cuban nationalism whose legacy is claimed by Cubans across the political spectrum. Martí reached out to blacks in general and to heroes of the Ten Years' War like Antonio Maceo in particular with the goal of uniting blacks and whites under a single Cuban identity. Meanwhile, a rhetorical sleight-of-hand that prefigured the Castro regime and the post-segregation United States was employed to put limits on black claims in the new Cuba. As Pérez aptly states, "Blacks could be admitted into the formulation of nation on terms of equality as defined by whites" (91). For Martí, these terms included a rebuke of any Black Nationalist tendencies. "The black man who proclaims his race, even if incorrectly as a way to proclaim spiritual identity with all races, justifies and provokes white racism," he said (quoted in Pérez 1999, 91). Attempts to suppress discussions of race and racial identity created the conditions for blacks to be seen as junior partners in the Cuban nation; they also allowed conservative elites who were concerned about black power to justify their turn to the United States as a way of protecting their interests from blacks. Martí's ideology was a critical part of the consolidation phase that followed independence. It allowed blacks to be "equal" parts of the nation as long as they agreed not to assert their racial identity. Pérez explains, however, that social structures remained racist, and in this context, racism and racial hierarchy were embedded within the concept of Cuban identity: "Cuba could not, under these circumstances, but default to racial categories, organized around assumptions of racial hierarchies in which white assumed a racelessness as it enjoyed a privilege of whiteness, while Cubans of color were obliged to obtain 'equality'" (91). De la Fuente makes a similar point: "National unity was to be achieved at the expense of racial identities, so the colonial discourse which stressed the incompatability of race and nation was somehow respected, although reconstructed and given a wholly different, inclusionary meaning. Afro-Cubans would have to choose between being black, in which case they served the colonialist purpose of portraying the nation as an impossibly, racially irreconcilable entity, or being Cuban, members of an allegedly raceless nationalist force. Any possibility for blacks to voice their specific grievances and discontent was therefore explicitly rejected as un-Cuban and unpatriotic" (1998, 44). It is important to note that whites were not asked to make the same choice. They were able to use discourses of "whitening" to maintain a veneer of black incorporation and their own sense of white identity. Afro-Cubans, they hoped, would disappear through whitening in the new Cuba and would be genetically and culturally incorporated into a white and modern nation (Helg 1990).

Spain and the United States exploited fears of black insurrection in order to attempt to weaken the independence movement. In response, obscuring racial differences became a method of presenting a unified Cuban front to both Spain and the United States. As Aline Helg delineates, these attempts had broad effects: They diffused the idea that blacks had been liberated by their own masters during the Ten Years' War; eliminated any idea that blacks should be compensated for mistreatment, suggesting rather that they should be grateful to whites; and promoted the idea that racial equality had been achieved in the Cuban military, thus denying black claims for proportional rewards based on participation (1995).

The myth of racial equality sought to hinder the development of a black consciousness and black demands. Blacks who did not buy into the myth of racial equality were attacked as ungrateful, dangerous, against the cause of national freedom and unity, and worthy of societal repression (Pérez 1999). Later, we will see how white Cubans responded with violence to Afro-Cubans who sought to articulate claims based upon race. The practice of repressing black demands while paying lip service to racial democracy and national unity, which later became a key feature of the Cuban Revolution's response to race, borrowed both pragmatically and ideologically from the discourse of the early days of the Cuban nation. Fear of black insurgency has been a constant feature of Cuban politics and a key *raison d'être* for consolidation for more than a century.

The Cuban independence movement was very conscious of the fear of black insurgency and its power to turn the white Cubans against the movement. Martí's statements reinforced the idea that blacks would behave themselves and subject themselves to white paternalism. This ethos was not limited to rhetoric; it also influenced how Antonio Maceo represented himself as a military leader. Far from being heroes among white civilians, Antonio and his brother José were mistrusted by the elected president of the civilian government, Salvador Cisneros, a white Cuban with ties to the aristocracy. Cisneros attacked the Maceo brothers and their troops, labeling them black racists, and suggested that they sought to grab power for themselves. He moved to remove black officers from their commands, which ultimately led to José Maceo's resignation and his death in a skirmish.

Until the white-led civilian authority became involved, promotions in the military had been made on merit alone. Afterward, civilians were required to approve all promotions. As a result, whites set guidelines that privileged whites with better educations and network connections, harming morale among black soldiers. The attacks on Antonio Maceo continued as he won victories and marched from the black-dominated east (Oriente) to the more urban and white western part of the island. Cisneros said: "[Maceo] considers himself as the unique chief, not only of Oriente but perhaps of all Cuba. Oh human miseries and ambitions!" (quoted in Helg 1995, 74). Maceo responded that his only demand was that his rewards and the rewards of his men be in line with their achievements. Colonel Enrique Fournier, an educated Afro-Cuban, was more strident and cynical even early in the war. He said, "The race of color, which is the nerve of this war, is going to sacrifice itself so that white Cubans [can] continue to exploit their superiority [over blacks]" (quoted in Helg 1990, 59). His words would prove prophetic, but the myths that the war had erased racial distinctions and been a boon for Afro-Cubans nevertheless gained currency.

In the wake of the Spanish-American War, the United States usurped the Cuban independence movement. Like their Cuban counterparts, leaders from the United States watched the rise of Antonio Maceo with consternation. When Maceo was killed in a minor skirmish after being ordered into dangerous territory and deprived of needed reinforcements by Cisneros (Helg 1995), *Harper's Weekly* felt "assured that the death of Maceo was favorable to the revolution because it averted the danger of a race war" (quoted in Franco 1993, 51). The black press in the United States, while initially supportive of U.S. intervention, soon saw the U.S. role as one of promoting segregation on the island (Hellwig 1998). This opinion was confirmed when the presence of U.S. troops on the island was followed by demands for segregation in both military and private accommodations (Serviat 1985).

Race and Repression: Consolidating and Creating the Cuban Nation

The period immediately after the War of Independence is known as the Republican period. Key features of Cuban white and black racial ideology and attitudes formed during this period. The Constitution of 1901 hinted at what Cuban racial politics would come to resemble. Reflecting elite resignation to the participation of Afro-Cubans in the polity, it granted equality to all males but did not officially mention race or ethnicity and did nothing to help the now-freed slaves. At the same time, specific policies were adopted to limit the "negative impact" of Afro-Cubans on Cuban society. The United States helped to impose an immigration law in 1902 that made immigration to Cuba by blacks and Chinese people illegal and encouraged European immigration, especially from Spain. This law, aimed specifically at Haitian and Jamaican migrants, was expanded and strengthened in 1906 (de la Fuente 2001). It was loosely enforced, however.

A movement to reduce the growth of the Afro-Cuban population and to use intermarriage to assimilate Afro-Cubans into a broader Cuban identity was supported by prominent social scientists. Francisco Figueras, who studied ethnicity, race, psychology, and culture, argued, "A race vegetating in childhood, the Africans brought to Cuba musical sense, exhibitionism, and lasciviousness, and their lack of foresight" (quoted in Helg 1990, 48). Figueras did save some criticism for the Spanish concerning their treatment of women, and he argued that slavery and the Spanish educational system had prevented Cuba from becoming modern, or, to define what he meant more specifically, from achieving modern capitalist development (Helg 1990). He suggested that Cuban society could be saved only by means of intermarriage and closer connection with the United States.

While Figueras is a minor (though important) figure in Cuban history, Fernando Ortiz looms much larger. His credentials as a racial liberal have made him an important historical figure in the story of blacks, whites, and the Cuban Revolution. The story of Ortiz's early work, however, is much more complex. In the early part of the twentieth century, Ortiz made the "progressive" argument for a largely social constructivist view of race (Helg 1990). What separated the races, he argued, was their culture. In Ortiz's view, all could reach the Anglo-Saxon ideal of civilization even though Africans began their quest at a point much further away from civilization than white Cubans did. Helg's paraphrase of Ortiz sounds like a modern U.S. comment on black cultural pathology: "[Afro-Cubas] were lascivious lovers, given to polygamy, and had no cohesive families; their religion led them to human sacrifice, anthropophagy and the most brutal superstitions" (52). For Ortiz, this general account of black primitivism explained black and white criminality in Cuba: Criminality was a result of the primitive African, who was altogether incapable of moral discernment, as Afro-Cuban culture involved witchcraft, music, dancing, and superstition. Moral rather than structural factors explained the gaps in opportunity; Ortiz wrote, "Today Cuban society psychically evolves in an imperceptible graduation from whites, who is placed by his talents at the level of the refined civilized man, to be the African black who, sent back to his native country, would resume his libations in the open skull of an enemy" (quoted in Helg 1990, 52). Importantly, however, Ortiz saw culture as mutable and held that over time blacks would fully become a part of the Cuban nation.

Segregation was primarily enforced through private institutions that managed schools, beaches, and parks. Professional organizations also racially policed membership. The largely Afro-Cuban revolutionary army was disbanded and replaced with a Creole-led army. Blacks were not nominated to national office. In response to such marginalizing policies, blacks developed their own organizations, and many who had supported the ideal of color-blindness began to favor the development of black organizations and mutual aid societies in order to protect the race and advance their cause. Rafael Serra, a companion of Martí's in New York, argued that the new integrated Cuba needed black organizations in order to move toward equality and worked to make them a reality (de la Fuente 2001).

Others took a more radical approach. Evaristo Estenoz decided to create an Afro-Cuban political party that advocated free education, state control of private schools, abolition of the death penalty, reform of the criminal justice system, and an end to the ban on nonwhite immigration. The organization was called the Partido Independiente de Color, and it was immediately attacked by the white establishment, which called it racist. Estenoz's attempt to hold open the space created by the wars of independence and to mobilize the black population toward equality ran square into the ideological and coercive forces of consolidation, as the state moved to repress blacks who had stepped outside of accepted boundaries of political activity. Ironically, both major parties of the time sought and depended upon black votes. In order to eliminate the competition, 200 leaders and members of the new party – which had 60,000 members by 1910 – were arrested. An electoral amendment, the Morúa law, that made black political parties illegal was used to justify the arrests (Helg 1995). Eventually, the party leaders were released, but their movement aroused widespread fears, and rumors about the rape of white women and black insurgency soon crisscrossed the island.

In 1912, the Partido Independiente de Color launched mass protests in the Oriente (eastern) Province, where there was (and is) the highest concentration of blacks and where there had been substantial losses of land. The protests violated the ideal that Cubans were all of one race, and the state used this ideal to justify brutal repression against what it depicted as black racists intent upon destroying the Cuban nation. With the support of the United States – and with the suggestion that the United States would intervene if the Cubans were not swift and brutal – the Cuban government brutally repressed the protests. The repression involved the police as well as white citizens who organized into militias in order to attack blacks and protect themselves (Helg 1995). More than 4,000 Afro-Cubans were killed by organized militias, while the Cuban and U.S. press announced that black attempts to upset law and order and rape white women had been averted (Helg 1995; McGarrity and Cardenas 1995). The black press across the United States condemned what it saw as the U.S. role in promoting segregation and racial violence on the island (Hellwig 1998). Some elements of the white Cuban press applauded the massacre, and some even urged the development of a secret militia like the Ku Klux Klan to maintain order and to terrorize black leaders. Other white leaders were upset at what they saw as a North Americanization of Cuban race relations. Black

Cuban leaders of the time were divided in their response, as well (Helg 1995). A black congressman, Martín Morúa Delgado, after whom the law that banned black political parties had been named, signed a declaration proclaiming that there was no racial discrimination in Cuba. Still others sought to organize along an integrationist line and maintain Afro-Cuban culture in the face of continued repression. Lynchings became more frequent as moral panic took over regarding black "witches," a fear that was based upon the work of Ortiz. Some Cuban newspapers applauded the lynchings as a progressive manifestation of North Americanization (Helg 1995). Racial violence was equally applauded, reviled, and denied.

Lourdes Casal, a respected Cuban scholar, wrote vividly of her family's recollection of the violence that occurred in 1912: "As a young Black Cuban, many things puzzled me about the complicated set of rules governing relations between the races in my country, particularly about the codes which regulated communications on race relations. I still remember how I listened, wide-eyed and nauseated, to the stories – always whispered, always told as when one is revealing unspeakable secrets – about the horrors committed against my family and other blacks during the racial war of 1912. A grand-uncle of mine was assassinated, supposedly by orders of Monteagudo, the rural guard officer who terrorized blacks throughout the island" (1989, 472). Casal discusses how the genocide in 1912 has been wiped from history but nevertheless continues to inform the political outlook and identity of Afro-Cubans: "The stories terrified me, not only because of their violence, but because my history books said nothing about these incidents. The racial war of 1912, in which thousands of blacks lost their lives, was, at best, a line or a footnote in the books" (472).

In order to maintain the myth of racial democracy, the fact of the brutal oppression – even while its impact lingered and remained in the collective memory of blacks – was denied. Eventually, the repression relaxed, and, culminating in 1927, restrictions against Haitian and Jamaican immigrants were eased as the Cuban economy transformed. Fears of a race war were soon sounded again as immigration accelerated, but the need for fresh labor took precedence. "Progressive" white elites like Ortiz hoped that the Cubans of African descent would be civilized, and most resigned themselves to a biracial Cuba. A powerful message had been sent, however: Racial movements would be brutally repressed. As a result, Afro-Cubans joined labor and other reformers responding to repressive and corrupt regimes supported by the United States (Franco 1993). The powerful and silencing attack that had been made on an independent black political voice made it much easier to claim there was no race problem in Cuba, and during the period after the massacre, it became official state doctrine that racial discrimination did not exist in Cuba. Thus, following the War of Independence, the state, aided by violence from regular citizens, the imposition of racist ideology, and the myth of racial democracy, managed to consolidate around an order that marginalized Afro-Cubans and blunted the possibility of equality.

The Development of Pan-African Sensibilities

In the decades before the revolution, Afro-Cubans and African Americans often found common cause in their responses to segregation and their negative relationships with whites and the U.S. government (Brock 1998). Black athletes, artists, journalists, and political activists began to reach across the ninety-mile divide. The friendship, collaboration, and mutual admiration of Nicolas Guillen and Langston Hughes, leading black poets of Cuba and the United States, respectively, demonstrate the perceived common interest between the two communities. Guillen's use of metaphors from the U.S. South in his poetry drew a connection between the anticolonial struggle in Cuba and the struggle against racism in the United States and Cuba, while Hughes's experiences in Cuba nurtured his belief in an authentic black cultural voice that transcended the limitations of segregation and represented a valuable cultural and social tradition (Ellis 1998). Journalists within the United States and Cuba drew upon one another's experiences to articulate key parallels in issues of gender and race. The Cuban women's magazine *Minerva*, for example, included articles on forging a black womanhood in the context of racial oppression in the United States and Cuba (Arrechea 1998).

These contacts, however, contained a certain amount of ambivalence. Both Marcus Garvey and the African Methodist Episcopal (AME) Church ultimately failed to win broad support in Cuba. The AME Church failed in its missionary efforts to recognize the salience of African-based religious practices for Afro-Cubans (Dodson 1998),

while the famous Black Nationalist Marcus Garvey was unable to convince a broad base of Afro-Cubans that they would be better off pursuing an overt separatist agenda that would have fused them organi-
zationally with Garveyites in the United States and Africa (Robaina
1998). His failure was due in part to the massacre of 1912 and
the Morúa law. The ambivalent relationships between citizens of the
United States and Cuba reflected central aspects of black diaspora politics as well as the precarious political position of Afro-Cubans. Their
legacy would be important in the post-revolutionary period.

Conclusion

The process of moving toward independence created openings for Afro-
Cubans, and the Afro-Cuban population claimed its freedom from slavery by fighting for Cuban independence. Following the regime change
and the creation of the new Cuban state, however, a conscious attempt
was made to consolidate the new regime and to limit Afro-Cuban influence. This attempt involved both the use of the ideology of racial
democracy and the spread of racist ideas like whitening. Racial violence, furthermore, was used as a means of ensuring that there would
be no black insurgency. Afro-Cubans were allowed to participate in
Cuban politics but were forbidden to create race-based organizations
or to challenge the hegemonic ideal of a race-blind society. In short, the
racial democracy that has been seen as a central feature of the Cuban
state was enforced between independence and the dawn of the Cuban
Revolution both by violence and by racist logics.

3

Race and Revolution

Transformation and Continuity

The Cuban Revolution was a watershed moment in Cuban racial history. Despite the huge changes it made to the racial landscape, however, many critical aspects of racial ideology remained the same after the revolution. The regime of Fidel Castro forged a racial ideology that was based upon pre-existing Cuban attitudes toward race, the practical circumstances of the moment, and a new vision for Cuba, combining old attitudes with a new state ideology: Marxism. But unequal pre-revolutionary access to education and economic resources, pre-existing racial ideology, inequality in housing and labor markets, and, after the collapse of the Soviet Union, unequal access to dollars all established the conditions for ongoing racial inequality. The war in Angola, which was caused by the geopolitical position of Cuba and the symbolic importance of military involvement in Africa, represented an opening of opportunities for blacks, and the subsequent Cuban economic collapse represented a significant retreat that will be explored in the latter chapters of the book in greater depth. Since the revolution, then, there has been a series of openings and consolidations that follow the race cycles theory, and alterations in race relations have reinforced a situation of inclusionary discrimination on the island.

This chapter examines the Cuban Revolution and its transformation of Cuban racial politics. It argues that the consolidation of the revolution, while institutionalizing important racial reforms, attempted to make racial problems invisible. It will draw on the growing literature about race and the revolution to create a synthetic account that develops the key theme of this literature – that the race problem was not solved by the revolution – but places the account into a theoretical context (Moore 1991; Sarduy 1993; Fernandez 1996; de la Fuente 2001). I agree with the major conclusion in the literature that the Castro regime used race as a tool of international policy while declaring the domestic race problem solved. This was a product of the state's need to consolidate at home. On the international stage, race became a central theme that the state used to rally domestic and international support in the context of a ferocious U.S. hostility toward the revolution and its policies.

Cuba on the Brink

During the years leading up to the revolution, Afro-Cubans were governed by a series of regimes that, in general, supported policies that marginalized blacks socially, politically, and economically. Ironically, Fulgencio Batista, the Cuban dictator, was himself a mulatto who claimed to be Indian rather than black. Batista's regime came to power during a period of economic stagnation, and it ruled by distributing patronage and the spoils of corruption to a broad base of supporters (Dominguez 1978). Education and social life under Batista were segregated in cities and rural areas by race and class. While lower-class blacks and whites lived and worked together, the middle and upper classes were entirely white, and they used informal segregation to prevent blacks' upward mobility. Blacks found themselves at a relative disadvantage in terms of labor relations and economic opportunity.

Even as U.S. investment increased and the economy of the country improved, blacks were largely left behind. In a survey of pre-revolutionary social conditions, Dominguez found that while the improvement in living standards benefited all Cubans regardless of race, sex, or age, those benefits were "shared unequally." "Whites profited the most," Dominguez explains, "and as a result, the gap in life chances between whites and blacks widened considerably" (1978, 75–6). Blacks tended to live in the poorest of tenements in Havana and to share worse living conditions than whites with similar incomes. Blacks were also imprisoned at higher rates; according to Dominguez, "whites were about one-third less likely to be convicted and imprisoned than one would expect from their share of the population, while blacks (excluding mulattoes) were two and a half times, and mulattoes were

TABLE 3.1. *Life chances by race (Zeitlin 1967, 69)*

	Employed 9 months or less before the revolution	Present weekly wage $40 or less	Skilled workers	Education third grade or less	(N)
Negroes	47%	46%	28%	39%	(36)
Whites	40%	34%	37%	28%	(116)

between 22 and 47 percent more likely to be convicted and imprisoned than their share of the population" (225). Zeitlin noted similar problems: "It is clear that proportionately more Negro than white workers are unemployed, received low wages, and had only minimal schooling before the revolution, while fewer of them were able to become skilled workers" (1967, 69; see Table 3.1).

Politically, blacks largely joined the Communist Party and other labor or populist organizations in an attempt to advance their cause. But this period was far from democratic; the polity as a whole exercised only limited democratic privileges, and blacks' access to the democratic process was more severely limited than whites'. A series of military coups resulted in regime changes, but each new regime made empty promises to aid blacks. Dominguez notes, "The ethnic cleavage was not reflected in the party system, and the parties were alike in opposing black affirmations of identity as well as in courting their votes. Blacks were underrepresented in organs of government in the pre-Revolutionary years, only achieving about 9% of the seats in the house and senate" (1978, 49).

The precarious balance that held Batista in power waned, however, as the upper and middle classes turned against him, and peasants and workers in the Oriente Province, many of them Afro-Cuban, joined a band of revolutionaries intent on ending his reign (Dominguez 1978; Casal 1989; C. Moore 1991; Perez-Stable 1993). This band of revolutionaries was led by a young man named Fidel Castro who changed the face of Cuba and made an impact that was felt the world over.

Race and Revolution

Since 1959, the revolution has continually faced a series of profound dilemmas. While race has been one significant issue, there have been others. As noted in Chapter 1, major societal issues that are essentially nonracial can interact with racial politics in profound ways. Major crises can create openings or opportunities for mobilization that previously did not exist. In Cuba, post-revolutionary crises have represented opportunities for the evolution of the revolutionary regime and shifts in the conditions of racial politics and racial hierarchy on the island. By looking at periods of crisis, we can explore how major processes within the revolution have interacted with race; though crises do not tell the whole story of race in Cuban society, they are the mechanism that has driven changes in Cuban racial politics.

The transition to the new regime, the consolidation after the Bay of Pigs invasion, the Cuban intervention in Angola, and the collapse of the Soviet Union have all been significant crisis points in Cuban history. The uneven patterns of opening and closure, along with the complexity of Cuban racial ideology, have created a situation of inclusionary discrimination in which blacks have been made an essential part of the state, Cuban national culture, and the Cuban national project but have remained unequal members within this context.

The powerful cycles of crisis and racial change began with the Cuban Revolution itself. The 26th of July Movement and its leader, Fidel Castro, triumphed over the forces of Batista and took control of Havana and the government in January 1959. Castro did not take the race issue very seriously before he came to power (McGarrity 1992); he felt it was necessary to make only vague statements about racial equality, securing the revolution's appeal to the white middle classes, who had begun to take a dim view of Batista. In his famous "History Will Absolve Me" manifesto (1953), which Castro issued after being captured by government forces following the failed attack on the military barracks at Moncada, point number twelve addressed the race issue. It stated that the 26th of July Movement would implement "adequate measures in education and legislation to put an end to every vestige of discrimination for reasons of race [or] sex, which regrettably still exists in our social and economic life" (quoted in C. Moore 1991, 7). While such a pronouncement may seem revolutionary, others had made similar claims, and Castro's manifesto avoided any bold and specific discussion of agrarian land reform, labor, education, and housing. His silence on these issues fell well short of his nationalist pronouncements about public utilities and other such matters (Patterson 1994).

Though he had a few blacks among his revolutionary cadre, Castro had little else to say about race that was positive. In fact, Castro and his movement used literature with racist caricatures of Batista in order to encourage support for the revolution. For the most part, blacks took a "wait and see" approach to the nascent revolution, as they had during regime changes in the years following the Spanish-American War (Rout 1976). Blacks who did join the revolution, however, often did so for explicitly racial reasons. Juan Almeida, a black man who was part of Fidel's inner circle before and after the revolution, stated, "I joined primarily because I felt the need to do something for my people, my country, and thereby to eliminate this damned racial discrimination" (quoted in North 1963, 37).

Almeida's hopes for the new government were not unfulfilled. The revolution created opportunities for profound reforms in race relations and for the incorporation of blacks at new and higher levels of Cuban society, and in the first months of the Cuban Revolution, the new leader of the Cuban nation made bold pronouncements on a variety of issues, including race. Yet it would be a mistake to characterize Castro's boldness as indicative of a new and consistent policy toward race. Policy contradictions were not unusual for the Castro regime: It was Castro, after all, who first sought to eliminate the Communist Party that had been a coalition partner with Batista and then announced the socialist character of the revolution (Zeitlin 1967; Perez-Stable 1993). And while Castro spoke glowingly of democracy, he also worked vigorously to consolidate power under his control and to avert democratic reforms (Dominguez 1978; Bunk 1994).

In the first months of the new regime, Castro's policies toward racial reform were similarly contradictory. The government attempted both to set out a radical new agenda on race and to protect important aspects of the status quo (McGarrity and Cardenas 1995). Castro and his followers hoped that a more equitable and prosperous economic system would eliminate racial problems by itself. They attempted to treat blacks as clients of the revolution and to contain their growing power and influence, maintaining the regime's image as a champion of blacks without causing fear and alienation among whites. In March 1959, Castro announced an initiative to end racial segregation while also managing to suggest that the problem was not serious. Castro's statements included a hallmark of Cuban race relations – a turn to the

United States as a basis for comparison: "In Cuba we do not have the same problem as, for example, in the South of the United States; there is racial discrimination in Cuba, but to a much lesser degree. We feel that our Revolution will help to eliminate those prejudices and injustices that remain latent" (quoted in C. Moore 1991, 15). A few months later, facing pressure from interest groups, private clubs, communists, and members of the radical labor movement, Castro began a more in-depth and nuanced discussion of the problem of race in Cuba, and he developed bolder policies that extended into 1962.

Nonetheless, the regime's contradictory attitudes toward race did not change. In March 1959, when Castro first addressed the race issue, he also specifically placed limits on the form that the revolution's response to it would take. Defining what would be a largely paternalistic view of Afro-Cubans, Castro stated, "One of the battles which must be increasingly made daily emphasized – what I may call the fourth battle – is that which will end racial discrimination in labor. . . . Of all the forms of racial discrimination, the worst is that which limits Cuban Negroes' access to workplaces. We must admit that certain sectors do practice such a shameful thing in our fatherland" (19). Castro further discussed the history and problems of blacks in terms of employment discrimination: "[Employment discrimination] is a thousand times more cruel [than social segregation], for it limits access to centers where one earns a living; it limits the possibilities of satisfying basic needs. Colonial society made the Negro work as a slave, demanded more of him than anyone without remuneration. Our present society (which some wish to call 'democratic') refuses to allow him to earn a living. Thus, while the colonizer worked him to death, beat him to death, we want our black brothers to die of hunger!" (19). While Castro went beyond the area of employment to condemn discrimination in education and recreation, he seemed to hope that integration could itself eliminate discrimination: "There is exclusiveness in recreational centers. Because Negroes and Whites have been educated separately. What is to be done? Simply to unify our public schools; afford our public schools all necessary resources" (20). Castro explicitly declined to consider any remunerative measures to make up for the years of exclusion and inequality, and he did not spell out a set of laws and legal protections that might have promoted equality. The Cuban leader preferred to leave these issues to individual consciousness and social sanction. He argued: "There should be no need to draft a law fixing a right inherent to human beings as members of society. Neither should it be necessary to legislate against an absolute prejudice. What we need is to curse and publicly condemn such men, who because of ancient vices and prejudices, show no scruples in discriminating against and ill-treating Cubans because of their lighter or darker hue" (20). Castro's comment shows that he was committed to a color-blind approach to the problem rather than to recognition of the stain that white supremacy had left on the country. Much like Martí's, Castro's concern for black racism equaled his concern for the historic oppression of Afro-Cubans.

While embracing and reassuring blacks, Castro also attempted to assure whites that blacks would not take over the country. In order to assuage whites' fears, Castro confirmed that blacks would owe strict allegiance to the revolution and would behave properly after being granted their freedom. Castro told whites that they would not be forced to interact with blacks in ways that made them uncomfortable. In a television appearance, his assurance was voiced in response to whites' fear that black men would go to white clubs and seek to dance with white women. Castro attempted to convince elite Cubans that blacks would be respectful and thankful for what the revolution had bestowed upon them and would not overstep their bounds. He said:

I did not touch this problem to open wounds but to close them; to cure them because these wounds have remained open for centuries in the very heart of our nation. So I am appealing to the ones as to the others for respect. And added to respect I am also appealing for sacrifice. And those of whom I will ask for the most respect, to be respectful, are precisely Negro Cubans on behalf of whom this battle against discrimination is being waged. For we are fighting to eliminate discrimination! And, gentlemen, this does not entail any foolishness about having people dancing with each other if they don't feel like dancing with that person. We intend to see to it that the most respectful ones will be, precisely, those Cubans who are today being defended by this Revolution. (25)

Castro saw blacks as clients of, rather than participants in, the revolution. This attitude was clear in other government statements; early revolutionary propaganda included an image of a young black child begging for a better future from whites, affirming in the process that blacks would not demand too much and would follow the rules of decorum established by whites. The accompanying text read:

I don't ask for much. I want to eat, get to know the taste of a pastry. The right to a glass of milk and a little bit of meat every day, to be healthy so, when I grow up, tuberculosis does not consume me. I want to play, to have a tricycle...to have a new toy. I want to study, to access books and a good school. In order for me to reach all that, it is necessary that my parents have a place to work. They don't want to send me to an institution. They want to earn what is fair in order to give me good toys, education, so when I grow up, I can be something besides a shoeshine boy, or a valet. If I become a good man, perhaps my intelligence will generate some respect and we all can get along and the races will understand each other. Perhaps when I become a man, people will have a clearer idea about life so that when one of my children goes by, instead of saying "there goes a 'negrito' [little black]," they will say, "*there goes a child.*" Isn't it true that I don't ask for much? (quoted in de la Fuente 2001, 271)

The symbol of the small child put a nonthreatening face on the push for progress on behalf of blacks. It also helped to eliminate the fear of miscegenation – in particular the fear that black males would have sex with white women – that had grown with Castro's pronouncements about social integration.

Despite his attempts to dampen whites' fears, however, whites continued to fret about racial change. Fears arose, for example, when Castro sent many young men and women into the service of the revolution to the Oriente Province, where the majority of the black population lived. White families with daughters in the literacy brigades worried that the girls would be taken advantage of sexually by black men; according to one study, "'One goes out and two come back' was the refrain" (Smith and Padula 1996, 84).

But whites were not the only ones to shape the revolution's policies on race; blacks were far from being passive observers. Even early on, black leaders, intellectuals, and Afro-Cuban citizens had distinct responses to the regime and distinct demands of it (Segal 1995). Blacks participated in the dialogue on race and posited themselves as a force that needed to be harnessed for the revolution. Carlos Moore notes that Juan Rene Bentacourt, the president of the black mutual aid societies' organization, the Federacion Nacional de Sociedades de Color (National Federation of Societies for Colored People), expressed support for Castro but also outlined a preferred course for the government that would address the race question in what he felt was the most productive manner:

It is impossible that anyone should believe, seriously and in good faith, that by ceasing to refer to "blacks" and "whites" the people will forget their existence, and racial discrimination will thus be liquidated by this miraculous method. If our black brother is to be freed from the centuries-old injustice that has endured . . . then Blacks and whites of good faith must be organized to this end, for only a social force, supported by a government of the generosity and prestige of the present one, can realize the heroic task of unleashing a new socioeconomic force. . . . We harbor no fears that Fidel Castro may forget his black brothers, or that he will stumble into the pitfall of non-productive and chauvinistic attitude regarding the racial question, for he is moved by the best of intention and is fully cognizant of the nature of this issue. (quoted in C. Moore 1991, 17)

Bentacourt's tone was both cautionary and hopeful, mirroring some of the optimism observed in public opinion.

And Bentacourt's optimism was not altogether misplaced; the policies of the Cuban Revolution related to race between 1959 and 1962 were important and powerful. Castro not only announced an end to racial discrimination but also launched an all-out effort to end illiteracy and another to implement land reform measures (Casal 1989; Bunk 1994; de la Fuente 1995, 1998). The focus of the revolution in its early years was on redistribution and collective work. These policies, along with the elimination of private schooling and discrimination in housing, went a long way toward improving the lives of Afro-Cubans (Dominguez 1978; Casal 1989). Rents were lowered, land reform was ongoing, and more employment opportunities were extended to blacks. In fact, Castro himself suggested that the capital be moved from Havana to Santiago de Cuba, a largely Afro-Cuban city, as a symbol of the priorities of the revolution. The revolution focused on extending assistance, services, and literacy to the poor in rural areas. Because a disproportionate number of blacks were poor, many benefited from these shifts and reforms. The government also opened up private beaches and parks to all Cubans regardless of class or color in order to promote integration, and it put pressure on labor unions that had histories of favoring friends and relatives of white workers to open up to Afro-Cubans.

TABLE 3.2. *Attitudes toward the revolution by race, 1962 (Zeitlin 1967, 77)*

	Favorable	Indecisive	Hostile	(N)
Negroes	80%	8%	12%	(50)
Whites	67%	13%	20%	(152)

These policies had a positive effect, even in their first few years. In 1962, in a limited survey, Zeitlin was able to establish that there was strong support in black public opinion for the revolution and that there had been significant gains in employment for black workers since the revolution (1967; see Table 3.2). An Afro-Cuban man in his sixties described the revolution positively: "While the revolution has not been perfect, it has improved the health and life of blacks substantially. Until the revolution, my family had no electricity or running water, education or health care. Since, we have enjoyed these services that were denied us before the revolution."[1] Blacks were hopeful, but they also wanted the race issue to be dealt with in a direct manner. Unfortunately, both ideology and the geopolitical position of Cuba would conspire against their hopes.

Revolution, Race, and Internationalism

It would be wrong to underemphasize the United States' impact on the shape and course of the Cuban Revolution (Patterson 1994). The U.S. stance and policy toward Cuba helped build Cuban nationalism, which led to the revolution and has shaped politics on the island after the revolution as well (Dominguez 1978; Patterson 1994). The United States has demonstrated a profound and open hostility toward Castro's revolution and in so doing has provided an important foil for the regime, which has cast itself as the defender of Third World sovereignty against the imperialist designs of the United States. The aggressive stance of the United States also provided a pretext for state consolidation and the unprecedented penetration of the state into spheres of Cuban social, political, and economic life.

---

[1] Interview conducted by the author. See Chapter 5 for more details about interview methodology.

The influence of the United States on race issues in Cuba – apparent from 1959 onward – was never more evident than in the wake of the Bay of Pigs invasion, which was carried out in 1961 by Cuban exiles with the support and consent of the United States (C. Moore 1991, 1995; Patterson 1994). An indirect effect of the U.S.-sponsored invasion was the Cuban state's consolidation of power; a notable aspect of this consolidation was the closing of the dialogue on racial issues and the jailing of many blacks who continued to push the question. The Bay of Pigs invasion thus both had a negative effect on the situation of blacks within Cuba and gave Castro a new rhetoric with which to position Cuba on the world stage. Organizations like the black clubs and mutual aid societies were closed, and Afro-Cuban religious groups were forced to register with the police (de la Fuente 2001).

After defeating the invasion, Castro also used the idea of black loyalty to the Cuban regime – rather than to a country that practiced racial *apartheid* – as a means of increasing support at home and embarrassing the United States on the world stage. His manipulation of race can be seen in his treatment and questioning of the black counterrevolutionaries who were captured in the ill-fated invasion. Consider the following account: "Castro himself questioned them. Angrily Castro told them they were guilty of treason on two counts: they had betrayed the country and betrayed their race" (Castro Speech Database). In a televised interrogation of prisoners, Castro pointed out to one prisoner that he could not attend clubs, school, or social events in the United States with the people for whom he fought. Speaking at a mass victory rally on May Day, the Cuban leader compared the lot of American blacks to that of Afro-Cubans. Black Cubans, he said, had willingly done battle to defend a socialist motherland, knowing "that they [might] fall, but never in vain, and that cause for which he falls [would] serve for millions of his brothers." American blacks, he said, were forced to die on behalf of white millionaires: "When a Yankee monopolist talks about the motherland, he is thinking about sending the Blacks of the South, the workers, to be killed to defend the motherland of monopolies. What kind of morality, what reason and what right does he have to make a black man die to defend monopolies, the factories and the monies of the ruling classes?" (quoted in C. Moore 1991, 119).

As the Castro regime sought to consolidate the revolution by means of anticolonial national rhetoric, black discontent and challenges to the regime's legitimacy were no longer tolerated. This did not end Castro's discussions of race completely, but it caused race to shift from being a domestic issue to being an international issue. Castro did not see a connection between Afro-Cubans and African Americans, but he saw the country of Cuba as a victim of the same oppression that the United States visited upon its black population. To Castro, then, the regime stood in for black Cubans on the international stage: Its fate with respect to the United States, in Castro's eyes, was coterminous with the fate of black Cuba. This powerful formulation linked Castro with black leaders worldwide and profoundly shaped policy on the island. Cuban social poets like Nicolas Guillen, who supported Castro and attacked the United States, frequently used an argument similar to Castro's. For many, racism was seen not so much as an internal Cuban problem as an expression of U.S. imperialism. Thus, the revolution's early dialogue on race ended in 1962, when the problem was declared officially solved.

Following the 1962 Cuban missile crisis, Cuba lacked leverage with the United States and the Soviet Union, and the government had serious concerns about sovereignty (Bunk 1994). The intervention of a superpower in Cuban affairs concerned the leaders of the Cuban regime as they searched for a way to maintain Cuban sovereignty and to advance the prestige of the regime domestically and internationally. Two issues proved powerful in Cuba's attempt to maintain sovereignty within the Soviet bloc and also to embarrass its very powerful enemy, the United States: race in the United States and the anticolonial struggle in Africa. These issues allowed Cuba to consolidate the state around a racial ideology that declared the race problem solved via Marxism and to argue that race was more of a problem in the United States than it was in Cuba.

Cuba became involved in Africa by first reaching out to Third World leaders like Kwame Nkrumah, Sekou Toure, and Patrice Lumumba. The Cuban effort was aided by the racist statements of the Chinese and the Soviets concerning their comrades in Africa. Nikita Khrushchev, for example, asserted in Paris that at least the Soviets and the French were both white (C. Moore 1991). This type of racial insensitivity allowed Castro to become the interlocutor between the Soviet and African regimes. Cuba positioned itself as the head of the cause of the anticolonial struggle, both militarily and discursively, that was to come. Castro forged alliances in Africa with anticolonial leaders and on several occasions invited them to Cuba. He spoke in no uncertain terms about ending racial and colonial exploitation (C. Moore 1991). In the course of pursuing internationalism, Castro also emphasized the regime's success on the race issue and its open defiance of the United States.

This policy would reach its peak in 1975 when Cuba committed 20,000 troops in defense of the leftist government of Angola against the UNITA rebels, who were supported by the white supremacist regime in South Africa. Castro also convinced the Soviet Union to commit equipment and logistical support to a war in which it had had no intention of involving itself. Race mattered in this intervention: According to Dominguez (1978), more than 50 percent of the troops in Angola were black, a far higher percentage than the proportion of Afro-Cubans in the armed forces. At the height of its involvement in the war, Cuba had as many as 50,000 troops in Angola, along with several thousand civilian personnel.

In the context of this intervention, Castro declared that Cuba was an "African Latin" nation that embraced both the black population and the cultural heritage of the former slaves. The statement was motivated by the mechanism of transnational politics, or, in this case, by the bilateral relations between Cuba and African nations. The declaration did not go unnoticed as Cuba went on to support the African National Congress in South Africa, the Marxist government in Mozambique, and other leftist movements on the continent. Fidel's fight on behalf of leftist anticolonialists came to be called the "Castro doctrine" (C. Moore 1991). The opening it created for domestic racial progress was not insignificant. Black representation was increased in organs of the party and in official positions, and blacks received substantial promotions in the military as a result of service (de la Fuente 2001). Cultural exchanges with Africa also reemphasized and brought new attention to Afro-Cuban cultural practices.

While pursuing an aggressive policy in Africa, Castro took aim at his hostile neighbor to the north. The United States' miserable record on human rights and the African American struggle for civil rights provided ready material for Castro to exploit. Black leaders of all varieties, who enjoyed seeing the forces of Jim Crow defeated a mere ninety miles from the southern United States, greeted the Cuban Revolution and Castro with a sense of optimism that no other world leader inspired in them (Reitlan 1999).

Castro had exploited African Americans' discontent effectively as early as September 1960, when he visited the United Nations. After arriving in New York, Castro's delegation was treated poorly by employees of the Shelbourne Hotel. Soon, members of Castro's delegation came up with an alternative lodging fraught with symbolism: the Hotel Theresa, a venerable institution of black Harlem. Castro's delegation was received warmly by the management and the people of Harlem (C. Moore 1991). Raul Castro announced: "A victorious enemy gave orders to close the doors of the hotels but must now watch impotently as the heroic population of Harlem opens its doors to our prime minister.... The truth, justice and the logic of the Cuban revolution have pierced the walls of lies..., winning over the hearts of twenty million oppressed Blacks in the United States" (quoted in C. Moore 1991, 79). Black leaders like Malcolm X, Robert Williams, and Adam Clayton Powell expressed support for Castro and the Cuban Revolution and visited him during his stay in Harlem. For these men, Castro represented a model white leader with the guts to challenge the hypocrisy of U.S. policy at home and abroad, and his challenge to the U.S. government represented a bold alternative to the glacial pace with which the United States was progressing on racial issues.

Castro's constituency in the United States supported his every move. When the U.S.-backed exiles invaded the Bay of Pigs, black leaders and organizations protested U.S. support of these groups (Segal 1995; Reitlan 1999). The principal black leaders of the day published a declaration that denounced the invasion as a "criminal aggression against the peaceful and progressive people" of Cuba and asserted boldly, "Afro-Americans, don't be fooled – the enemies of the Cubans are our enemies, the Jim Crow bosses of this land where we are still denied our rights" (quoted in C. Moore 1991, 113). At the U.N., African nations supported Castro, while only South Africa joined the side of the United States. As Carlos Moore aptly notes, this established the triangle of American-African-Cuban relations that affected politics in all three places (1991).

As the next chapter will discuss, the Castro regime reached out specifically to black activists during the turbulent 1960s, offering them asylum as well as opportunities to make state visits that embarrassed the United States and confirmed Castro's credentials as a supporter of black rights worldwide. Cuban internationalism served Cuban racial ideology: Internationalism allowed the Cuban Revolution to externalize racial problems and the battle against racism. The regime's ideological battle against racism was about combating U.S. imperialism and capitalism more than it was about any real domestic agenda. Even in the 1960s, discussions of Cuba's racial problems turned quickly from assertions that the domestic problem had been solved to a critique of the United States. Nicolas Guillen recounted in a 1962 article in *Granma*: "In his speech in the city of Santa Clara, Fidel Castro spoke of racial discrimination and its absence from Cuba since the triumph of the Revolution." Guillen cited racist practices during the Republican period and said that Cuba had had a strong relationship to the U.S. South. He noted: "The Republic was run by a collection of marionettes who responded to the strings pulled from Washington, and the descendants of Maceo found it difficult to even exist alongside the descendants of Martí." Racism was consciously externalized, a move that supported the ideas both that capitalism was the problem and that in many ways the Cuban nation was and would continue to be an inclusive one. One article explicitly tied U.S. capitalism to the problems in South Africa (Benitez 1980). Other articles attacked U.S. aggression in Grenada as racist. In *Granma* on February 26, 1984, Luis M. Arce wrote: "The invasion of Grenada also spotlights something that the Reagan administration would rather hush up in this election period: the administration's contempt for the black population of the United States because the invasion was also a hidden manifestation of racism.... Reagan realized the danger, the grave danger involved in the rapid and easily established links between the Grenada Revolution and different sectors of the black community in the United States who identified with their Caribbean brothers and sisters based on their common roots, culture, language interests and demands."

Coverage in *Granma* of U.S. black leaders also focused on their internationalism and solidarity with anticolonial and socialist struggles. An article on Marcus Garvey stated: "Garvey understood that racism was an instrument of oppression and manipulation of the black masses, as he understood that the limitations of US bourgeois democracy could not provide a solution to this problem; he rejected their attempt to present Africans as people without history. His focus on race did not prevent him from seeing class differences and he generally directed himself to the poorest sectors of society." The article went on to praise Garvey for his letter in support of Lenin: "In making his statement Garveyist nationalism distinguished itself from ordinary bourgeois nationalism which would never have gone as far in praising Lenin as Garvey did, in exalting socialism and the important role of the peasant class in revolution" (Guillen 1985). The article concluded that this is what drew the ire of the FBI and that Garvey's work had been halted in Cuba by the Morúa law, which branded the UNIA as racist and banned black organizations.[2]

Accounts of Malcolm X emphasized similar issues of Black Nationalism, and Black Power was lauded for its support of the Cuban Revolution and its avoidance of bourgeois nationalism (*Granma*, June 25, 1967). An account about SNCC makes the point: "On several occasions SNCC has made clear its militant stand in favor of the peoples of Asia, Africa, and Latin America who are struggling for liberation in line with this position; early this year Stokley Carmichael – in the name of SNCC – signed a declaration of solidarity on the part of the U.S. Negro movement with Puerto Ricans fighting for their independence, specifically with MPI [the pro-independence Movement of Puerto Rico]." In the same article, Martin Luther King Jr. is portrayed as limited by his failure to develop a thoroughgoing critique of capitalism and his advocacy of nonviolence, but his stance against the Vietnam War and his tendency to mingle with the masses are seen as positive signs that distinguish him from the NAACP and the Urban League. Even King's assassination was condemned by all major mass organizations of the Cuban Communist Party, and the riots that ensued in the United States were covered in great detail. It was just this kind of domestic mass protest that the externalization of the race problem was meant to contain.

Black Crackdown and State Consolidation

While trumpeting the cause of black empowerment in the United States and Africa, the Cuban regime had to decide what role Afro-Cubans

---

[2] The Morúa Law was passed before the racist massacre of 1912 not only to justify that violence but also to prevent the UNIA from gaining a foothold in Cuba.

would play in politics at home. Specifically, the question of whether blacks would be allowed to make demands and claims on the state as a group or whether it would be preferable to suppress outgrowths of independent black identity was raised. This question collided with discussions about whether the government and party would operate as a mass party or a vanguard party (Dominguez 1978; Eckstein 1995). The idea of incorporating black mass organizations within the party was a logical possibility, but it was seen as a potential challenge to Castro's core group of revolutionaries. The fear of black insurgency appears almost to have been a holdover from the ideology of Martí and others; it predated the revolution and harkened back to the origins of the Cuban nation. In this context, despite international commitments to Black Power, Castro used a mix of pragmatic and ideological concerns to justify the elimination of any independent black voice or critique of the revolution. The decision was driven not only by economic difficulties but also by attempts to consolidate the state following the Bay of Pigs invasion in April 1961; it drew on a Marxist reduction of the race problem to class and on Latin American exceptionalists' denial that racial problems existed in Cuba.

Despite its commitment to antiracist movements in Africa and the United States, then, the regime made it clear that Cuban expressions of black culture and political identity, such as Afro-Cuban religious practices and black fraternal organizations, were "backward" (Eckstein 1995; Segal 1995). This argument was based on the Leninist ideal; the hope was that Afro-Cuba would be progressively assimilated into a more rational tradition, that archaic cultural expressions like Afro-Cuban religions and ethnic identity would be exchanged for a Cuban national identity based on "raceless" Marxist ideology (Casal 1989; McGarrity and Cardenas 1995; C. Moore 1995). In the interest of racial harmony, Afro-Cubans were supposed to abandon their unique cultural and racial identity. Blacks would be included in the Cuban national project, but state promotion of black culture was shifted from the synthetic representations for tourists that were a hallmark of the Republican period to the authentic representations of Afro-Cuban religion, dance, and music that came to be considered part of the Cuban national "folklore" (de la Fuente 2001). As folklore, the practices were not considered to be an active part of Cuban national development following the revolution. Other aspects of black culture and organization were banned outright, including black mutual aid societies and Afro hairstyles, while members of Afro-Cuban religions were not allowed to join the party and had to register with the police in order to perform religious rites.

An attack on black organizations began in the 1960s following the Bay of Pigs invasion, when members of organizations began to be watched and sometimes arrested (Segal 1995; Ibarra 1998). The justification for closing the clubs drew upon Marxism and Latin American exceptionalism, arguing that because racial discrimination no longer existed, clubs and organizations for blacks were no longer necessary (de la Fuente 2001). Religious believers, gays, and blacks with strong cultural or Black Power beliefs – all seen as "different," as threats to Cuban unity, and as signs of weakness that might be exploited by counterrevolutionaries – were targeted by the security forces of the regime (Covarrubia 1999). Conformity to the doctrine of the revolution and the Western rationalist tradition was demanded. De la Fuente notes that in September 1961, following the invasion, more than 170 black organizations were shut down by authorities in Havana. While some blacks supported the actions of the regime, others fought to maintain their organizations in order to continue a racial dialogue.

Suppression of independent black voices reached its height in the late 1960s and early 1970s. In 1967, shortly before the World Cultural Congress (to which leading Afro-Cuban figures were not invited), a group of black cultural and political figures approached the revolution to address the concerns of Afro-Cubans. According to Carlos Moore, the group included leading black cultural and political figures like Rogelio Fure, Nancy Morejon, Nicolas Guillen Landrian (the filmmaker), Sara Gomez, and Walterio Carbonell, among several others. Minister Llanusa Gobels labeled the position taken by these leaders "seditious" and declared: "The revolution would allow no sort of activity that would 'divide' the people along racial lines. The government and the party were solely authorized to theorize on matters of culture and only hidden enemies of the revolution could bring up a subject that had been resolved since 1959" (1991, 309). Of those who met with the minister that day, several, including Guillen and Carbonell, were arrested. Their attempts to exploit the opening created by the revolution were rebuffed. The only black Cuban allowed to attend the World Cultural Congress was the poet Nicolas Guillen. Several activists and writers at the congress, however, talked with blacks who complained about the top-down nature of the party and the fact that although educational access was equal, the disadvantages produced by years of discrimination still limited opportunities for blacks. In 1971, the first Congress on Education and Culture proclaimed the socialist revolution to be "itself the highest expression of Cuban culture," and it went on to call the Afro-Cuban Abacua brotherhood a "focus of criminality and juvenile delinquence" (102).

The crackdown on black activism was not limited to an intellectual elite. Three separate popular movements emerged among Afro-Cubans, and all of them were crushed by the police. The first movement, the Movimiento Liberacion Nacional (MLN), grew out of frustration about the state's handling of black culture. The MLN launched one strike against the regime and was gathering explosives and weapons for another when government security officials discovered its plan and jailed its leaders. Moore claims that the group had no connections with the CIA or the exile community, but the threat it posed cleared the stage for the regime to make swift attacks against other black organizations. We cannot be sure that Moore's claim is true, but it is clear that the action taken against the MLN set a precedent for the treatment of future black organizations.

The second movement, the Movimiento Black Power of 1971, borrowed liberally from the diaspora for inspiration, both in name and substance. According to Carlos Moore, the works of Frantz Fanon were the movement's inspiration, and the members of the Black Power movement in the United States were kindred spirits (1991; Segal 1995). Members of the Movimiento Black Power were forced to recant their Black Power beliefs; some were rewarded with positions, while others were jailed or forced into exile. This mix of carrots and sticks maintained the hegemony of the state and eliminated grassroots alternatives to the regime.

A third movement, the Afro-Cuban Study Group, began as a group that shared an interest in African American culture, particularly in soul music and information sources like *Ebony* magazine (C. Moore 1991; Segal 1995). The group was diasporic in focus; it sought to connect with and learn more about black people, history, and movements worldwide. In 1974, its members were deeply disappointed by the failure of the government to allow the publication of Cheikh Anta Diop's

Afrocentric treatise on ancient history, *Blacks in Antiquity*. The Greeks, a cornerstone of the regime's school curriculum, were seen to have been particularly maligned by Diop. In the words of officials, Diop's work "'Negrified' Greek history and 'Negroized' the ancient Egyptians" (quoted in Moore 1991, 313). This episode demonstrated the ideological and cultural danger that an Afrocentric reading of history presented in the context of the revolution. The group members who sought the publication of Diop's work were castigated for promoting "racism" and for "a lack of firmness and loyalty to revolutionary principles" (314). Despite this setback, the group grew more popular for its devotion to popular music and black culture; the police soon stepped in to abolish the flourishing, alternative black public space. Moore tells the story as follows: "Barroso, one of the main participants, was taken by surprise. His Vedado home was entirely surrounded by groups of police. They were armed to the teeth and had lots of special assault rifles. They carried strong flashlights and bullhorns to summon him out. These young people were taken from their homes, in a way quite reminiscent of what we saw in the newspapers of how the [U.S.] police hunted down, surrounded the homes, and flushed out unarmed Black Panthers" (315–16).

At the same time that Castro was promoting anticolonialism in Africa and providing asylum to black activists victimized by the repression of the U.S. government, then, the nonconformity of Afro-Cuban activists and their grassroots approach was perceived to be a profound threat to the regime. The threat of U.S. intervention provided a pretext for limiting blacks' opportunities to express their identity, their culture, and their critique of racial politics on the island. The blatantly counterrevolutionary activity of the MLN, mixed with the regime's ideological commitment to a "raceless" polity and its fear of U.S. intervention, provided a powerful excuse for closing the race question and labeling black organizations potentially divisive.

Dominguez wrote in 1978, "The revolution has claimed to have solved the race problem; it has therefore become subversive to speak or write about its existence" (225). Domestically, the government needed to consolidate power and to mobilize the masses behind issues that promoted national unity. This involved developing and backing mass organizations that would support the revolution rather than promote independent critiques of it (Casal 1989; Eckstein 1995; McGarrity and

Cardenas 1995; Smith and Padula 1996). Racial problems were seen as potentially destructive to both the Marxist project and to the nationalist project.

The Gains of the Revolution

It is important to remember that the regime hung its claim to having solved the race problem on some tangible achievements. While racial hierarchy remained in place in Cuba, several structural changes improved the status of blacks. In nearly every case, however, these achievements were limited in ways that reflect the inclusionary discrimination prevalent in Cuban society. By 1961, the revolution had eliminated private schools and made a substantial investment in ensuring literacy and an adequate education for all (Dominguez 1978; Casal 1989; Eckstein 1995). Casal reports, however, that "visitors . . . noticed underrepresentation of blacks in high-powered schools (such as the Lenin Vocational School, where a grade school average of 98% plus is a prerequisite for admission) and overrepresentation of blacks at the INDER (National Sports Institute) schools" (482). Blacks also represented about 9 percent of the party and parliament. While there is a substantial debate as to what degree that 9 percent was an improvement over the pre-revolutionary regime, it is clear that black participation in local organizations expanded and black influence increased (Dominguez 1978; Casal 1989). Profound limitations remained on the ability of blacks to bring racial issues into play, however, and the highest levels of the government and party remained largely white.

In general, the revolution has failed to meet the demand for adequate housing, but housing reforms and the granting of ownership to former tenants have created a situation in which more blacks own their houses in Cuba than in any other country in the world (McGarrity and Cardenas 1995). While there is ample evidence that blacks continue to be overrepresented in older, less desirable neighborhoods and have fewer opportunities to trade up for newer or larger homes (see Chapter 4), Cubans now more than ever live in integrated neighborhoods and have cross-racial friendships. In 1976, as a result of the implementation of reforms in the area of health and welfare and the expansion of resources, Afro-Cubans also became one of the healthiest black populations in the Americas, approaching the life expectancy of whites

TABLE 3.3. *Estimates of life expectancy by race in Cuba, Brazil, and the United States, 1980s (de la Fuente 1995)*

Country	Whites	Blacks	w-b
Cuba (1981)	71.2	70.2	1.0
Brazil (1980)	66.1	59.4	6.7
United States (1980)	74.4	68.1	6.3

TABLE 3.4. *Literacy rates by race and sex in the population of Cuban ten- to nineteen-year-olds, 1899–1981 (de la Fuente 1995)*

Year	Total	White male	White female	Total whites	Nonwhite males	Nonwhite females	Difference
1899	43.1%	40.8%	45.4%	34.8%	29.8%	39.4%	8.3%
1907	69.5%	69.1%	70.0%	66.9%	63.2%	70.3%	2.7%
1919	63%	60.6%	65.6%	56.6%	51.2%	62.0%	6.3%
1931	75.6%	72.7%	78.6%	71.5%	66.8%	76.1%	4.1%
1943	74.5%	71.3%	77.9%	69.5%	65.4%	73.6%	5.0%
1953	72.4%	NA	NA	NA	NA	NA	–
1981	99.1%	98.9%	99.3%	98.8%	98.6%	99.1%	.2%

(see Table 3.3). The literacy rate among Afro-Cubans, finally, improved dramatically (see Table 3.4).

A final example of inclusionary discrimination can be seen in the 1981 census. While taking casualties and committing more black troops to Angola, the Cuban government elected in 1981 to collect racial statistics for the first time since the revolution. It has been argued that this measure was taken to convince Afro-Cubans that the regime was making progress on the race issue in the hope that they would support the endeavor in Angola with their lives (Adams 1999).

We must remember that racial statistics are always a product of the social, political, scientific, and economic exigencies of the moment and of the enumerators (C. Moore 1991; Nobles 2000; de la Fuente 2001). Just as race is a pseudoscientific construct that has no existence outside of its social and political context, census taking has been part of the "science" of race making, or creating what we understand to be race. There is no such thing as an "unbiased" account of race, only counts that reflect the bias of their sociopolitical moment. Because research on race was generally prohibited by the regime, there is little data save observations to counter the claims of the census.

The ambiguous instructions for categorizing race given to its mostly white enumerators combined with the lingering impression that Cuba would be best represented by being more white to produce a very interesting count that did not reflect what by all accounts should have been an explosion of the black population due to a hemorrhage of whites via exile, an increase in black fertility, and a decrease in mortality. There is substantial evidence, moreover, that the black population was miscounted prior to the revolution (C. Moore 1991). Nevertheless, the numbers revealed Cuba to be 66.0 percent white, 12.0 percent black, 21.9 percent mulatto, and 0.1 percent Asiatic (Comite Estatal de Estadisticas Oficina Nacional del Censo). Some have pointed out that someone like Jesse Jackson would be considered mulatto, while Tiger Woods and Colin Powell would be designated as Asiatic or white. Thus, even people who in many contexts would be perceived as black – or who might refer to themselves as black – were counted by the census as mulatto, or even white, in many cases. The figures served the purpose of minimizing calls for race-specific policies and the threat of black identity politics, and they granted legitimacy to the regime for dealing so fairly with a relatively small minority and incorporating it in various aspects of national life.

In 1986, in the wake of the Angola mobilization, Afro-Cuban numbers in the parliament and other major organs of the party were expanded (Adams 1999). The levels of Afro-Cubans increased first to around 25 percent in 1980 and then, in an increase of 89.1 percent, to a level of 35.5 percent in 1986 (Adams 1999, 263–4). The new "Afro-Latin" nation of Cuba again improved opportunities for blacks in education and government, opening positions even at high political levels. This process lasted until shortly after the war in Angola ended, at which point it was interrupted by perhaps the most serious crisis the revolution has faced to date: the collapse of the Soviet Union and the threat of U.S. invasion. By 1991, black representation in parliament was back to levels around 20 percent below its height only five years before (Adams 1999).

Despite this decrease in black representation, there were a number of major symbolic gains for Afro-Cubans. In 1981, Tamayo Mendez, an Afro-Cuban, became the first Latin American to go into space. He was a hero as a Cuban for having achieved this honor, but it was also symbolically important that he was black. Cuban athletes also distinguished themselves on the international stage, especially at the Olympics. In 1992, Afro-Cuban long sprinter Ana Fidelia Quirot, named Fidelia after Fidel Castro, cemented Cuba's visibility in women's athletics. She became an even bigger story in 1996 when she won a silver medal after recovering from severe burns received in a household accident.

The gains of Cuban athletes were not limited to women or to track and field. Afro-Cuban high jumper Javier Sotomayor achieved great heights throughout his career. Sotomayor won several world championships and a gold medal in the Barcelona Olympics of 1992. He is also the current world record holder in his event. Cubans have also participated in, and in some cases dominated, amateur boxing, with Afro-Cubans Félix Sávon and Teófilo Stevenson being two of many Cuban boxers who are world renowned for their excellence in the sport. Their success is seen as a triumph of the revolution, as Cuba has frequently been at the top of competition in terms of medals per capita at the Olympics. The fact that blacks are powerful symbols of national pride while their access to other avenues of power and prestige is limited demonstrates the inclusionary discrimination of the regime.

A survey conducted by the Cuba Center for Anthropology (1995) indicates that while blacks have greatly benefited from the revolution, they are less likely than whites to believe that there has been "a lot of progress" on racial issues or that more whites support racial equality than did before the revolution. While these gaps reflect the racial hierarchy to some degree, it is worth noting that a majority of Cubans across groups believe both propositions, though there is more support for the idea that things have improved in general than for the idea that the attitudes of whites have improved.

Rectification and the Special Period

When the policies of the regime were thrown into flux by transformations in the Soviet Union, race politics in Cuba shifted again. In 1986, in the wake of Gorbachev's *glasnost*, the Castro regime turned inward and convened the Third Party Congress, inaugurating what was called the "process of rectification of errors and negative tendencies." This process was linked to the chain of crises and critical events connected to

TABLE 3.5. *Cuban attitudes toward racial progress under Castro (Ramos 1998, 108)*

	Racial discrimination		Attitude of the white population		
Skin color	A lot of progress	Not much change	More whites are for racial equality	Fewer whites	No change
Blancos (white)	80.9%	19.1%	62.0%	10.0%	28.0%
Negros (blacks)	75.0%	25.0%	50.0%	12.5%	37.5%
Mestizos	70.6%	29.4%	68.7%	18.8%	12.5%
Total	76.1%	23.9%	60.5%	13.2%	26.3%

the war in Angola and the Cuban commitment to a free South Africa. Of even greater consequence was the Reagan administration's aggressiveness in Latin America and the Caribbean, which included the invasion of Grenada in 1983, the attempt to overthrow the Sandinistas in Nicaragua, and support for the military governments of El Salvador and Guatemala against pro-democratic, socialist insurgent movements (Bengelsdorf 1994; Perla 2003).

In response to these external threats, the Cuban government charted a rhetorical course exactly opposite the plan taken by the Soviet Union. The aggressiveness of the Reagan administration prompted the Cuban Revolution to implement popular reforms and move toward mass defense mobilization (Begelsdorf 1994). These reforms became known as "rectification." The rhetoric of rectification called for more redistribution and fewer market reforms in order to justify the austerity that resulted from the rising costs of imports from COMECON (Eckstein 1995). The political scientist Carollee Bengelsdorf describes the reformulation of defense strategy that rectification involved:

The original impetus for Rectification in this analysis was the 1983 invasion of Grenada. Here the absence of Soviet response made it crystal clear to the Cubans that they were on their own facing a far more hostile and actively aggressive White House and this required a structural rethinking of military strategy. The new strategy was designed around *guerra popular*: the organization of massive numbers of people into territorial militias (involving something more than 2 million people, that is, roughly one-fifth of the island's population) rather than sole reliance upon a professional army. The dramatic nature of the change was evident on a number of levels. First, given their experience with "people's war," Vietnamese military advisors were substituted for Soviet counterparts. Second, the people's war strategy fell under the direct jurisdiction of the Party rather than the army. (1994, 143)

This strategy required popular reforms that would mobilize political support for the regime among the masses. The political scientist Hector Perla, in his work on the Sandinista response to Reagan's policies in Nicaragua, calls a similar response "revolutionary deterrence." Perla argues that the Sandinistas implemented popular reforms, developed an unconventional civil defense strategy, cultivated international support, and sought the help of friends and allies in the United States to counter the administration's policies (2003). In the case of Cuba, racial and economic reforms became a way of creating needed domestic support and rallying international support for the regime.

These policies marked a clear break from Soviet-style administration. "While Gorbachev may have perceived that reforming the Soviet system might lead to a more humanitarian and thus efficient socialism," Planas has argued, "Castro foresaw that the reforms could also undermine institutional Marxism-Leninism" (1993, 242). Fidel criticized members of the regime for becoming too capitalist and for "teaming up with capitalist hucksters . . . playing at capitalism, beginning to think and act like capitalists, forgetting about the country" (quoted in Planas 1993, 258). Thus a trend toward economic growth at the expense of redistribution that had begun in the early 1970s was reversed.

While preparing Cubans for the hard economic times ahead, Castro attempted to float another issue to the population that would in the near future be hit hardest by the economic austerity on the horizon: Afro-Cubans. Fidel and Raul Castro made speeches at the Third Party Congress in which they argued that racism was still persistent in Cuba and that blacks were underrepresented in major positions (de la Fuente 2001). Castro, who had stated in an interview with Jim Lehrer just a year earlier that "neither racial discrimination nor discrimination due to sex" existed in Cuba, changed his tune. He commented: "The correction of historic injustice cannot be left to spontaneity. It is not enough to establish laws on equality and expect total equality. It has to be promoted in mass organizations, in party youth. . . . We cannot expect women, blacks, mixed-race people to be promoted spontaneously.... We need to straighten out what history has twisted" (quoted in de la Fuente 1998, 62).

The opening created by the war in Angola and the growing U.S. threat fostered a new discursive environment that encouraged the discussion of racial reforms even as the regime attempted to consolidate around a new order. For the first time, Castro floated the idea of the possible use of "positive discrimination," or affirmative action, that would serve to soften the harsh blow that would soon come to Castro's most loyal group of supporters, Afro-Cubans. His announcement was greeted with substantial ambivalence, however. Gisela Arrandia Covarrubia, a Cuban researcher and activist on issues of race on the island, expressed concern about the proposed policies: "The method of numerical participation is not enough, and may produce an adverse reaction. This is due to the fact that if the person who makes this promotion is a racist, he or she will promote someone who is known to be incapable of exercising that power, therefore creating in society a negative attitude toward the incorporation of Afrocubans. This unfavorable reaction will reach both whites and Blacks. The latter will reaffirm their guilt complex, based on their supposed inferiority. On the other hand, we know that skin color is not enough to modify conduct, and like Frantz Fanon said, there are Blacks with white souls" (1999). Her argument demonstrates Afro-Cubans' concern about the motives behind the regime's change in policy.

Few of the reforms promised in the process of rectification were implemented. Quite the opposite, the regime sought to open Cuba to foreign investment. It seems to have used rectification to mobilize public support behind it in preparation for the austerity of the "special period" that soon arrived. The "special period in times of peace" (a reference to the depth of the crisis and how it might be likened to war) began in the midst of the rectification process. In 1989, the collapse of the Soviet empire and the cessation of Soviet subsidies meant almost immediate austerity for Cuba. The economy imploded, and growth rates soon dipped to negative levels. The people of Cuba felt the real effects of living in an underdeveloped country. The rug was pulled out from under the golden age of Cuban socialism, shelves quickly were emptied of food and medicine, blackouts became commonplace, and life in Cuba became quite desperate. Massive numbers of Cubans took to rafts (*balseros*) in order to make the ninety-mile trip to Miami in search of food and basic necessities. As predicted by the race cycles model, the special period resulted in greater racial inequality and a retreat to the ideology of inclusionary discrimination. The regime's earlier denials of the existence of racism, moreover, have encouraged racist explanations for the growing inequality.

Market-based policies and foreign investment appeared to be the only way to bail out the sinking ship of Cuban socialism. Cuba first allowed tourists to visit and encouraged joint ventures with foreign countries to promote tourism. It remained illegal for Cubans to possess or use dollars, however. The term "tourist *apartheid*" expressed Cubans' frustration at being denied access to the wealth and goods that could be attained with dollars but were barred to them. Except for those who worked in tourist areas, Cubans were not allowed to shop in the stores or enter the hotels and beaches set aside for foreigners. At the height of the economic collapse in 1994, this law resulted in riots in which groups of Cubans, most of them black, stormed and looted a store full of goods for tourist consumption. In response, the regime legalized the use of dollars and the receipt of remittances from abroad. In order to encourage economic activity, it also allowed Cubans to open small private enterprises. This experimentation with capitalism created a dual system, or dual economy – a heavily regulated peso economy and a limited free-market capitalist economy.

As Chapter 5 will demonstrate, the forces unleashed by these economic reforms were profound. Black and gray markets quickly emerged. Tourist dollars and remittances flowed in greater numbers to whites who had relatives abroad or who appeared to have a "better presence" for work in the tourist sector. Most blacks could obtain dollars only through gray or black market activity like prostitution and the illegal sale of goods. Tourism and remittances became the two largest parts of the Cuban economy. By 1996, modest growth had been restored, and the depths of the crisis were behind the regime. What remains is a new social and economic inequality among Cubans based upon access to dollars. As order was restored, the regime sought both to expand access to dollars and to put greater controls on the Cuban economy. The Chinese model of state-controlled capitalism and joint ventures between foreign investors and organs of the regime like the military was seen as the means of getting the country back on its feet.

Petty capitalism was greatly reduced by means of greater government regulation.

The capitalist intervention was such a drastic departure from the basic logic of the state that it failed to produce the gains that the race cycles model might have predicted. The regime could not get through the crisis by expanding opportunities but instead had to allow for interventions that increased social and racial inequality. Many began to grumble about resurgent racism and race-based economic inequality, and the regime has had few if any answers. Though there has been some recognition of the problem, the regime, relying on Latin American exceptionalism and Marxism, has tended to downplay the growth in racial inequality, stressing that the pains of the special period "were shared by all."

On the other hand, Afro-Cuban cultural and religious expressions have been better tolerated and accepted as the regime has sought both to market them as Cuban attractions and to allow for more freedom in everyday life to cope with difficulties. The renaissance in Afro-Cuban music and arts has been felt worldwide as the opening of Cuba to the outside world, accompanied by an opening within, created larger stages for representations of Afro-Cuban culture. Blackness became an important commodity that could be sold in international markets. Again, blacks have faced inclusionary discrimination: Marketed as a central part of Cuban culture, they have found their life chances declining. The special period, as predicted by the race cycles model, has caused increasing racial inequality.

Conclusion

This chapter has demonstrated that the problem of race within the Cuban Revolution is a product of both the previous regime and the ideological and pragmatic limitations placed on the pursuit of racial equality. While great progress was made in race relations during the early years of the revolution, stagnation soon followed. Black Nationalists ascribed this stagnation to the racist motives of the Castro regime, and Marxists denied its existence for some time, but by Castro's own admission, the problem of racial hierarchy persisted. The complex motives and interests of the state, in conjunction with the geopolitical position of Cuba, state crises, and Cuban racial ideology, created a situation of inclusionary discrimination. In keeping with the race cycles model, the Castro regime, seeking to consolidate the state following a crisis, drew upon Marxism and pre-existing racial ideologies to suggest both that the race problem was not serious and that blacks represented a danger to Cuban advancement and national unity.

The Cuban discussion of race frequently shifted from a domestic discussion to an international one that challenged both the United States and the Soviet Union, positioning Cuba between them and the Third World. Limits on political organizing protected Cuban sovereignty from potential incursions, while Cuba's role as the window to Africa for the communist bloc and as a close ally of the black movements in the United States protected it from both the Soviet Union and the United States. The need to portray Cuba as a racial paradise to allies in Africa and the United States, however, limited the domestic dialogue about race. Cuba's interest was in maintaining credibility on the issue by declaring the problem solved and preventing unwanted discussion or activism that might interrupt its relations with Africa or its use of race to embarrass the United States.

The international involvement in Angola again opened the issue of race domestically by creating a need to mobilize in order to meet the challenges of war. Following the conflict, the state closed the dialogue as it turned its attention to the devolution of Soviet support. The looming economic crisis and U.S. threat again opened discussions about racial issues, but decisions about how to address the new Cuban economy and overcome the "special period" ultimately silenced issues of race and increased racial inequality.

All of these factors come together to form the often contradictory and uneven policies, rhetoric, and practices that have conspired to maintain racial hierarchy in Cuba. Race has been shown to have interacted with and diffused itself into most major debates surrounding the Cuban state and the regime, both before the revolution and after. At the same time, international factors have played a critical role in the formation of racial politics, shaping both the racial environment in Cuba and Cuba's role in the world.

4

Match Made in Heaven or Strange Bedfellows?

Black Radicals in Castro's Cuba

In September 1960, after being snubbed by the staff members of a posh Manhattan hotel while visiting the U.N., Fidel Castro and his entourage made their way to Harlem to stay at the venerable Hotel Theresa. There, Castro was greeted by people shouting, "Fidel, free American Negroes too!" "Fidel, turn Harlem into another Sierra Maestra!" and "Fidel si, Ku Klux Klan no!" (quoted in C. Moore 1991, 80). The crowd's warm reception was matched by the respect and interest with which the Cuban leader was received by a broad spectrum of black leaders. A few days after Nikita Khrushchev visited Castro in Harlem, Malcolm X paid Fidel a call. Later, Castro delivered a now-legendary speech before the U.N. General Assembly in which he stated his friendship and closeness with black America. He proclaimed: "Before coming to the United States we already enjoyed great sympathy, but now it has increased even more. American Negroes have grasped one great human truth: that everyone is happy in Cuba" (82).

While the mainstream media in the United States was suspicious and condemnatory of the Cuban Revolution, the U.S. black media followed the revolution closely and generally supported it (Gosse 1998). To blacks in the United States, the revolution appeared to have created a far more fluid system of race and class than the system that existed in the United States, or, for that matter, anywhere in Latin America. As in other Latin American countries, intermediary racial categories such as mulatto seemed to mediate between black and white. But Fidel Castro's communist regime also reduced class differences and outlawed racial discrimination (Robaina 1993; Sarduy and Stubbs 1993). The regime's commitment to eliminating class difference and its support of revolutionary regimes in Africa and elsewhere also proved attractive to African American activists (Moore 1991; Newton 1995).

Many Black Nationalists felt positive about the improvements in literacy and the gains in quality of life that Afro-Cubans had made. As a result, some nationalists – they would come to be called revolutionary nationalists – strongly supported the Castro regime, believing that it modeled the ability of revolution and socialism to eliminate racial inequality. Others, noting the persistence of racial discrimination in Cuba and the regime's repression of racial dialogue, argued that the Castro regime was not innocent of racism. These individuals – who would come to identify themselves as cultural nationalists – clung tightly to an ideal of black self-determination, emphasized its absence in Cuba, and rejected as unacceptable a paternalistic, white-led regime that focused primarily on class (C. Moore 1991). Cuba proved to them that multiracial coalitions and Marxist ideals were incapable of producing racial equality.

The differences in opinion over Cuba mirrored debates about the direction of the Black Nationalist movement in the United States. Revolutionary nationalists criticized cultural nationalists for their failure to consider important issues like class and gender and for their support of right-wing black regimes in Africa. Cultural nationalists argued that revolutionary nationalists' willingness to emphasize the categories of class, gender, and sexual orientation directed attention away from racial oppression, which they believed was the single most important type of oppression within the United States and around the globe (Newton 1995; Dawson 2001). At stake in the nationalist disagreement was the question of what role white liberals and radicals would play in the Black Power struggle: Revolutionary nationalists were open to building coalitions, but cultural nationalists rejected white participation in the movement completely.

Castro established a relationship with Black Nationalists when he visited the United States that has lasted until the present day. Were black militants and Castro strange bedfellows or a match made in heaven? While this chapter will show that the question is a vexing one, I contend that the experiences of U.S. black activists in Cuba not only demonstrate the ideological differences among them but also allow us to see the strengths and limitations of Cuban racial politics. The regime's relationship with black activists from the United States provides a lens through which to view the inclusionary discrimination of the Castro regime. This chapter first discusses the historical development of Black Nationalism, exploring how ideas about black identity, self-determination, and the role of other categories like class have been transformed by historical events. Next, it analyzes the stories of five Black Power activists who visited Cuba: Robert Williams, Stokely Carmichael, Eldridge Cleaver, Angela Davis, and Assata Shakur. Using these stories, I will demonstrate how the "race question" in Cuba created dilemmas that contributed to the divergent development of revolutionary nationalism and cultural nationalism, and I will analyze how these dilemmas contribute to our understanding of the peculiar features of race and politics in Cuba.

Historical Development of Black Nationalism

Black Nationalism has been a major ideological rallying point for blacks throughout the diaspora for at least 200 years (Moses 1978; Dawson 2001). Black Nationalism as an ideology developed within the United States, but it drew heavily on international exchanges, events, and interactions (Gilroy 1994; Hanchard 1994; Dawson 2001). A set of core principles defines Black Nationalism. To varying degrees, nationalists believe that white supremacy is a global and central organizing principle of the modern world, that blacks must develop autonomous institutions to combat it, and that race is a salient and primary identity (Dawson 2001). Over time, however, nationalists have disagreed about how much emphasis should be placed on each of these core principles. Hence, some have argued for the complete separation of the races because "whites are too tied to the psychological and material benefits of white supremacy to ever make good coalition partners." Others, according to Dawson, found it important for whites to organize within white communities (2001). Some adopted a "race first and only" philosophy, while others argued that – in addition to race – class, gender, and sexuality are salient identities. Despite these differences, up to the 1960s, Black Nationalists saw themselves as adhering to a fairly unified ideology.

Black Nationalism underwent a series of transformations over time. In the eighteenth and nineteenth centuries, nationalists advocated a militant response to slavery and racial inequality. Nationalists like Edward Blyden, Bishop Henry Turner, and others proposed emigration to Africa as another solution (Moses 1978). Emigration would not mean a return to a glorified African civilization, however, but an opportunity to introduce Africa to Western civilization. For its reliance on Western civilization, the early Black Nationalist movement has been characterized by Moses as "Anglo-African" nationalism.

In the early twentieth century, Marcus Garvey formed the largest Black Nationalist organization in history; it reached Africa, Latin America, North America, and the Caribbean. Garvey argued that white racism was a permanent feature of the United States and that blacks had to emigrate to Africa in order to liberate the continent from European colonialism and build a great, new African civilization. Garvey's appeal was based on black pride. In contrast to racist stereotypes, it promoted a positive view of people of African descent. Garvey exalted the accomplishments of African civilization and believed future black achievements could be modeled on African examples.

At the same time, however, Garvey clung to what is often perceived to have been a Western worldview (Moses 1978; Robinson 1991; Hutchinson 1995). Garvey's promotion of black pride and his push for emigration to Africa were radical, but his views on gender and economic issues were relatively conservative for his time. Unlike many of his contemporaries, Garvey believed in capitalism and in a Christian conception of gender and sexual roles. The African Blood Brotherhood led by Cyril Biggs challenged Garvey's faith in capitalism. Harlem Renaissance writers, interacting with the negritude movement, also questioned the Western moral values that were the basis of much of Garvey's thinking on social issues (Robinson 1991). What was unique about Black Nationalism in the latter part of the twentieth century was its explicit rejection of Western values.

Debates about capitalism and social issues reemerged in the 1960s, however, and fostered a split among nationalists. Garvey's themes of African pride and "self-help" were picked up by the Nation of Islam (NOI), and the NOI transmitted these ideals to other "cultural nationalist" groups (Dawson 2001). Elijah Muhammad, the founder of the Nation of Islam, based his movement in part upon the ideas of Garvey and other religious nationalists of the early twentieth century (Haley 1991, Dawson 2001). The Nation of Islam held that whites in general, and white liberals in particular, were inherently too tied to the psychological and material benefits of racism to ever deal fairly with blacks (Haley 1991; Dawson 2001). NOI members believed, furthermore, that only separate black institutions that focused on economic and moral development internal to the black community could succeed. With the rise of its spokesman Malcolm X, the Nation of Islam became a powerful nationalist counterpoint to the civil rights movement (Haley 1991). It provided the ideological foundation for the development of other nationalist organizations throughout the 1960s.

The Nation of Islam's focus on male rites of passage and the development of black masculinity borrowed heavily from Islam, but it also drew from Christian conservatism. This influence survived in groups that rejected Islam for what they claimed was a more authentic "African" worldview. Organizations like the US organization, whose leader, Ron Karenga, developed the modern Afrocentric holiday Kwanzaa, have made male rites of passage their central focus and have adopted conservative views about gender and sexuality. Although in the nineteenth century these conservative social values were identified by Black Nationalists as the best of Western civilization, twentieth-century nationalists would call the very same values distinctly African (Dawson 2001). The NOI and other nationalist organizations have gained strength by emphasizing these values in their attempts to convert prisoners and others. Malcolm X himself was recruited by the NOI in prison.

Malcolm X's split with the Nation of Islam was the foundation and inspiration for the later development of a more powerful and vocal nationalist movement. While Malcolm X's shift from a race-first philosophy to a more internationalist perspective was catalyzed by the accusations of infidelity against Elijah Muhammad, his pilgrimage to Mecca was the creative force behind his new beliefs (Haley 1991). During his pilgrimage, Malcolm X came to believe that interracial coalitions could work together for racial justice. His new conception of internationalism emphasized that colonized states and people around the world had to rise up and form coalitions to fight for social justice and racial equality. He promoted coalition and fellowship with the newly independent nations in Africa in particular: "I think the single worst mistake of the American black organizations, and their leaders, is that they have failed to establish brotherhood and communication between the independent nations of Africa and the American black people. Why, every day, the black African heads of state should be receiving direct accounts of the latest developments in the American black man's struggles – instead of the US State Department's releases to Africans which always imply that the American black man's struggle is being 'solved'" (347). Malcolm X also embraced Kwame Nkrumah, the president of Ghana, who was known for his Pan-Africanist and socialist beliefs. Malcolm X's flirtation with the socialist world led him to meet with and speak positively of officials from communist China and Cuba (Haley 1991; C. Moore 1991) and to support the Arab world and the possibility of interracial cooperation.

Malcolm X, who had once criticized white liberals, began to believe that some might become allies in the fight for racial justice: "Each hour here in the Holy Land enables me to have greater spiritual insights into what is happening in America between black and white. The American Negro never can be blamed for his animosities – he is only reacting to four hundred years of the conscious racism of the American whites. But as racism leads America up the suicide path, I do believe, from the experiences that I have had with them, that the whites of the younger generation, in the colleges and universities, will see the handwriting on the wall and many of them will turn to the spiritual path of truth – the only way left to America to ward off the disaster that racism inevitably must lead to" (Haley 1991, 341).

Malcolm X's assassination ended the development of his vision, but the Black Panthers developed a secular version of his international-ist perspective. The Black Panther Party for Self Defense, founded in 1966 by Huey Newton and Bobby Seale, was formed in response to police brutality and the need for traffic control to protect small children from speeding cars (Pearson 1994). Later, the party developed children's schools, breakfast programs, and many other services that spread across the nation. In addition to dealing with practical issues, however, the party fostered intellectual and theoretical activity. Huey Newton and others borrowed liberally from the works of Mao Tse-tung, Frantz Fanon, Kwame Nkrumah, Karl Marx, Che Guevara, Malcolm X, and others to form a unique ideological perspective that sought to negoti-ate the space between the disparate positions of Black Nationalists and

Marxists (Cleaver 1969; Route 1991; Pearson 1994; Brent 1996). The party favored community control of both public resources and government functions. Panther-style internationalism asserted that urban ghettos were equivalent to colonial states, that whites and others could help the cause by organizing within their own communities, that violent revolution was acceptable if it was needed to protect the community, and, finally, that the most desirable form of social organization was democratic socialism (Pearson 1994; Newton 1995). These beliefs fueled the party's growth and its practical, service-oriented activities.

Ideology distinguished the Black Panthers from their contemporaries who espoused nationalism based on the NOI model. Newton and the Panthers explicitly rejected much of existing Black Nationalism as being impractical, reactionary, and myopic in its single-minded focus on race. In his writing, Panther minister of defense Huey Newton explicitly attacked what he called "reactionary nationalism" and began the process of defining "revolutionary nationalism" in response to what he felt were the failings of the NOI model: "There are two kinds of nationalism, revolutionary nationalism and reactionary nationalism. Revolutionary nationalism is first dependent upon a people's revolution with the end goal of the people being in power. Therefore to be a revolutionary nationalist you would by necessity have to be a socialist. If you are a reactionary nationalist you are not a socialist and your end goal is the oppression of the people" (Newton n.d.). Newton labeled as reactionary the focus on culture and behavior that characterized what would later be called "cultural nationalism"; he claimed that cultural nationalists conflated culture and race with class and materialism (Haskins 1997). Newton believed that both class and race were central to understanding oppression in the world and that black control of institutions and government did not necessarily result in freedom or better conditions for blacks.

As the Panthers visited other countries, their faith in socialism grew stronger. Right-wing black leaders such as Mobutu Sese Seko in Zaire, who in Newton's estimation oppressed the working class, proved to them that black political control was not sufficient in itself to liberate African people. In an interview, Newton criticized the boxer Muhammad Ali for supporting a "Fascist Mobutu in Zaire" and commented on events in Angola: "As far as Angola in relationship to blacks in the United States, I think it was a fantastic conscious-raising event because blacks and political people in general, black – I'm speaking of blacks in particular, black political people – and the masses now understand that everything black is not necessarily good. For a long time, with the black nationalist movement, the cultural nationalists, only – only demanded independence for African countries, and had no understanding that it's possible to have a conflict among black people, political conflict" (Newton n.d.).

Newton made these statements from Cuba, where he became increasingly convinced that socialism was central to eradicating racism. This point of view, which saw socialist regimes as implicitly positive, fueled the Panthers' use of socialism as an organizing principle (C. Moore 1991). Cuba became both an ally of the Panthers and their shining example of socialism's ability to eliminate racial inequality. The Panthers embraced white radicals, supported the socialist regime in China, and made gender and sexual equality core components of Panther ideology (C. Moore 1991; Robinson 1991; Newton 1995).[1] Thus, Newton and revolutionary nationalists saw the black community as differentiated, while cultural nationalists clung to a conception of African unity that sought to bury differences of gender and class under the rubric of a universal black identity. This ideological difference led to difficult and sometimes violent conflicts among nationalists.

The first major split with cultural nationalists came as a result of the severed relationship between the Panthers and Stokely Carmichael. Carmichael joined the Panthers after leaving SNCC and the civil rights movement to further develop his slogan, "Black Power" (Pearson 1994).[2] Carmichael was initially optimistic about his relationship with the Panthers because the organization drew significant grass-roots attention to the idea of a more militant response to racial inequality. As we will see later in the chapter, however, Carmichael began to criticize the Black Panthers' socialist leanings following his visit to Cuba. Carmichael charged that the Panthers who visited Cuba

---

[1] Theory and practice were very different realms for the Panthers. Newton wrote extensively on gender equality and the need to practice tolerance of gays and lesbians in the African American community. The Panthers' poor record in terms of personal violence against women, however, is well documented (Pearson 1994).

[2] Carmichael suffered a nervous breakdown after the police crackdown on the civil rights march in Selma. His experience there converted him away from nonviolence and coalition building and called him to assert a Black Power perspective (Pearson 1994).

failed to see the ongoing presence of racism on the island (Pearson 1994). Carmichael also argued that Cuba was proof of the inadequacy of socialism; in doing so, he suggested that the white left would remain racist. In response, the Panthers published propaganda suggesting that Carmichael had become a CIA informant. The split between Carmichael and the Black Panthers spawned further conflicts between the Panthers and cultural nationalists and within the Panther organization itself.

The argument between revolutionary nationalists and cultural nationalists – particularly between the Panthers and the US organization led by Ron Karenga – eventually turned violent. The bitter battle began with Huey Newton's pronouncement that cultural nationalists were misguided. Utilizing Fanon's ideas about the relationship between culture and oppression, Newton attacked African American culture as a product of the experience of oppression. "The black man's culture bore the marks of oppression," he wrote. "The black man could wrest his manhood from white society only through revolutionary political struggle – not through posturing, dress, or reviving African cultural roots" (1995, 76). The US organization responded that the Panthers were blinded by Marxist ideology, which Karenga considered to be a tool used by liberal whites to detract attention from the true, racial struggle. The FBI's counterintelligence program used agents and false written threats to bring about a violent conflict between the two organizations that ended in the shooting deaths of Panthers "Bunchy" Carter and John Huggins on the campus of UCLA (Pearson 1994; Brent 1996). Ultimately, the war with the FBI destroyed the Panthers, and it would take until the early 1990s for cultural nationalists to recover.

The initial division that set the stage for the violence and turmoil was, as noted above, a disagreement about race and politics in Cuba. As discussed in Chapter 3, Castro embraced the idea of racial equality and became a symbol of radical revolutionary activity throughout the African diaspora. Castro also expressed deep and lasting support for African Americans in their fight for racial equality. In visits to the United States in the early 1960s, he openly courted African American support with fiery speeches, such as his challenge to Adlai Stevenson in 1961: "I would like to ask Mr. Stevenson, what would happen if the government of the United States, which claims to be the champion of democracy, dared arm not only the Negroes of the cotton-fields of the

South, but the Negroes here in Harlem? I dare you: arm them and let's see if they exercise the right to vote or the right to pull the trigger to liquidate existing racial discrimination in the United States" (quoted in C. Moore 1991, 112). This type of rhetoric convinced radicals, liberals, and many others to support Castro. As we saw in the previous chapter, however, Castro attempted to prevent the development of black political movements in Cuba at the same time that he was a beacon for racial justice on the international stage. While he has embraced the ideals of racial equality, his regime has explicitly attacked the expressions of black self-determination that are the central features of the struggle for racial equality. This contradictory behavior became apparent in the relationship between the Castro regime and Black Power activists; the problem of racial equality and self-determination in Cuba helped to crystallize the differences between revolutionary nationalists, who saw Castro's regime positively, and cultural nationalists, who criticized it.

African Americans' Experiences in Castro's Cuba

The late 1960s were years of great turmoil within the United States. African Americans formed mass movements to fight for civil rights and racial justice and were met with violent repression by government forces (Pearson 1994; Dawson 2001). Frustrated that peaceful protests were countered with violence, many young activists turned to militant forms of nationalism (Cleaver 1968; Planas 1993). They sought to defend the African American community against police brutality. These young activists' challenge to authority prompted violent clashes with police that resulted in the prosecution of activists, including Huey Newton, William Lee Brent, Assata Shakur, Eldridge Cleaver, Robert Williams, and others (Newton n.d.; Cleaver 1969; Pearson 1994). The FBI and local police organizations arrested and imprisoned people whom they considered to be dangerous activists (C. Moore 1991; Pearson 1994; Haskins 1997), and some activists, including Fred Hampton and Bobby Hutton, were killed in the ensuing clashes. Others like Geronimo Pratt, Huey Newton, Eldridge Cleaver, Angela Davis, William Brent, and Assata Shakur were jailed and faced lifelong imprisonment on charges of murder, robbery, or attempted murder. In order to avoid facing trial in a legal system that rarely provided justice for

African Americans, many of the accused fled the country as political refugees (C. Moore 1991; Pearson 1994).

Some black activists fled to Cuba because they felt the island was a safe haven from U.S. authorities; it had no extradition treaty with the United States. Cuba was easily accessible, and it symbolically represented defiance of the United States in the Western hemisphere. Other black activists sought safety in countries like Ghana, Algeria, and Sweden, but Cuba became a central hub even for those en route to other places, because black activists and the Cuban government shared an enemy and the common purpose of exposing U.S. repression. Activists who arrived in Cuba expecting to find a racially equitable society found, however, that the reality was much more complicated. The successes and failures of racial politics in Cuba forced these individuals to reassess their perspectives and, as a consequence, their feelings about race and politics in Cuba.

Robert Williams

In 1961, Robert Williams became the first prominent black leader to flee to Cuba. Williams faced an arrest warrant after his units, which were organized to provide self-defense for the black community in Monroe, North Carolina, got into a shootout with the state's National Guard (Cohen 1972; Tyson 1999). Williams had already visited Cuba and campaigned for the acceptance of Cuban ideals; he had argued that the United States should allow black leaders to visit Cuba to see how discrimination was eradicated (Cruse 1984). Williams also stated prior to his exile that he would rather be used as a pawn by Cuba against U.S. imperialism than as an Uncle Tom who white-washed Jim Crow (Tyson 1999). Williams arrived in Cuba, then, with the understanding that the island nation had solved its race problem. Though he was an honored guest in Cuba, his honeymoon with the Cuban state would not last forever (Cruse 1984; C. Moore 1991).

Williams maintained a strong Black Nationalist, separatist strain in his beliefs, which he espoused while in Cuba (Cruse 1984; C. Moore 1991; Tyson 1999). This brought him into conflict with the Cuban government, which had explicitly forbidden the existence of autonomous black organizations and political organizing. Williams also became annoyed with the regime's paternalistic treatment of Afro-Cubans. As a result, Williams was chastised by the chairman of the Communist

Party in Havana. According to Williams, the chairman articulated the regime's fear that Williams's beliefs might inspire Black Nationalism in Cuba. He said: "Williams, we want you to know that the Revolution doesn't support Black Nationalism. We believe in integration, in White and Black workers struggling together to change capitalism into Socialism. Black Nationalism is just another form of racism. Cuba has solved her race problem, but if we went along with your ideas about black self-determination in the United States, it wouldn't be long before somebody would start demanding that our Oriente province should become a separate black state and we are not going to let that happen" (quoted in C. Moore 1991, 255). Williams believed that black agency and autonomy were crucial in the struggle for racial equality, but he was forbidden to promote them in Cuba. He had run up against the bitter paradox of Cuban Marxism, which suppressed race-based organizing in order to build Cuban national identity.

Following his conversation with the party chairman, Williams picked up and left for China, where his faith in communism would not be muddied by Chinese racial politics. In 1967, Williams declared that "power in Cuba was in the hands of a white petite bourgeoisie" (255). He asserted: "I find many of [the Cuban communists and U.S. Communist Party members in Cuba] to be very notorious racists. Any Afro-American who believes in self-defense and labors militantly for human rights is branded a black racist and considered ripe for liquidation" (quoted in Tyson 1999, 293). Williams continued to criticize the race situation in Cuba from his home in China, and he later talked with black revolutionaries like Carmichael about Cuba. His move prevented him from seeing, however, that the conflict he encountered in Cuba was with his communist beliefs rather than with the regime. The lack of blacks in China, or of any group that Williams identified as black, made it easy for him to ignore the conflict between a Marxist perspective and his identity politics.

Stokely Carmichael

Using his usual strong rhetoric, Carmichael articulated his philosophy of Black Power in 1965: "When you talk of 'black power,' you talk of bringing this country to its knees. When you talk of building a movement that will smash everything Western civilization has created. When you talk of 'black power,' you talk of picking up where

Malcolm X left off. When you talk of 'black power,' you talk of the black man doing whatever is necessary to get what he needs. We are fighting for our lives" (quoted in Haskins 1997, 16). Carmichael's set of beliefs was based on what he called "a closing of ranks," which he considered to be the only effective strategy for black advancement. It demonstrated his leanings toward cultural nationalism. Like other cultural nationalists, Carmichael believed that "closing ranks" meant repudiating coalitions with whites. He argued: "Coalition's no good. 'Cause what happens when a couple of Negroes join in with a bunch of whites? They get absorbed, that's what. They have to surrender too much to join. . . . Black people got to act as a black community, and the Democratic and Republican Parties are completely irrelevant to them. I know we're gonna be on our own. But we've learned, in the past six years of trying to redeem the white man, that we don't have any alternative now but to go this way" (47).

Carmichael's emphasis on community control and his leadership ability made him an attractive ally to the Panthers (Haskins 1997). Their coalition initially utilized the SNCC leaders' organizational abilities and the Panthers' street savvy. In 1967, as a leader of SNCC, Carmichael embarked on a world tour following his conversion from a civil rights–based politics to a Black Power ideology. The first major stop was Havana, where Carmichael addressed the Organization for Latin American Solidarity. When he arrived in Cuba, Carmichael had not yet completely cut ties with a revolutionary nationalist perspective; the split between cultural and revolutionary nationalists was not yet complete. But Cuba drove the final wedge between him and the Panthers, cutting off the possibility of cooperation across the ideological divide.

Carmichael was warmly received in Cuba; Castro shouted, "Stokely, *esta es tu casa!*" (quoted in C. Moore 1991; Reitlan 1999). Castro also attempted, however, to preempt the growth of any native Black Power movement in Cuba. He stated: "It is from the black segment of the American population that the revolutionary movement in the United States and its revolutionary vanguard will emerge. It is not because of racial problems that this movement has emerged, but because of a social problem, that of exploitation and oppression" (quoted in C. Moore 1991, 257). Castro's repudiation angered Carmichael, who liked and respected Robert Williams and leaned toward Williams's nationalist ideology. But the final straw was the suggestion by members of the Cuban government that the respected Robert Williams, who had recently left Cuba for China, was a CIA informant. This lie led Carmichael to attack the Cuban state and reject Marxist ideology completely in 1968 at a speech on the campus of UCLA that was attended by Angela Davis, several Panthers, and their rivals, members of the US organization. He announced: "Now then that brings us to the point of this thing about communism and socialism. Let's get to that once and for all. Communism is not an ideology suited for black people, period, period, period. Period! The ideologies of communism and socialism speak to class struggle. We are not just facing exploitation. We are facing something much more important, because we are the victims of racism. Neither communism nor socialism speak[s] to the problem of racism. And racism, for black people in this country, is far more important than exploitation. We must therefore consciously strive for an ideology which deals with racism first. That's what we recognize. . . . It is our humanity that is at stake; it is not a question of dollars and cents" (quoted in C. Moore 1991; Pearson 1994).

As a result, Carmichael was declared "Persona Non Grata in Cuba" (C. Moore 1991, 260). Carmichael's repudiation of white progressives was incompatible with the Cuban government's ideology. Carmichael likewise split with the Panthers over their relations with white progressives and their use of Marxist-Leninist philosophy. Because of his views about Marxism and Cuba, the Panthers accused Carmichael of being a pawn of the CIA (Newton 1995). They defended the Cuban government in a criticism of Carmichael: "Although some critics of the Black Panther Party have implied, namely Stokely Carmichael, that we have taken the position that if socialism is instituted that racism automatically ceases, we have never held that position. What we say is that in a socialist society the conditions are more favorable for a people to begin to struggle to eliminate racism. . . . Some members of the Black Panther Party used Cuba as a means of escape from fascist suppression in Babylon and they are alive, well and free today. It would not be in the interest of Cuba or the world revolution to begin to launch attacks at Cuba because they have not been able to eliminate all forms of racism in the ten years since their revolution began" (quoted in Foner 1995, 37). Here, we can see the party defending Cuba for pragmatic reasons without wholeheartedly accepting the Castro regime's claims on the issue of race. Carmichael's assessment of racial politics in Cuba was filtered through the lens of ideology, and his visit to Cuba sharpened the distinction between him and the Black Panthers. This conflict highlighted the central ideological struggle among Black Nationalists in the United States, which was also an underlying struggle in Cuba: the struggle between a Marxist perspective based on class identity and an approach that emphasized race as the primary political identity to the exclusion of others.

Eldridge Cleaver

Eldridge Cleaver was a street hood turned political activist. He became known for his amazing speaking and writing abilities, which he developed during his years in prison. Cleaver began his career as a cultural nationalist when he converted to Islam in prison. A follower of Malcolm X, Cleaver was heartened by Malcolm's rejection of the doctrines of the Nation of Islam (Cleaver 1968). As he saw it, "there were those of us who were glad to be liberated from a doctrine of hate and racial supremacy." He wrote: "The onus of teaching racial supremacy, and that is the white man's burden, is pretty hard to bear" (16; Rout 1991; Haskins 1997).

Upon leaving prison, Cleaver became impressed with the Panthers and disillusioned with the Nation of Islam. He began to look beyond cultural practices for a solution to the race problem. "The Negro's basic situation," he said, "cannot really change without structural changes in America's political and economic system" (quoted in Haskins 1997, 87). This insight led Cleaver to embrace both socialism and the use of extreme violence. When Huey Newton, wounded in a shootout with the police, faced the death penalty for murder, Cleaver remarked, "There is a holocaust coming . . . the war has begun . . . the violent phase of the black liberation struggle is here, and it will spread. From that shot, from that blood, America will be painted red" (38). Soon after Newton's arrest, Cleaver and Little Bobby Hutton were attacked by the Oakland police, leaving Hutton dead – a martyr to the Panther cause – and Cleaver wounded. Cleaver formed a Panther alliance with the white Peace and Freedom Party. He also embraced an internationalist perspective, supporting Castro, Ho Chi Minh, and others in connection with extreme radical white forces (Cleaver 1969). Facing prosecution for his shootout with the police, however, Cleaver was forced into exile. He had powerful enemies, including the FBI and the governor of California, Ronald Reagan (Pearson 1994).

On Christmas Day 1968, Eldridge Cleaver, the most famous member of the Black Panther Party, secretly arrived in Cuba. He remained for five months, under the impression that Castro would commit to training a group of black revolutionaries in Cuba. Cleaver also sought to build a chapter of the Black Panther Party in Cuba. Such an organization would have been a substantial threat to the regime's policy of preventing the establishment of race-oriented organizations. Cleaver was never allowed to start an organization or train forces, and he soon became impatient with the Castro regime. He began to question its commitment to racial equality and was given a book of Cuban history by Communist Party officials. From it, he learned about the black revolutionary Antonio Maceo, who fought side by side with the "Cuban George Washington, José Martí" (Rout 1991). Cleaver felt that Maceo was representative of the hidden racism in Cuba. He stated later: "People said José Martí was the brain and Antonio was the brawn. That is bullshit because Martí died almost immediately after the war began, so there was nothing he could have said to carry the movement through. The white Cubans historically were constantly trying to sell out blacks, to keep them from coming to power. That's the main historical fact" (quoted in Rout 1991, 105). For Cleaver, learning about Maceo was "part of the process of solving the problem we had there" (105).

Following an incident with a young woman that led Cleaver to believe he was going to be set up on a rape charge, he was accused of trying to blackmail a Cuban official. In the belief that the Cubans were out to get him, he began to stockpile weapons and to gather together a group of Afro-Cuban hijackers, whom he baptized the Cuban wing of the Black Panther Party (Rout 1991; C. Moore 1991). Cleaver even let it slip to the Reuters news agency that he was in Cuba and alive in order to protect himself from assassination or incarceration (Rout 1991). Shortly thereafter, Angela Davis was to arrive in Havana. Carlos Moore suggests that the party wanted to end the public relations fiasco that the defection of Williams to China, Carmichael's repudiation, and the growing conflict with Cleaver had created. Many scholars have suggested that the Cuban government wanted to avoid the possibility that Cleaver might meet with Angela Davis and change her mind – and the minds of other African Americans – about Castro (Rout 1991; C. Moore 1991). Whatever the reason, before Davis arrived, a ticket to Algeria materialized along with the message that Cleaver's wife was already there (C. Moore 1991; Rout 1991; Pearson 1994). Cleaver, who had concluded that Cuba was like the San Quentin penitentiary, continued on to Algeria.

Later, Cleaver said: "The white racist Castro dictatorship is more insidious and dangerous for black people than is the white racist regime of South Africa, because no black person has illusions about the intentions of the Afrikaners, but many black people consider Fidel Castro to be a right-on white brother. Nothing could be further from the truth" (quoted in C. Moore 1991, 261–2). Cleaver also later criticized Castro's indiscriminate use of black troops in Africa as an attempt to send blacks away from the country, give the appearance that he was on the side of blacks, and neutralize dangerous elements within the country. Reflecting on this period of his life, Cleaver felt those in the party had forgotten their nationalism (Rout 1991). By nationalism, Cleaver clearly meant a race-first philosophy that was skeptical toward the intentions of white Marxists, including the Cuban government. Cleaver's Cuban experience, then, directed him away from revolutionary nationalism and back toward the cultural nationalist "race first" perspective.

Angela Davis

Consistently throughout her career as an activist, Angela Davis sought to understand the nexus among race, class, and gender. Unlike many others, she leaned toward orthodox Marxism before she became involved with various Black Nationalist groups. Her interactions with nationalists like George Jackson and Stokely Carmichael caused her to question both Black Nationalism's treatment of gender and its criticism of socialism (Davis 1974). The central question for Davis was how to understand race in the context of other identities.

When Davis distributed copies of George Jackson's *Soledad Brother* to women in prison, she emphasized: "In the past he had seen black women as often acting as a deterrent to the involvement of black men in the struggle. But he had since discovered that this generalization was wrong" (62). She also criticized a number of cultural nationalist groups for their gender politics. She said of Karenga's US organization: "I became acquainted very early with the wide spread presence of an unfortunate belief among some Black male activists – namely to confuse their political activity with an assertion of their maleness. They saw – and some continue to see – Black manhood as something separate from Black womanhood. These men view Black women as a threat to their attainment of manhood – especially those Black women who take initiative and work to become leaders in their own right. The constant harangue by the US men was that I needed to redirect my energies and use them to give my man strength and inspiration so that he might more effectively contribute his talents to the struggle for Black liberation" (161).

Davis felt uneasy about excluding whites from the movement. She argued explicitly that "when white people are indiscriminately viewed as the enemy, it is virtually impossible to develop a political solution" (150). She became distressed by Carmichael's views of socialism, which led to a rift between them. She recalled, "I was distressed to discover that among some of the black leaders there was the tendency to completely dismiss Marxism as 'the white man's thing.'" "It had become clear to me," she wrote, "that in order to achieve the goals of the black liberation struggle, it would have to become part of a revolutionary movement embracing all working people" (150–1). She hoped that Carmichael's visit to Cuba would bring him around to agreeing with her point of view: "I was encouraged to learn that Stokely was about to make a trip to Cuba. Once he saw black, brown and white people constructing together their socialist society, he would be compelled, so I thought, to reexamine his own position" (151). Following his visit, however, Carmichael hardened his position against Cuba, and his UCLA speech drew the wrath of Davis, who wrote: "His speech was all the more disturbing because I knew that he had been in Cuba the preceding summer and had been warmly received wherever he went. I knew for a fact that Cuba had unequivocally demonstrated to him that socialism alone could liberate black people. Now that he was back in the US where the official propaganda made socialism less popular, he was opportunistically reversing his position" (168). Committed to a revolutionary identity, Davis was unwilling to believe that Carmichael's criticism of socialism and Cuba could be anything but opportunism.

After joining the Communist Party, Angela Davis made her first trip to Cuba in October 1972. Her observations of racial politics in Cuba validated her conversion to Marxism and her involvement in the

Communist Party. In Cuba, Davis was allowed to address mass rallies, a privilege that was extended to few visitors (Davis 1974; C. Moore 1991). The positive reception she received convinced her of the warmth and nobility of the Cuban people and of the power of Marxism put into practice. In her autobiography, Davis obscured racial difference in favor of presenting a picture of a unified class and national identity in Cuba. "Wherever we went," she wrote, "we were immensely impressed by the results of the fierce struggle that had been waged against racism after the triumph of the revolution. The first executive decrees of the new government had been to abolish segregation in the cities, brought to Cuba by corrupt capitalists from the United States" (1974, 210). Davis assumed that because of its belief in Marxism and its public support of racial equality, the Castro regime would not promote discrimination in Cuba. Her analysis of racism in Cuba was materialist: "It was clear to us – Kendra, Carlos and I, the three black members, incessantly discussed it – that only under socialism could this fight against racism have been so successfully executed" (210). Davis seems to have been unaware of some of the repressive measures against black identity and Black Power that had been taken by the Cuban government. In fact, she unwittingly broke down some of these barriers. It has been said that as a result of Davis's visit and her popularity, blacks who wore Afros ceased to be harassed by government officials (C. Moore 1991).[3] Ironically, Davis pushed the boundaries of state hegemony in Cuba by expressing black pride through her hairstyle, not her words.

Assata Shakur

Assata Shakur began her career as an activist rather unremarkably. There was little evidence to suggest that she would eventually become a revolutionary nationalist and a rebel on trial for murdering a police officer. Shakur was a working-class college student concerned, above all, with trying to improve herself through education (Shakur 1987). Along her route to revolutionary nationalism, she first experimented with traditional liberal civil rights beliefs and then with cultural nationalism. Her experience with cultural nationalism led her to change her name, and her name change was the first step in a journey that led

---

[3] Later, in 1992, the barriers to religious observance would be broken by yet another African American visitor, Jesse Jackson.

her to envision a black nation for the first time. She recalls: "My mind spaced out on the idea and in a minute I was imagining red, black, and green buses, apartment buildings with African motifs, black television shows and movies that reflected the real quality of blacks' life rather than the real quality of white racism. Sure enough, I liked the idea of a black nation, but it seemed too farfetched" (184).

As she studied, however, she came to see the struggle in class terms, or at least as a struggle against capitalism. This brought her into conflict with her cultural nationalist friends, who clung to a race-first perspective: "I got into heated arguments with sisters and brothers who claimed that the oppression of Black people was only a question of race. I argued that there were Black oppressors as well as white ones. Black folks with money have always tended to support candidates who they believed would protect their financial interests. As far as I was concerned, it didn't take too much brains to figure out that Black people are oppressed because of class as well as race, because we are poor and because we are Black" (190). Her belief in socialism conflicted, however, with her feelings about the paternalism of white communists: "I could not stand the condescending paternalistic attitudes of some of the white people in those groups. Some of the older members thought that because they had been in the struggle for socialism for a long time, they knew all the answers to the problems of black people and all the aspects of the black liberation struggle" (191). Her disaffection with the white left led her to embrace only selected aspects of revolutionary nationalist beliefs: "Although I respected the work and position of many groups on the left, I felt it was necessary for black people to come together to organize our own structures and our own revolutionary political party. I believe that to gain our liberation, we must come from a position of power and unity and that a black revolutionary party, led by black revolutionary leaders, is essential" (191). Shakur's beliefs, then, could best be described as an amalgamation of revolutionary nationalism, black feminism, and cultural nationalism. These beliefs would shape her analysis of race in Cuba.

Shakur's career as a soldier in the Black Liberation Army caused her severe legal troubles. Her tumultuous career as a revolutionary led to two arrests on trumped-up charges of bank robbery (she was later acquitted) and ended with her arrest and conviction for allegedly murdering a state trooper. In 1977, Shakur daringly escaped from prison in

New York and fled to Cuba, where she still lives. Shakur's history in the struggle and her membership in the Black Liberation Army have made her a celebrity in Cuba, where she appeared on the dais at the 26th of July rally in 1997 with fellow black radical Kwame Toure (Stokely Carmichael), who was visiting Cuba to receive cancer treatments.[4]

In discussing Cuba, Shakur has criticized her nationalist past. "Without a truly internationalist component," she says, "nationalism was reactionary. We have fought imperialism as an international system of exploitation, and, we as revolutionaries need to be internationalists to defeat it" (267). Her embrace of an internationalist perspective indicates that since moving to Cuba, she has adopted a more Marxist position. In her autobiography, Shakur tells the story of a former soldier who fought in Angola for African liberation and who was repulsed by the idea that his daughter had chosen a black man as a husband. The man eventually accepted the relationship and his grandchildren. Shakur uses this narrative to identify racism in Cuba with personal prejudice. Shakur also argues that racism in Cuba is different historically from racism in the United States. When she arrived in Cuba, Shakur "was most interested in learning what had happened to blacks after the triumph of the Revolution" (269). The initial response she received was similar to that heard by Davis. People commented to her, "Racism is illegal here in Cuba" (269). Shakur argues that the Cuban government has, for the most part, "been committed to eliminating all forms of racism." She writes: "There were no racist institutions, structures, or organizations, and I understood how the Cuban economic system undermined rather than fed racism" (270). Thus, for Shakur, the absence of formal discrimination is evidence of the absence of racism. She does not explore whether there is any institutional basis for racism or question whether Cuban discrimination laws are enforced.

Instead, Shakur focuses on the lack of agency and identity among Afro-Cubans, ignoring the state's role in limiting black organizations and black critique of the regime. Shakur most systematically criticizes black Cubans who seem not to identify as black. This stance

---

4 Despite its earlier conflicts with Carmichael, the Castro regime eventually became more tolerant of Carmichael's politics. Though he was living in Africa, he was welcomed in Cuba for cancer treatment. Carmichael did not address any mass rallies in Cuba, and he died of cancer in Africa shortly after his visit.

makes her feel uncomfortable, because black pride has been such an important part of her political development and, she believes, of the struggle against racism. Shakur was puzzled when a black friend told her, "I am not African, I am Cuban." She feels that black identity has been displaced in Cuba by identities based on nationality or racial mixing. Shakur writes that she sees little value in the category of mulatto: "I can't imagine any type of political movement based on a mulatto identity" (271). Shakur has remained convinced that Afro-Cubans must develop black agency connected to black identity in order to end what racism there is in Cuba, or even to struggle with the government toward this end.

Conclusion

Encounters with the racial ideology of the Castro regime have forced Black Nationalists to make difficult choices. The cases discussed in this chapter demonstrate that generalizations about Black Nationalists' experiences in Cuba are difficult to make. While Angela Davis's visit to Cuba confirmed for her the validity of her revolutionary nationalist beliefs, Eldridge Cleaver's period of exile in Cuba convinced him to abandon revolutionary nationalism for cultural nationalism. Robert Williams became convinced that the Cuban regime was racist but clung to his revolutionary nationalist ideology in China. Stokely Carmichael, attracted to some aspects of revolutionary nationalism when he went to Cuba, ultimately rejected it because of the racism he identified on the island. Assata Shakur's blended cultural, revolutionary, and feminist nationalist ideology shifted in a more Marxist direction after she fled to Cuba, but she has remained critical of Afro-Cubans' identity politics.

What all of these cases demonstrate clearly, however, is that Cuba played a central role in defining revolutionary and cultural nationalism in opposition to each other in the 1960s and 1970s. The primary feature of this split was a difference of opinion about racial self-determination. Through the lens of Marxism, revolutionary nationalists saw the potential of white-led regimes such as the one in Cuba to end racial inequality, and they began building coalitions with white radicals. Cultural nationalists rejected this strategy. Though the conservatism of cultural nationalism has often paralyzed the movement in the United States, the cultural nationalists' focus on race and self-determination was central to their ability to criticize Cuban racial politics. Revolutionary nationalists were able to build pragmatic political coalitions and expand their vision, but they were ultimately unable to develop a critique of some of the problems of racial inequality within Cuba. Forcing activists to choose between Marxist politics and ideals of racial self-determination, Cuba became a point of divergence for Black Nationalism that ultimately helped to destroy revolutionary nationalism.

Nationalists' experiences in Cuba also demonstrate the boundaries of Cuban racial politics. The visits from black activists pointed to both the strengths and the weaknesses of the Castro regime's racial policies. The absence of constant dialogue and self-criticism about race produces stagnation in any society; when positive steps for racial change are not continually being taken, economic shifts are likely to produce setbacks for racial equality. Cuban identity has been figured in decidedly European terms, with Afro-Cuban culture and Chinese culture relegated to the arena of folklore. Afro-Cuban and Chinese organizations have been discouraged and repressed. Mutual aid societies and cultural organizations that engaged in political advocacy prior to the revolution have been destroyed. Without these institutional spheres for analysis of the race problem, the capacity for continued racial improvement has been severely limited, and inclusionary discrimination has come to characterize race relations in Cuba.

5

Race and Daily Life in Cuba During the Special Period

Part I: Interview Data

On a hot March afternoon in Havana, a Cuban friend and I entered the Havana Libre Hotel and waited to meet with two other friends. We sat at the bar and tried to order drinks. The bartender refused us service, however, and asked us to leave, whereupon a security guard soon followed and escorted us out of the hotel. It bears mentioning that my friend and I are black. My friend, "Pedro,"[1] is a dark young Cuban man with sharp features that denote his origin in Santiago de Cuba. In island terminology, he is an "Oriental."[2] The type of rude treatment we received would not have been out of character in 1950s America – or in 1950s Cuba, for that matter – but it seemed strange to be at the receiving end of it in Cuba today, in a society in which people of all colors live, work, love, and celebrate – for the most part, together. How, then, can I explain a Jim Crow experience in what appears to be a rainbow society?

Angry and confused, my friend and I left for another establishment. I asked Pedro what had happened. He gave me an explanation that others seemed to agree with: "We are both black and well dressed. I am clearly an Oriental and therefore lower class. You are black and dressed in American clothes. We are, in their eyes, hustlers, criminals.

---

[1] All names of Cubans I interviewed, including that of Pedro, have been changed in order to protect the identities of the speakers.

[2] "Oriental" refers to Cubans from the eastern part of the island, most specifically those from Santiago de Cuba, the area with the highest concentration of blacks.

Blacks are not supposed to have the cash for nice clothes, because we do not have relatives in Miami or good jobs that pay dollars. People will always think we are either hustlers or athletes."

Beyond the general challenges that measuring experience poses to any social scientific endeavor, race is a particularly vexing problem. It is discursive and ideological. It has no existence outside of a set of social definitions and practices (Stepan 1991). In the case of Cuba, defining who is black and how that "fact" affects life chances is a moving target. The state's policies of declaring the race problem solved and at the same preventing research on the subject create substantial barriers for researchers (Casal 1989; de la Fuente 1995; Helg 1995; Covarrubia 1999). The type of data often used to establish and measure racial inequality within the United States simply do not exist for Cuba.

This chapter represents a first step in overcoming the problems of data collection that plague the study of race in Cuba. It draws on in-depth interviews with forty-four Cubans collected over approximately ten months on the island. The interviews lasted from approximately thirty minutes to two hours and involved Cubans from all walks of life. The Cubans interviewed lived in several geographical regions: Six lived in the city of Matanzas, two in Veradero, six in Pinar del Rio, ten in Santiago de Cuba, and twenty-three in Havana. There is not sufficient variation to classify this as a representative sample of opinions across the country or in any particular region. The interviews are illustrative, however, and they provide evidence to support the argument that despite significant progress, a structure of racial hierarchy remains in Cuba. In order to protect the identities of the people interviewed should my research materials have been seized, the interviews were not recorded.[3] Notes were taken in shorthand during the interviews. I frequently asked speakers to repeat what they had said so that I might capture quotations of the kind that appear in this chapter.

My interview subjects showed little reticence about discussing race and their lives in Cuba. The interviews generally began with

---

[3] Research on race, while gaining acceptance, is still looked upon with suspicion in Cuba. Some of the comments contained in this chapter are of an extremely sensitive nature. The accuracy of the accounts and speakers must be balanced with the need to protect the confidentiality of the respondents. I have taken great pains to do so.

conversations about the current economic and political situation. With older subjects, more time was spent reflecting on life before and throughout the revolution. With younger subjects, I focused on the current situation and the future of the island. I was invited back to talk more with many of the people I interviewed, and in particular with the interviewees in Havana, where I spent the majority of my time. Over the course of several interviews, I was able to reflect, to inquire about new information, and to foster unhurried and detailed discussions.

The use of interviews has both advantages and disadvantages. The primary disadvantage is the difficulty of obtaining a representative sample that allows for the type of coding and statistical inference favored in political science research. In contrast to surveys, open-ended interviews do not systematically test a series of stock variables in a controlled environment. But much has been written about the difficulty of examining racial attitudes and about the limitations of survey research in this area. Both survey research and the literature on political behavior in political science tend to focus on snapshots; the literature has prioritized single moments as they are represented by survey responses (Zaller 1993). Michael Hanchard explains: "Most survey studies of political behavior with an interview component are concerned with political preferences at moments of choice (elections, referendums, etc.) rather than with the more critical task of attempting to locate conscious attitudes about politics based upon personal experiences. This is a crucial prerequisite for a comprehensive understanding of racial politics and political cultures in multiethnic politics" (1994, 27). We are unable to understand from survey data how and why people arrive at their expressed attitudes, and we cannot observe how they reason about any given topic.

The weaknesses of the survey research approach, however, are the strengths of in-depth interviews. Open-ended in-depth interviews allow researchers to explore how specific life experiences and information shape attitudes and opinions about race that are complex and often contradictory. While it is certainly helpful to have "objective" measures of how race structures life chances, it is equally important to understand to what degree individuals *believe* that race structures their life chances. This is the factor that allows us to assess the political salience of race. Because race is itself an ideological construct, a true measure of its impact on attitudes and behavior is more likely to be found in subjective discussions than in a review of available data.

The interview data I collected allowed me to combine an analysis of the structure of racial hierarchy on the island with a consideration of how Afro-Cuban agency interacts with this structure. In *Domination and the Arts of Resistance: Hidden Transcripts*, James Scott suggests that state hegemony comes in thin and thick varieties. States that have won only thin hegemony must attempt to convince subordinate groups that "the social order in which they live is natural and inevitable"; the members of these groups often feel resignation and ambivalence toward the state. Subordinate groups which live under states that have achieved thick hegemony, on the other hand, possess a far-reaching false consciousness that produces consent. Hanchard, relying on Gramsci, explains why leaders rarely need to utilize coercion to maintain order: "Once a dominant group assumes leadership – that is, the development of political, intellectual, and cultural influences that correlate with their economic power and coercive powers – the principal tasks become those of compromise and brokerage, the ability to influence and persuade recalcitrant or even oppositional groups under a new political rubric" (19). The "new rubric" in the case of Cuba is a reliance on a unified national identity that obscures difference and externalizes racial problems.

I argue in this chapter that the Cuban state has achieved only a "thin" hegemony that must be reinforced through coercion, cooptation, and the skilled manipulation of symbols. If the state's hegemony were complete – if it had managed to produce a false consciousness among subaltern groups – there would be no gap between the official story on race and the opinions of the person on the street. If there were no hegemony or coercion, on the other hand, social movements would quickly erupt in an attempt to make the official story meet the on-the-street reality. Instead, there is a middle ground in Cuba; alternative points of view operate around and beneath the official story. Robin Kelley and James Scott identify this middle ground as "infrapolitics" (Scott 1990; Kelley 1994). Robin Kelley writes: "Oppressed groups challenge those in power by constructing a 'hidden transcript,' a dissident culture that manifests itself in daily conversations, folklore, jokes, songs, and other cultural practices. The veiled social and cultural worlds of oppressed people frequently surface in everyday forms of resistance – theft, footdragging, the destruction of property – or, more rarely, in open attacks on individuals, institutions or symbols of domination" (8).

Cuban infrapolitics involves participation in the black market: The illicit trade in gasoline, foodstuffs, consumer goods, sex, drugs, and cigars is a means of survival for many Cubans. To the extent that Cubans link their economic dislocation to failures of the government and the government's racial policies, black market participation is not only a form of survival but also a form of resistance to the new order – not simply to the Cuban state but also to some extent to foreign tourists, the Soviet collapse, the U.S. blockade, and other external factors that are perceived as more proximate causes of dislocation than the Cuban state. Despite the power of the state and its banning of alternative institutions, then, many Afro-Cubans hold and express alternative points of view about racial politics on the island and engage in illegal activity as an outlet for these impulses. The case of Cuba demonstrates how powerful infrapolitics can be (Eckstein 1995).

Some clear patterns emerged from my conversations with Cubans from a variety of walks of life. After reviewing briefly the circumstances of Cuba's "special period," the following discussion considers the relationship between race and the tourist industry, remittances, the black market, unemployment, the sex industry, access to legal employment, law enforcement, housing, and issues of culture and identity. Next, it analyzes Afro-Cubans' attitudes toward racial politics itself and toward the United States. Finally, it considers whether any of the other three major theories of racial politics that I have discussed in this study is able to account for the racial situation in Cuba as well as the race cycles model does. The chapter will demonstrate (1) that Afro-Cubans often perceive race as a significant and increasing determinant of life chances in Cuba; (2) that the new economic order has contributed to a step backward in terms of racial equality; (3) that the black market and migration are forms of resistance to economic displacement and that they are perceived through a racial lens; and (4) that racial politics in the United States and the U.S. embargo have a profound impact on racial politics on the island. These facts are evidence of the persistence of racial hierarchy in Cuba, and they demonstrate that the gains of the revolution have not been durable.

The Special Period

Between 1989 and 1991, the collapse of the Soviet Union and COME-CON led to severe economic hardship for Cuba. Even earlier, the Soviet Union had begun to demand hard currency from Cuba for trade and to slash aid and loans to the Castro regime. Without favorable trade relations with the Soviet Union, the Cuban economy virtually came to a halt. Castro declared the period "a special period in peacetime" (Eckstein 1995). The collapse of COMECON exposed the underlying weakness in the Cuban economy; Cuba had long depended upon imports for food, energy, and key agricultural inputs. A committed socialist in Havana named Julio made this point: "We call this the 'special period,' but it is not. What we have today in Cuba is the 'real' period. Our internal economy is very weak. We are dependent and poor. Cubans are accustomed to a lifestyle that is not sustainable given the economic fundamentals of our country."[4] In response to the collapse, the Castro regime introduced a sweeping set of reforms. These reforms included austerity measures that cut food allotments, salaries, and electricity supplies as well as access to other products, health care, and government subsidies of drug costs. Unemployment benefits were slashed, and many state industries shut down. In order to obtain hard currency and stimulate investment, the Castro regime also opened the island to tourism and to limited foreign investment. Resources were shifted from the population to provide comfortable conditions for tourists, and with the growth of tourism, dollars – once illegal – became commonly used on the island (Eckstein 1995). They soon became the preferred currency.

The impact of the legal use of dollars on the island has been profound. In 2002, the government established a managed float between the Cuban peso and the dollar at 20:1. Goods that can be purchased using pesos are heavily subsidized, but goods that must be imported are not, and they can be purchased in dollars only. Thus, the island can be said to have two economies: a dollar economy and a peso economy. Those with access to dollars are able to purchase a wider array of goods, including some necessities like medicine, clothing, and cooking

---

[4] Unless otherwise noted, all quotations in this chapter are taken from the interviews I conducted on the island.

oil. In a sense, then, Cuba today has not one population, but two: those with dollars and those without.

Life on the island of Cuba is currently very difficult for many people. The lack of adequate employment, housing, income, and basic necessities has created severe problems. Government rations and the buying power of the Cuban peso have been greatly reduced. Unemployment has risen sharply, and salaries in many areas do not meet the minimum needs of the employed (Eckstein 1995). Severe housing shortages, particularly in Havana, make it necessary for several families or generations to live in small apartments together. Illegal migrants from the countryside live in shantytowns that ring the city of Havana. Gainful employment is extremely difficult to obtain. (Because of the erosion of the peso's buying power, "gainful employment" in Cuba today must involve either payment in dollars or access to goods and services as perks of employment.) The transformation from an economy of broad distribution to one with scant resources has been disadvantageous to many Cubans, black and white alike. Afro-Cubans, however, tend to believe that blacks have more limited access to dollars and to gainful employment than whites do.

Tourist *Apartheid*

The connection between tourism and dollars is close. Currently, tourism is the number one sector in the Cuban economy, providing hard currency for both individuals and the government (Eckstein 1995). The tourist industry primarily involves joint ventures between European and Canadian companies and CUBACAN, an arm of the Cuban military created to develop private enterprise. It is very lucrative, but unfortunately it has created a host of problems for Cubans, including a growth in prostitution, inequality, and racial tension.

The term "tourist *apartheid*" was coined in the early 1990s when the Cuban government began to open the island to tourists. Only tourists could stay in the hotels set aside for them, and only tourists could shop in special "dollar stores," where goods unavailable elsewhere on the island were sold. Cuban citizens could enter these institutions only if they were escorted by tourists, and they were barred from owning or trading dollars. In 1993, during the darkest days of the economic crisis, when food shortages were widespread, Cuban citizens broke into several stores at prominent hotels. A young Cuban named Luis described the events of those days: "It was the summer of 1993. People were angry and hungry. Groups began to break into stores near the Malecon, and they began to loot. During that time, Cubans were not allowed in the dollar stores. The police quickly descended upon the looters and broke up the riot. Even Fidel himself came down to the Malecon to help bring order to the situation. Later, it became legal to possess dollars and shop in dollar stores. However, for Cubans, security is very tight, and you are not treated well in many places. This is especially the case for us black Cubans, who are perceived to be thieves and hustlers." Luis's comment points to the frustration that Cubans felt about the existence of a gap between the dollar economy and the peso economy. In response to the riot, the government allowed Cubans to handle and use dollars.

But while the line between the two economies has become softer, race now serves as a dividing line. Employment in the tourist industry is very lucrative. A bartender at a famous tourist spot in Havana told me, "Here I can make almost $300 a week. In most other jobs on the island, you cannot make that much money in a month." A university professor named Marisol confirmed his statement: "I make about $40 a month [converted from Cuban pesos at 20:1]. People who work with tourists can make almost ten times that amount. Even with rations and government subsidies, I can barely make ends meet. Many people with training and skills have left their jobs to work with tourists." Much like that of the Soviet Union, the Cuban economy is inverted. Jobs in areas like medicine, education, engineering, and construction pay very poorly, while labor in the service industry – because it brings with it access to hard currency and foreign exchange – pays very well.

Race seems to play a role in determining who is able to work within the legitimate sectors of the tourist industry. Ricardo, an Afro-Cuban assistant manager of a hotel outside of Havana, explained: "The foreign corporations do not in general want to hire blacks. Part of it is information. Many of the openings are spread through word of mouth. I think there is a perception that the hotels and the tourists prefer whites, therefore whites get asked to apply. I try to spread the word to blacks when there are openings, but many of them do not get hired, and many cannot make it through the interview process. Many are simply discouraged and do not try anymore. I found out about this job because I had a friend who was being hired. I studied business and management in Spain. I believe I am much more qualified than my counterparts."

Ricardo's account suggests that the perceived "tastes" of European tourists and hotel executives may be limiting opportunities for blacks. It also points to an information gap that puts blacks at a disadvantage when it comes to finding jobs in tourism. Similar sentiments were expressed by others, who indicated that it is difficult for Afro-Cubans to find employment in hotels. A young black woman named Lorena stated: "It is impossible for blacks, and to a large degree for mulattos, to get jobs in hotels that pay dollars. Even if you are educated and attractive, you cannot find work. Europeans have 'refined tastes' and prefer white Cubans. Life is much harder for blacks as a result."

A former government official named Francisco who worked in international affairs described the problem as multidimensional. He said the tastes of European tourists, administrative insensitivity to the problem, and corruption all play roles in excluding blacks from the tourist sector of the economy. "The administration, in its zeal to boost tourism and investment, has sought to cater to the tastes of European tourists and investors," Francisco told me. "That is, they have sought to make the country appear more 'European' and at the same time utilize Afro-Cuban culture as an exotic allure. Because the government has never clearly realized that the problem with this is that blacks remain in inferior sectors and far from power, they have not worked to ensure that blacks are included in the industry other than as entertainment." Thus, perceptions of European tastes interact negatively with the regime's failure to integrate Afro-Cubans into the political economy of the island. But the problem goes deeper than this. "There have been problems with corruption in the hotels," Francisco told me. "Some have paid for their positions. In Veradero, there were recent arrests surrounding this problem. Since blacks do not have equal access to dollars in the form of remittances that whites have, this compounds the problem." I interviewed others who confirmed the existence of corruption and the fact that remittances from relatives in foreign countries provide some Cubans with a needed economic boost.

Remittances

Remittances represent the second-largest portion of the Cuban economy. These payments come to Cubans from friends, family members, and associates who are living and working in foreign countries. Though the racial dimensions of remittances are not initially apparent, they become clear when one examines the demographics of the Cuban exile community. The vast majority of Cubans living off the island reside in the United States. The 1990 census showed that 92 percent of the Cuban American population is white. Thus, it logically follows that the distribution of remittances flows primarily to white families in Cuba. Remittances help the Cubans who receive them to meet their basic needs and to acquire goods that are available for purchase only with dollars. An Afro-Cuban woman named Yolanda described the variety of ways in which remittances foster inequality: "Blacks have fewer relatives in Miami. We do not get remittances. For example, if you get remittances you can start a business, have nice things, and occasionally it takes money to pay to get a job at a big hotel. Some jobs cost money if you want them. The people who make the hiring decisions often take dollars in exchange for aid getting the job. Without dollars, it is hard to get medicine, clothes, an apartment, and good food. It is especially hard to find a nice place to live. There is a terrible housing shortage here in Cuba. My husband and I have no hope for finding our own apartment. We have to live with our families." Blanca, a former member of the Cuban parliament from Havana, stated: "There have recently been cases of arrests for corruption and selling positions. In most cases, it was individuals with access to dollars from remittances who were paying to obtain positions in tourism. It is true that few blacks have access to remittances. Also, the licensing to start a *paladare* or to have tourists stay in your private home is expensive. They require dollars and a large home. Few blacks have these things and are underdeveloped in terms of the new Cuban economy. In this area, I think the gains of the revolution might truly be in jeopardy."

In short, Afro-Cubans face a substantial disadvantage when it comes to the nascent free enterprise system in Cuba. Their skin color limits their access to the tourist economy and its rewards, while Afro-Cubans lack the resources – namely remittances – to begin government-sanctioned small businesses, which are spreading across the country. In the small town of Viñales, a white male business owner explained: "*Paladares* [small home-based restaurants] are growing. We are just learning markets and how to make dollars. We make many mistakes and it can be difficult to please the government, but we are still better off than other workers. I make more here than a group of doctors and teachers combined. But I would not have been able to start the business without remittances from relatives in Miami. They really made this possible." The dollars from Miami fund illegal businesses as well. A white Cuban who operates a covert furniture repair, building, and garment factory in the courtyard of a small apartment building in Pinar del Rio told me: "I got the money from my brother who lives in Miami. He has been there for over twenty years and sends me a healthy remittance. I was able to buy materials and stolen machinery on the black market that allowed me to create my business. I am able to pay the residents here to use the space and to keep quiet. I buy materials and pay my workers with the profits. The remittances help me make money and help during the slow periods. Without that money, this would not have been possible, and I would be among the poor. With help from my brother, I am successful and providing many things I needed for my clients."

The Black Market

The ease with which this business owner is able operate an illegal shop points to the ubiquity of the black market and its relationship with legitimate enterprises. The black market is a part of everyday life in Cuba, and it is difficult to survive or to advance economically without participating in it. The black market is a site of resistance as well as the vanguard of the new economic order (Eckstein 1995). For the purpose of this chapter, I define the informal economy as being constituted by economic activity that is officially illegal, occurring without the sanction of government licensing or outside the official channels of a state enterprise. Such activity is known colloquially in Cuba as "business."[5] This term describes a range of activities from renting a room to foreigners without a license to selling stolen gasoline. Many goods, such as bread and gasoline, are skimmed from state supplies and sold on the black market outside of the system of rationing. The black market is conducted exclusively in dollars and is many Cubans' primary means of supplementing sagging incomes and meeting basic needs. The pervasiveness of the informal sector of the economy is a

---

[5] The term in Spanish is *negocios*. The concept of this kind of corruption is so popular it has found its way into the lyrics of Cuba's most popular salsa band, Los Van Van.

response to the slow rate of change within the formal sector and the inability of the formal sector to meet the demands of the population as a whole for goods and services.

Exchanges of needed goods and cash often involve a series of barter transactions, cash transactions, and a complicated system of networks, credit, and obligations. Involvement in the black market is so much a part of everyday survival on the island that the government turns a blind eye to it. Francisco, the retired official, said: "We know that the majority of the population is involved in some form of illegal trade. However, we understand that some of this activity is necessary, given the embargo and the special period, for the survival and comfort of our people. At the same time, trade in things like illegal drugs and corruption of officials will not be tolerated." Thus, within limits, "business" is tolerated. Eckstein notes that the growth in free markets has had important effects. She explains, "Market reforms reduce the share of the surplus directly appropriated by the state, in allowing enterprises to retain some of the profits they generate and in allowing small scale private activity that is difficult to monitor and tax" (1995, 10).

While remittances and salaries paid in dollars can create business opportunities in the black market, much black market activity is bred from poverty and discontent. Frustrated with the shrinking buying power of salaries and subsidies, many Cubans seek some means of economic mobility. The black market – an exit from official economic activity – is fed by the government's attempts to liberalize sectors of the economy. Eckstein explains: "In diversifying labor's economic options to improve productivity and consumer producer satisfaction, the government created new bases for quiet defiance of state regulations. When it permitted sideline activity, workers manipulated the reforms to their own advantage. Aggregate output improved, but the state's ability to regulate what was produced and the revenue thereby generated suffered" (11). Thus the black market in Cuba has become a form of infrapolitics, or everyday resistance (Scott 1990; Kelley 1994; Eckstein 1995).

Afro-Cuban disadvantage in official economic spheres, however, does not automatically provide for Afro-Cuban advantage in the informal sector of the economy. Rather, the "new" private economy has tended to reinforce racist distinctions. Afro-Cubans are more likely to be engaged in less desirable forms of black market participation – petty crime, hustling tourists, and prostitution, for example – than whites are. Their participation in such activities reinforces associations between race and criminality. Arturo, a white Cuban, explained to me in stark and basically racist terms, "Look, Chico, I am a business man. I sell gasoline, bread, and other goods. While it is illegal, I think it is legitimate. I work out of my home and operate a small business. The blacks are the ones who are out on the streets selling counterfeit cigars to tourists. They are lazy and are just as likely to rob you as they are to do real business. It takes time and commitment to build a small business here, even an illegal one. The police harass blacks because they are more criminal and violent; it is simply their nature. I am not racist; this is a matter of proven, social scientific fact."

Afro-Cubans assert that they participate in the less desirable sectors of the black market because of their lack of capital and access to resources. A black hustler named Lazaro, who sells counterfeit Cuban cigars in Havana (which he claims are authentic), argued: "You can steal some cigars or roll your own. I know selling to tourists is dangerous, but I have no other choice. You have to have a good position to get access to large quantities of cigars, food, or gasoline. The police attempt to protect the tourists, and it is hard. But I do not have the money or the position to do anything else. If you look at the *jineteros*,[6] you will see that most of them are black. We are not bad people; we just cannot get into a better business or find better jobs." Blacks are not only pushed into unemployment by the lack of jobs; they are also pulled into the black market by the diminished buying power of government wages and the attraction of the dollar economy. Blacks' exit from labor markets is often a rational decision based upon the evaluation of a series of alternatives.

The Sex Industry

A similar push-pull dynamic often draws women into the sex industry in Cuba. Since Cuba opened to Western tourists in the early 1990s, the sex industry has flourished. For many young Cuban women, the sex industry provides access to dollars for necessities in an economy

---

[6] Translated literally as "jockeys," the term is more accurately translated into English as "hustlers."

where other work provides substandard wages. It also provides access to luxuries in the form of stylish clothes and expensive nightclubs that are open only to those with dollars. These factors, combined with evolving attitudes about sexual freedom, make the sex industry a viable choice – even an attractive choice – for many young Cuban women. Teresa, a black woman who "dates" foreigners, told me: "There is very little work for young people in Cuba. Even if you have a job, it is hard to make enough money to eat. I like to eat, and I like nice things. I do not receive any remittances, and I am not able to get a job in the hotels. Dating foreigners is fun, and it is good business." Another young woman, Maria, argued: "I could get a job and make twenty dollars a month. I would still have several boyfriends. Since I am young, I prefer to date tourists. They can give me money, gifts, and I get to go to really nice places and have nice things. There is no comparison."

Teresa's and Marla's use of the term "dating" underlines the range of activities that can be characterized as prostitution. Many women exchange gifts or money for sex, and any observer can see that their activities range from very subtle to blatant. There are women who stand on the street, seeking tourists who have rented cars or who are riding in taxis. Some young women seek entry into discos and other clubs in order to meet men. Many claim that they simply date foreigners and that there is no direct exchange of sex for money. Teresa described her view of these activities: "I like to go to nice places; El Commodore, the Havana Cafe, they are beautiful places where beautiful and rich people can be found. Sometimes I find a rich Italian or Spaniard, and we will date while he is here. He is my boyfriend for the time. Yes, he will give things and sometimes even send gifts and money after he has returned home to his wife. But I am not a prostitute. I just like to date foreigners."

There is, nevertheless, a sharp line of demarcation in Cuba between young women who will date tourists and those who will not. Young women who are concerned with negative perceptions of themselves or who have Cuban boyfriends will not date tourists. A young student named Mercedita explained: "If you don't want to be called a prostitute, you do not date foreigners. If you do, you are automatically suspected of doing so for financial reasons. If you do not want that stigma, you avoid dating foreigners. This is the case for men and women." The power of that stigma was confirmed while I was shopping in Cancun.

A female Cuban store clerk explained to me that she had married a Mexican businessman, then claimed repeatedly and adamantly that she was not a prostitute.

Race is one of many salient factors in analyzing the sex industry in Cuba. While women of all colors are represented in the industry, it appears that the more profound economic pressures on Afro-Cuban women drive them into the industry in greater numbers. But there is also a demand specifically for black and mulatto women. Many Italian, British, Canadian, and German tourists seek women of color as an exotic alternative to the women at home. A Canadian man told me: "The men like me who come here look for mulattos and black women. They are different and more exotic than the women at home. Besides, they are simply sexier and more hot than Canadian or European women." Even Mexican men from the upper classes regularly have bachelor parties in Havana, where darker Cuban women are highly sought after. One young woman, Milagro, explained: "The tourists want something different than the wives they have at home. They like us lusty island women, particularly the blacks and mulattos." Teresa said: "There are European, Canadian, and a few men from the United States who come here to live out their fantasy of being with a woman of color. They are afraid to do this in their own country."

Racial stereotypes about the sexuality of women of African descent are not confined to men from Western capitalist countries, of course. They are also reinforced by centuries-old attitudes and customs on the island. It is not unusual to hear references to the sensuality of black women in popular music. An older white Cuban man told me, without blinking, "Black women and mulatto women are simply more hot-blooded, more sexy than white women or European women. They have a different way of moving that stirs the soul."

The perception of black women as both poor and sexually available has a substantial negative side, however. Police harassment and ridicule is a way of life for many women working in the sex industry, but black women are more vigorously targeted by police. They are often stopped when entering hotels unescorted and are harassed and asked for their *carnet* (identification) by police officers on the street. As Ricardo, the hotel executive, noted, "Black women are in the first case more obviously Cuban and not likely to be legitimate guests of the hotel, and they also can hurt the image of the hotel." I observed an embarrassing incident in which security personnel stopped the teenage daughter of a visiting African dignitary in the lobby of the Hotel Nacional. After she told them who she was and showed her room key, she was allowed to enter, but the point had been made: In Cuba, race is a marker of participation in the sex industry. Alejandro de la Fuente notes that in public discussions of prostitution, women of all colors are darkened or racialized: no matter their color, they are referred to as "black" (2001). This situation suggests how identities based on race, gender, and sexual identity intersect.

Legal Employment Outside the Tourist Industry

Many Afro-Cubans feel that there is substantial discrimination in the employment offices of ministries that are able to provide their workers with more substantial economic resources. Afro-Cubans argue that they are largely confined to low-wage, direct service government positions; they can get jobs as primary care physicians and teachers, but not positions of bureaucratic power. Carlos, a young Afro-Cuban physician in Havana, stated: "It is difficult for us to get jobs in the ministries or in tourism. The best jobs are reserved for those with 'revolutionary merit,' who most often happen to be white. Don't get me wrong. If you work really hard and participate in volunteerism, you can be okay. But only whites are considered to have the highest level of merit. They get the very best jobs because of this." The limitations on obtaining employment are subtle rather than blatant. Carlos commented: "No one will say, 'You can't have the job because you are black.' It is always discussed in terms of merit. In Cuba and especially in Havana, it isn't so much bad to be a black, but there are advantages to being white – rich relatives, perceptions of merit, and many other things that you just can't count. Many don't hate blacks, but they still see whites as better." The regime's failure to institute affirmative action programs that would include minorities has contributed to the perception that there is subtle employment discrimination and that nothing is being done about it.

Emilio, an official in Santiago, suggested that many whites can draw on privileges and resources that date back to before the revolution: "It is hard to deal with this problem. I am white, and I can honestly admit that I have had advantages. My family was well off before

the revolution. After, I went to school with the child of the woman
who used to work in our house as a domestic servant. But how can
we expect to achieve the same things? My parents were middle-class,
they knew people, were educated and able to pass on resources to me
even within the socialist system. Blacks have not had these advantages." Unlike Carlos, however, many white Cubans conclude that
Afro-Cubans' problems are rooted not in inequality of opportunity,
but in black deficiency. Another official in the Ministry of the Interior,
Miguel, told me: "Blacks simply do not work hard. They have simply been enjoying the gains of the revolution that were given to them
by Fidel. They simply do not work hard to maintain the revolution.
They are by nature lazy. The proof is all the young men in Old Havana
'working' as hustlers. They do this because they are simply too lazy
for hard work." Perceptions of the impact of race and racial attitudes
profoundly structure the dialogue about unemployment, merit, and
disadvantage in Cuba. Popular psuedoscientific explanations are used
to justify the persistence of the gap between blacks and whites, and
such explanations serve to absolve the government of responsibility
for solving the problem (Tyson 1999).

Police

By all accounts, blacks are disproportionately represented among
Cuba's prison population. Ray Michalowski argues, moreover, that
"there is some overrepresentation of dark-skinned Cubans in the lower-
income sectors of the society, and some indication that these Cubans
may suffer slightly higher victimization rates for interpersonal violence
and minor theft." The prevalence of blacks as both criminals and victims of crime reinforces negative stereotypes, and, in a vicious cycle,
these negative stereotypes cause blacks to be imprisoned at higher rates
than whites. In fact, Cuban criminal statutes allow individuals to be
imprisoned for "social dangerousness" or activities "manifestly against
the norms of socialist morality" (de la Fuente 2001). De la Fuente notes
that in the mid-1980s, a brief period for which data exist, blacks were
7.6 times more likely than whites and 3.4 times more likely than mulattos to be declared socially dangerous, and they represented 78 percent
of all individuals jailed for this reason.

Blacks also report being singled out for harassment by police. Police
officers, along with many citizens of Cuba, see Afro-Cuban men as

likely to be violent criminals or robbers in the same way that they see
young black women as likely to be sex workers. This is especially the
case in cities like Havana, Santiago de Cuba, and Veradero, particularly
in areas tourists frequent. In tourist areas, police frequently stop and
interrogate blacks, a practice supported by Cuban law, which, scholar
Ray Michalowski notes, "places few formal limits on police discretion
to stop or interrogate citizens" (1993). In my travels, I was frequently
the target of these stops. My passport was usually enough to redirect
police officers' questioning to whether I was a Cuban American seeking to cause trouble. One time, I was accused of shoplifting a *Time*
magazine from the Hotel Nacional. On another occasion, while shopping in Havana and in Santiago de Cuba, I was asked to leave my bag
with security personnel, while a white Cuban and a white American
were not asked to do so. The people I interviewed reported having
had similar experiences. These experiences demonstrate that there is a
perceived connection between race and Cuban-ness: Foreigners are perceived to be white, while Cubans are perceived to be black. Blackness
is associated with criminal behavior.

Many of the young Afro-Cubans I spoke to complained about police
harassment and comments they regularly hear from their fellow citizens. Dyami, a young Afro-Cuban female lawyer, complained: "Blacks
are blamed for everything bad in Cuba. If you describe a crime to
someone, the first question they will ask is, 'Were they black?' This
is a common response to anything. There is an attitude that us [*sic*]
blacks are lazy, stupid criminals, and people say it. They will often
talk to you about it and try to say that you are a 'good black,' but of
course the others are all bad. Because of this, it is hard for blacks to
get good jobs; we are often suspected of being criminals or hustlers,
and it is hard for us to make a good living here in Cuba." There is a
conventional wisdom that blacks are more prone to violence and criminality than whites. Miguel, the Cuban official, told me: "It is simply a
sociological fact that blacks are more violent and criminal than whites.
They also do not work as hard and cannot be trusted. You are very
smart, and it is a pity you are black, because it will be very hard to
overcome the damage your people do." Such casual racism as Miguel's
is not considered to be racism by many whites.

Class and city of origin are also involved when Afro-Cubans are
judged on sight by police officers and other Cubans. Blacks from
Santiago de Cuba are perceived as potentially more dangerous when

they are found in Havana and wearing "nice" clothes. My friend Pedro explained: "I just bought a new pair of gym shoes, Nikes. Because I am black and an Oriental, everyone will call me a hustler. The people in my neighborhood call me a hustler. They say nasty things about me because I am black and have dollars. Because I am an Oriental, I also get stopped by the police. They want to make sure that I should be in Havana and that all my papers are in order. People who look like me from Santiago de Cuba are supposed to be lower-class and are not from Havana. I work hard for my money, but people think I am a pimp because I am black and from Santiago de Cuba."

Housing and Migration

The pattern of racialized thinking that Pedro describes is reinforced by housing inequality; though there have been improvements since the revolution, Cuban housing patterns reflect the durability of racial hierarchy on the island. Housing segregation is not enforced by legal barriers but by housing patterns that are vestiges of the pre-revolutionary era, evidence of the regime's failure to implement a system that would equalize both income and access to resources, including housing. While all housing in Cuba is in great need of capital and revitalization, the housing crisis is particularly sharp in older urban areas. Both the housing shortage and the sagging housing infrastructure create ugly and overcrowded slums.

It would be too simple to say that there is absolute housing segregation in Cuba. There are blacks who live in more fashionable neighborhoods and whites who live in very poor areas. When one examines wealthy neighborhoods, however, it is clear that they are largely white areas. Havana neighborhoods like Veradero and Miramar, for example, contain mostly large, single-family homes, many constructed in the 1940s and 1950s, that are primarily occupied by whites. A few Afro-Cubans live in smaller houses in these very fashionable areas, but most live in apartment buildings. The population density of these areas is light compared with those of less-fashionable Central Havana and Old Havana. Blacks live in crowded tenements where what were once one- or two-bedroom apartments have been carved up into three apartments. Some, called "ovens," have makeshift ceilings and floors that convert a single-floor unit with a high ceiling into two units on two floors. Often, several generations of a family live in one of these units.

Squatters' camps ring the areas surrounding major cities such as Havana and Santiago de Cuba. These are shantytowns occupied primarily by Afro-Cubans who have fled the countryside in search of dollars and better economic prospects. The failure of the government to develop market incentives for agricultural production, along with the pull of tourist dollars in the big cities, fuels the migration. Though the government officially does not allow individuals to migrate without permission, it has been difficult to stop them (Eckstein 1995).

Housing inequality affects Afro-Cubans' success in the "new Cuban economy," in which a large home in a fashionable area becomes a central asset for improving family income. The Afro-Cubans I interviewed commented on the problem of housing inequality and segregation, which they saw as a source of disadvantage. One Afro-Cuban man explained: "Most of the jobs and nice houses are in Miramar and Vedado. There are some blacks in these areas, but if you notice, they live in small places. This is left over from the revolution. Whites who had money and connections immediately before the revolution have maintained their property. While each person can only own one house, in some cases a white husband and wife will each own a relatively large family home. They can rent one to Cubans and tourists and use the extra space in the other for a *paladare*; this provides a huge economic advantage."[7] A young Afro-Cuban nurse named Laura talked about the housing problems in very stark terms: "There is simply no housing available. In my neighborhood, Central Havana, there are mostly blacks, and we live crowded in a very small apartment, two or three generations at a time. My husband and I live with my parents and grandparents in a four-room apartment. People say race is not an issue, but there are few whites in my neighborhood, and few blacks in nicer neighborhoods with newer buildings. Blacks simply do not have the connections to get better housing." The argument that advantages prior to the revolution transferred into the post-revolutionary period was confirmed by a young black engineer named Marcos, whose family

---

[7] When these interviews were conducted in 1997–8, *paladares* were a growing part of the Cuban economy. Since then, government taxation and expanding alternatives have reduced their numbers.

resides in a large house: "I have a car, and we live in a house that generally only white people have. My family was middle-class before the revolution. They were lucky for blacks."

One retired black man explained that the racial difference in housing has complicated causes, and he argued that some progress toward equality had been made since the revolution: "The problem is houses must be traded rather than purchased. There are cash transactions on the side, but you also must have either a large amount of cash or a worthy property to trade. Those whose families owned property before the revolution have an advantage when it comes to the best housing. Blacks have not been able to get access to larger homes because of a lack of resources and connections, not segregation laws. There is a housing shortage, but housing is much more evenly distributed than before the revolution, when there was legal segregation and greater inequality. I suppose it is all relative." While young Afro-Cubans struggle with housing inequality that is exacerbated by the general housing shortage, then, most people recognize that the housing situation has improved since the revolution.

Black Consciousness

The literature on race in Latin America has frequently questioned why there has been relatively little organization around issues of race in Latin America as compared with that in the United States, and in particular why there has been no black civil rights movement in Latin America. Two basic theories have evolved to answer this question. The first hinges on the concept of Latin American exceptionalism. This point of view holds that race is simply not as salient a social category in Latin America as it is in the United States. The other theory is that hegemonic forces have made subaltern groups in Latin America *believe* that race is not a salient social category. Supporters of this theory have investigated the degree to which "black consciousness" – by which I mean the degree to which blacks see themselves as sharing a common culture, history, and set of life experiences that are unique and connected to the construct of race as it has been historically understood – must exist before a race-based movement can flower. I argue that while there has been a hegemonic attempt by the Cuban state to minimize the salience of race and black consciousness in Cuba, Afro-Cubans still perceive many aspects of their lives to be connected to race. While Afro-Cubans believe they are a fundamental part of the Cuban nation, they also see themselves as having a specific set of experiences and a history that sets them apart.

The degree to which Cubans believe that race is a central factor in their lives appears to correlate with the degree to which they believe that Afro-Cuban identity is a separate variant of Cuban identity, a separate and distinct cultural, social, and political category. Many Afro-Cubans see race as a central factor in their lives and identify as black in a way that distinguishes them from their white Cuban counterparts. Though the regime has held that such expressions are inherently separatist, individual comments seem to indicate the opposite. A considerable number of the Afro-Cubans I spoke to see their identity and experience as unique, but at the same time they see their fate as linked to the fate of Cuba as a whole and the Cuban Revolution in particular. They believe that the state has failed to deliver on promises of equality and the principles of the revolution, and this belief involves an implicit rejection of the hegemonic idea that race no longer structures life chances in Cuba. While racial identity and racial categories are fluid and situational in Cuba, they nonetheless have powerful social consequences.[8]

But Afro-Cuban attitudes toward race vary greatly; they range from the opinion that race no longer matters in Cuba to the argument that the country is fundamentally racist. The Afro-Cubans I interviewed tended to embrace – and to rank – multiple identities. Cristina, a lawyer from Santiago de Cuba, said: "I think of myself as both Cuban and black. It is confusing how many in the United States seem to think of themselves as black or white first and American second. I am Cuban. We are all Cuban, but at the same time there are differences." A few of the Afro-Cubans I spoke to, however, clearly agree with the official line that race is no longer important and that those who seek to explore race are themselves racist. One young Afro-Cuban woman in Havana, Felicia, grew uncomfortable with my probing questions and said: "Why

---

[8] Here, I do not place "race" in quotations. While recognizing the epistemological problems of race as an analytical category, we can nonetheless come to understand the social, political, and economic meanings and consequences of race and racial categories in similar situations. In stark contrast to Mara Loveman (1999), I do not believe that such discussions of the construction of race leave us unable to deploy race as an analytical category.

are you asking about race? You must simply be racist. Race is not a problem here in Cuba. We are all Cubans and are not worried about race at all."

Others claimed their racial identity as their central identity. Marcos, the young black engineer, explained: "Life is much harder here for blacks. We are discriminated against, and this makes life even harder." The young nurse, Laura, reflected: "There is a lot of racism in Cuba, and all of us blacks know it. We are discriminated against and need to stick together." This opinion was echoed by the retired government official, Francisco, who argued: "Racism is ingrained in the Cuban psyche. You hear terms like bad hair to refer to black hair every day. Other things like opinions that blacks are lazy, blacks are criminal, and other racist opinions are a part of the Cuban lexicon. These terms denigrate blacks and blackness. There is a blatant and unthinking racism that is a part of Cuban life and has been since slavery." Racist jokes and sayings are a common part of the Cuban lexicon, and they frequently go unchallenged (N. Fernandez 1996).

Interracial Marriage

The idea that race mixture eliminates racial discrimination has been central to Latin American exceptionalist discussions of race in Cuba. While intermarriage complicates the process of racial categorization, however, it does not eliminate the problem of racial hierarchy. Multiple categories, far from rendering racial distinctions meaningless, reinforce the idea of a racial hierarchy. They create a continuum of racial distinctions, with whites at the top of the list in terms of social, political, and economic capital and with blacks at the bottom. An Afro-Cuban doctor named Camillo explained to me: "Race is a problem here. Race mixture only creates other categories and a means to whiten your children. But everyone knows that it is best to be white and worst to be black."

The category of mulatto, moreover, is not durable, in the sense that it is rare for someone to consistently be called a mulatto or to consistently refer to themselves as mulatto. A young Afro-Cuban teacher, Tomas, explained: "Sometimes people consider me to be black; sometimes I am mulatto. It depends on the person and the context. I consider myself to be both. I think of mulatto as a category of black. The important thing is that I am not white." The same is true of blacks who have Chinese ancestry, who are often referred to as *el chino* or *la china*. While this term recognizes their ancestry, it does not "whiten" the people to whom it is applied. A secretary told me: "Because of my eyes from my Chinese ancestry, I am known as *la china*. But I am thought of as black." The binary division between black and white is the most durable form of racial categorization, while highly fungible and unstable categories range in between.

Despite widespread intermarriage, skin color remains a symbol of whether or not one has married well. Marrying someone of a lighter complexion is considered a step up, while marrying someone darker is often considered a step down. This dynamic is played out when family members either accept or reject an in-law based on racial characteristics. The anthropologist Nadine Fernandez argues: "The close knit and deeply interwoven relations among family members made the interracial couple (for white women) a direct affront to family loyalty. For the Afro-Cuban families of the men in these relations, the concern seemed to center on how their sons would be humiliated by the white family and the fear that the relationship would threaten or compete with Afro-Cuban family solidarity. White families whose sons were in interracial relationships did not couch their protest as family betrayal, but rather located the problem in the production of mixed race children" (1996). Since the nineteenth century, Fernandez argues, the ideology of interracial relationships in Cuba has largely remained the same.

Carla, a young white nurse who married a black doctor, was cut off from her family. She described how old racist customs clashed with revolutionary ideals: "My family owned a plantation in Camaguey. My father supported the revolution, but the rest of his family moved to Miami. My father did not like capitalism. However, for years his family owned slaves on their sugar plantation. We are Spanish and part of the upper classes. Even though my husband is a doctor and a very good man, my family does not accept our relationship. My father has black friends, but could not accept a black into the family. He is still very racist, and it is a very difficult situation for us. I live with my husband's family and do not talk with my family much." Similarly, the black teacher, Tomas, explained the problems he had with his white wife's family: "It is difficult to be black in Cuba. The darker your skin, the worse things are. For instance, my wife is white. Her grandmother

TABLE 5.1. *Do you think interracial marriage is advisable?*
(Ramos 1998, 103)

Color of the respondent	No	Yes
Blanca (white)	68.0%	32.0%
Negra (black)	25.0%	75.0%
Mestiza	29.4%	70.6%
Total	44.8%	55.2%

did not want us to get married and referred to me as a 'nigger' and a 'monkey.' We live with my family and do not have much contact with her family. They hate me because I am too black. But most of all they know that it is harder for blacks to get good jobs with tourism and in the ministries. They worry about me being able to provide for ourselves and any children we might have."

A survey conducted by the Center for Anthropological Studies at the University of Havana confirmed that Cuban whites still have substantial concerns about interracial marriage and relationships. Table 5.1 shows that whites, far more than mestizos or blacks, have concerns about the propriety of interracial marriage. White attitudes are almost the mirror image of blacks' on this critical issue.

Intermarriage is not a prerequisite for sensitivity to the experiences of blacks. An interracial couple I spoke with separately had very different understandings of the racial situation in Cuba. The husband, Fernando, a white mechanic, argued: "There is no racism in Cuba. We are all brothers and sisters, and everyone is treated the same." His wife, Olga, a nurse, had a decidedly different view of the situation. "There is a lot of racism in Cuba, and it is everywhere," she told me. "Blacks are treated worse than whites." Intermarriage is, in fact, largely compatible with the structure of the Cuban racial hierarchy, which places whites at the top and blacks at the bottom.

Afro-Cuban Culture

Conceptions of *mestizaje* and race mixture are performed in Cuban popular culture. The music of groups like Los Van Van or the emergent international popularity of the Afro-Cuban All Stars has reemphasized the preeminence of Afro-Cuban rhythms, styles, and musicians in the national culture of Cuba. While the revolution sought to distance itself from race-specific pronouncements at home, Afro-Cuban music has in many senses formed the public face of Cuba. To a large degree, forms of music like son and salsa have been "nationalized" despite being distinctly black – perhaps because they are distinctly black and Cuban simultaneously.

Afro-Cuban culture has been viewed both as backward and as an integral part of Cuban national identity. The state has attempted to assimilate aspects of Afro-Cuban cultural expression at the same time that it has labeled other aspects as "primitive folklore." Several Afro-Cubans I spoke to, including a number of artists, felt that the cultural history of Cuba was being harmed in this process. An artist in Havana said: "There has been an effort to incorporate Afro-Cuban culture as 'folklore' for tourists. The problem is, it is seen as part of the past identity of a now integrated and equal Cuba. So, we can all dance a little salsa, or say a devotion to Saint Lazarus, but the struggle is gone. Black culture is about the history of the Afro-Cuban struggle. But the history is still living, it is not dead."

A dancer and musician in Matanzas expressed similar concerns: "Our culture is presented as primitive, backward, anachronistic, not as a living, breathing culture and struggle that defines us as a people. It has been absorbed for tourist consumption." So while tourism has helped to popularize and make Afro-Cuban cultural forms lucrative, those involved in the commodification of the culture have sought to present it as a primitive form that has little modern significance. An artist and Santeria practitioner in Santiago de Cuba explained: "They want to deny our existence as a people. Blacks are simply museum pieces of the new and old Cuba. Our struggle is glorified in the past and denied in the present and the future. Museum pieces have no life of their own or struggle. They are simply there to look at."

Another musician reported: "People like salsa and it has become popular. But people still look down on Santeria and other black cultural expressions. When these expressions become popular like salsa, they call them 'Cuban.' Rock music is accepted, and the government promotes groups and concerts. This is the case with jazz and salsa. However, rap is seen as subversive. The same is the case with reggae, because this music is a new, authentic black cultural form. I love rap, and others do too." In the years since I conducted my interviews, hip hop groups like Los Orishas and others have gained prominence performing music that simultaneously expresses frustration about the current economic and social situation in Cuba, condemns materialism, and expresses a strong sense of nationalism. Ultimately, however, the state's attempts to limit the modern expression of black identity and the growth of any struggle for racial equality have been compatible with the commodification of Afro-Cuban culture.

Raising the Race Question

Despite the widespread feeling among Afro-Cubans that race is a serious problem, there is no consensus about what might be done about it. In fact, while Moore suggests that hegemony most profoundly affects assessments of racial inequality as a problem, my interviews indicate that it more powerfully acts to prevent individuals from conceiving of solutions. The government line – that an aggressive program to eliminate racial hierarchy would cause division, chaos, and sociopolitical disorder in hard times – was repeated to me in a number of interviews. Even those who were the most critical of and adamant about the existence of racial hierarchy repeated this point of view. The argument against aggressive racial debate supports the notion that race can be a destructive and divisive topic and suggests that the government and Cuban people are too busy with the "special period" to undertake such a massive project of reform.

Blanca, a white Cuban woman in Havana who served as a locally elected member of parliament, described the ongoing problem of racial hierarchy and then explained why, at this point, very little will be done about it:

Cuba was one of the last societies to end slavery. The type of exploitation that occurred here is something we all recognize. The discrimination and exploitation occurred until the revolution. What has been difficult is figuring out what we should do about the problem of inequality. For example, after the revolution the daughter of the black woman who had once cleaned my family's house was now able to attend the same school that I attended. This was a great triumph. But at the same time, I had an advantage. My parents were educated and knew people. We had books in the house. They helped me immensely. My friend and I were not likely to have the same level of merit. What we have not yet worked out is how to deal with this problem without ruining our unity as a nation. While the black problem is significant and has remained so, the problems we face as a nation are far greater.

As Blanca's comment indicates, the problem of race is frequently cast as an issue of "special interest" that cannot be part of a program of improving Cuban society in the context of hardship. This way of thinking about the problem can be contrasted with the role of the Federation of Cuban Women (FMC, Federacion de Mujeres Cubana) in agitating for women's equality through the courts and throughout society. A black representative from the FMC explained to me why there is little need for a black organization to perform a similar function within the party as the FMC performs for women:

Racism remains, and blacks are still behind. However, discrimination is more subtle, and positive institutions like education help a lot. We are trying to push for more race research and understanding about the problem. However, because racism is officially illegal but widely practiced, there is a taboo about talking about race. If you bring up racial issues, many will accuse you of being racist and the cause of the problem. Cubans are very sensitive when talking about race. If you mention race, you are thought to be divisive and possibly racist. However, I do not see a separate black organization along the lines of the FMC. We do not want to separate ourselves from the people. We are not interested in being divisive. However, we do not want to be invisible either.

Francisco, the most critical black government official living in Havana whom I interviewed, concluded that in the context of U.S. policy and the special period Cuba simply cannot afford to deal more actively with the race problem:

This problem continues today. The revolution's major weakness has been a direct confrontation on racial issues. When Fidel talks about race, he speaks as if he has a lack of oxygen. The only message is that whites should not apply discriminatory criteria. However, everyone knows that they do. The primary response is to turn the issue of nondiscrimination to an issue to be worked on through the development of ideology and individual consciousness rather than government action. Fidel has called on us to "trust the power of individual consciousness." This is very weak compared to the efforts in other areas. The problem is the question of how to deal with this problem and maintain a unified Cuban society. Our position in the world and vis-à-vis the United States demands unity. The race issue here is potentially explosive, and there are powerful interests who do not want to see change within the party. Further, though we all know the group in Miami is primarily composed of white racists, you cannot underestimate the ability of the United States and these groups to exploit any division within Cuban society.

The Comparative Case

As Francisco's comment suggests, perceptions of racial politics in the United States play a key role in racial politics in Cuba. Perceptions of racial insensitivity and injustice in America, and in Miami in particular, provide Afro-Cubans with a reason to support the current regime. The individuals I spoke to who were the most critical of the Castro regime were also most likely to conclude that things would be worse under the leadership of the Miami exile community or in the United States. The Castro regime benefits from this attitude: Those who feel that race is no longer a problem largely credit the regime for solving it, and those who feel that race is a problem feel that the regime has done a better job than any alternative regime could do. A young male engineer, Marcos, told me: "I know that I won't be able to get a job as an engineer that will make it possible to make a living. I am smart and work hard like many other blacks, and we are still shut out. I am not a counterrevolutionary, but I think it's a problem. The government is starving blacks. They do it because they know that things are worse for blacks in Miami." An older custodian in Santiago de Cuba explained, "The revolution has done so much for us blacks.... Race is not a problem here as it is in the United States."

Several of the people I spoke to, including Marcos, had strong feelings about the problem of race in the United States. One young teacher from Havana said: "I saw Rodney King and the riots in Los Angeles and Miami. In the United States, blacks are treated worse than dogs. There is racism and discrimination here in Cuba, but black people are not being beaten and shot in the streets." Her comment offers proof that the events that profoundly affect African American opinions about race have similar force in Cuba. A black attorney said frankly: "My family has a problem with race, and the country does as well. However, though the police are bad and it can be hard to find work, it is far worse in the United States."

A former government official explained: "Despite the racism and the fact that many blacks in high positions are just symbols, blacks will never fail to support the revolution. The revolution advanced blacks far past any other order or the proposition of leadership by those in Miami. They know that things would be worse if the whites in Miami returned to Cuba." The historian Laurance Glasco noted that migrants to the

United States who return to the island report experiences of rampant racism that affect how Cubans see the United States and perhaps their own situation on the island (1998). The Castro regime is the benefactor of the inability of the United States and the Cuban exile community to achieve more racial equality and avoid racial incidents. One can only imagine that the incidents of racial violence in the United States have reinforced these perceptions.

Conclusion

In this chapter, I have explored the character of race relations in Cuba today, using the lived experiences of common Cubans as my guide. The chapter offers a micro-perspective on the broader race cycles conception of racial politics. It demonstrates that the advances of the revolution toward racial equality are being threatened in the context of the economic collapse that characterizes Cuba's special period. The increasingly unequal distribution of resources renders the lives of blacks more precarious in economic, social, and political terms. The privations of the current dollar-based economy disproportionately affect Afro-Cubans, who for historical, structural reasons have unequal access to dollars. The interviews I conducted suggest that there is a growing economic gap between blacks and whites, as whites have access to better opportunities in private enterprise and employment.

Racist attitudes persist on the island, moreover, influencing both how police carry out their jobs and how families interact with one another. In discussions of the sex trade, the black market, and similar topics, this chapter has demonstrated that race interacts in Cuba with categories like class and gender in ways that make it profoundly difficult to establish the independent effects of each. In fact, the level of colinearity is so profound that race often becomes a sign of class position, criminality, and "revolutionary merit." Racial disadvantage in Cuba often involves issues of class, gender, and geographical bias that mutually reinforce one another.

As the race cycles model predicts, the economic downturn in Cuba has been accompanied by a closing of opportunities for blacks and a return to pre-existing racial ideology. Inclusionary discrimination is alive and well in Cuba today. It describes both the persistence and the character of racial inequality in Cuba. Race relations are characterized by the existence of a flexible hierarchy and fluidity as well as by structural disadvantage, nonlinear progress, and the evolution of negative conceptions of blacks.

It is important to note how this picture differs from that depicted by scholars who follow other predominant schools of thought – Black Nationalism, Marxist exceptionalism, and Latin American exceptionalism. I have argued that the regime has not necessarily promoted racism, but that it has allowed structures that reproduce inequality to go relatively untouched. The relative inequality of blacks is a result of passivity as much as it is a consequence of activity. This chapter has shown that blacks in Cuba have unequal access to networks and other resources that allow for upward mobility. Many Afro-Cubans have no access to the cliques that allow for promotion in the Communist Party, to hard currency from relatives abroad, or to other resources that whites carried from the pre-revolutionary to the post-revolutionary era. Proponents of Latin American exceptionalism argue that structures of advantage did not exist prior to the revolution and thus cannot exist after it. Marxists argue that the revolution, by eliminating class, eradicated racial inequality at the institutional level and to a large degree at the level of individual consciousness. This chapter demonstrates that Marxism closed the gap but did not eliminate it, and that the implementation of a mixed economy with market-based elements has exacerbated these inequalities as well as racist attitudes.

Black Nationalists argue, furthermore, that racial problems are a product of overt racism at the highest rungs of the party rather than the result of structural disadvantages. The people I interviewed, however, argued clearly that structural disadvantages existed before the revolution and that while prejudice is still a problem, ongoing inequality is more the result of state inaction than it is the result of overt prejudice. In Cuba today, racial exclusion and racism are quite compatible with the economic and social order. In the context of an economic crisis, state hegemony has reconstituted itself around a general denial of racism that – given obvious and observable inequalities – tends to support racist attitudes about blacks.

The Marxist and Latin American exceptionalist models are implicitly linear. They insist that improvements in race relations are durable, and that race relations progress consistently toward greater equality. The tendency of scholars to see linear improvement is powerful. It colors discussions about race relations within the United States, Brazil, South Africa, and Cuba. History has tended to show, however, that transformations in the political economy can produce significant setbacks in race relations. If those who subscribe to the Latin American exceptionalist model or the Marxist exceptionalist model are correct, the structure of racial hierarchy in Cuba should have withered away by now. I argue, by contrast, that the gains of the revolution, while substantially closing the gap between the races, failed to eliminate it altogether. This failure, in the context of economic crisis, produced growing inequality that can be partially explained by persistently negative perceptions of blacks and the relative advantage of whites. At the same time, the catalysts are not completely internal. The decline of the Soviet Union, the tightening U.S. embargo, and the impact of foreign tourists and capital have all worked to undo the gains of the revolution in the area of race. These forces are bringing the problem of racial hierarchy into sharper focus and will most likely continue to do so in the future. In the meantime, however, a lack of credible alternatives binds Afro-Cubans to the fate of the revolution.

6

Race and Daily Life in Cuba
During the Special Period

Part II: Survey Research

In the spring of 2000 and the spring of 2001, I had a unique opportunity to conduct surveys regarding racial attitudes in Cuba. While survey research on race has its limits, as discussed in the previous chapter, the surveys I conducted in Havana allowed me to produce statistical measures of the salience of race in Cuba and to investigate to what degree racial politics in Cuba conform with the theories of Marxist and Latin American exceptionalists and Black Nationalists or with the alternative: inclusionary discrimination.

Most important, the surveys enabled me to conduct a broader test of many of the arguments I made in the previous chapter, which were based on in-depth oral interviews with a relatively small sample of Cubans. Using the surveys, I was able to test the following propositions: Racial categories are coherent and salient in Cuba; race affects Afro-Cubans' life chances; the new dollar economy is racially stratified; racism continues to exist among Cuban whites; blacks continue to support the regime because of its past successes and their mistrust of other alternatives; and the economic downturn has exacerbated Cuban racial differences, producing differing perspectives among blacks and whites on the Cuban economy and social life.

If the Marxists and Latin American exceptionalists are correct, there should be few differences of opinion across racial lines, and racism should almost be nonexistent in Cuba today. All Cubans should be equally attached to the nation and should see Cuba's as an open society in which few differences are based upon race. Black Nationalists argue, on the other hand, that racial politics in Cuba reflects palpable white racism. They assert that blacks should generally exhibit a false consciousness, that they should believe that racism is not a problem. In contrast to these arguments, I maintain that racism can exist alongside perceptions of inclusion and the sense among blacks that they are better off in Cuba than anywhere else.

Methods

In this chapter, I analyze data collected in Cuba that address some of the questions posed in the previous chapters. Native Cuban interviewers were hired and trained to collect the statistical data. Three hundred and thirty-six people from Havana were surveyed in the first sample and 244 in the second sample. In the second sample, I made a concerted effort to oversample blacks, and the interviewers asked a number of questions about black consciousness.

Because of the sensitivity of conducting race-related research in Cuba, it was necessary to operate with extreme caution to protect interviewers and respondents. A snowball sampling procedure was used.[1] The team of Cuban interviewers was asked to begin with contacts in various neighborhoods. They found willing subjects in each place and asked them to direct us to others who might be willing to participate in the survey. Using this technique means that the sample does not represent a single network but multiple points of entry. While the technique does not produce a randomized sample, it was the best we could do in the highly restrictive research environment. Special efforts were made to achieve racial, neighborhood, and income variability within the sample. Respondents were interviewed at their homes. All interviews were conducted in Spanish. Each sample was collected in five days, and the survey response rate was more than 95 percent.

There has been only one other sample of public opinion on race conducted in Cuba in the past forty years by U.S.-based researchers (de la Fuente 2001). That sample, gathered by Alejandro de la Fuente, did not include standard measures of racial attitudes used by social scientists. Also, the data explored by de la Fuente do not contain statistical

---

[1] The snowball sample was necessary in order to ensure confidentiality and the safety of those interviewed.

controls or tests of significance, and de la Fuente has not made his data widely available. These omissions seriously limit the inferences other researchers can make from de la Fuente's sample. In addition to de la Fuente's work, several Cuban research units have conducted survey research in Cuba. We do not know how many people were sampled by these researchers, however, or to what degree the samples are representative. Also, the raw data have not been made publicly available, rendering it impossible to subject the data to a range of statistical tests. The researchers' reports do not tell us even whether the results are statistically significant.

The survey results presented in this chapter include statistical tests for significance, controls, and variation. In an effort to reflect the flexibility of racial hierarchy in Cuba and the existence of multiple racial categories, many of the discussions of survey results that follow employ race as a continuous rather than a categorical variable, exploring how movement in one direction or the other on the racial spectrum affected survey responses. When it was impossible for me to take this approach, I broke the analysis into three categories, leaving whites and blacks at ends of the spectrum and collapsing all those in the middle into a category denoted as mulatto (or mestizo, in the case of some of the data from Cuban researchers). The data presented here are a significant improvement over current knowledge of race and public opinion in Cuba. Placed in the context of analogous data from the Cuban scholars' surveys and of the conclusions I drew from my interviews (discussed in Chapter 5), the transparency of the data collection and the statistical techniques that I have employed allow us to draw more firm conclusions than has previously been the case.

Racial Categories and Hierarchy

Racial categorization has often been discussed in the literature on race in Latin America. Some theorists contend that the multiplicity of racial categories and widespread race mixing mean that racial categories in Latin America are fluid. Others conclude not only that the categories are fluid but that fluidity makes racial categorization less salient, effectively eliminating the existence of racism in some Latin American nations. Still other scholars have argued that multiple racial categories allow for some fluidity but create pigmentocracy – racial

TABLE 6.1. *Intersubjective racial categories and skin color in Cuba*

Measures of race	Correlation
Interviewer-rated racial category and skin color	.907**
Interviewer-rated skin color and self-rated skin color	.934**
Interviewer-rated racial category and self-rated racial category	.947**
Self-rated racial category and self-rated skin color	.887**

hierarchy based on skin shade and the African-ness of facial features (Hanchard 1994; Sidanius et al. 2001).

For this study, the interviewers asked a series of questions to address the issues of racial categorization and hierarchy. First, the interviewer ascribed a skin color gradation and a racial category to the interviewee. Then, the interviewee was asked to choose a racial category and a skin color gradation for him- or herself. We used six categories for the close-ended racial category question: *blanco(a)*, *jabao(á)*, *trigueño(a)*, *mestizo(a)*, *mulatto(a)*, and *negro(a)*. This technique borrows significantly from the work of Kronos and Solaun (1973), but it has been modified in response to many of the critical questions raised by Carlos Moore about the "inaccuracy" of racial statistics in Cuba. I wish to argue not that race is real but rather to show that we can significantly test the intersubjective reliability of racial categorization. That is, we can come to know if racial categories are salient to individuals, as well as whether they are apparent to viewers. We can test the relationship between the interviewer's perceptions of racial categories and individual self-perceptions.

The survey results indicate that there is a strong correlation between skin color and racial category (see Table 6.1). While racial category is not reducible to skin color and may include things like eye color and hair type, skin color is a strong and powerful predictor of racial category. Also, despite the use of numerous racial categories by the interviewers, there was a strong degree of agreement between self-described racial category and the category ascribed by the interviewer. This indicates that racial categories are seen to be quite distinct, despite the fact that they exist on a relatively fluid continuum. While many social scientists have taken to putting the term "race" in quotation marks, especially in the context of Latin America, it is clear from the

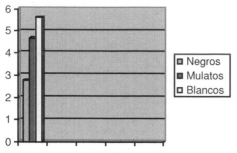

FIGURE 6.1. Perceived status of racial groups

survey that it is incorrect to assume that race mixing and the existence
of multiple racial categories in Cuba make race a confusing and poorly
understood construct in daily life. Cuban racial categories are quite
distinct, and people are able to discern who fits into what category.

The next question the surveys explored is whether there is a racial
hierarchy in Cuba. The survey asked respondents to rate the perceived
status of *negros*, *mulattos*, and *blancos* on a seven-point scale. Status
was not defined in specific economic or social terms but was left to the
interviewee to ascribe. The results in Figure 6.1 show that perceived
status is ranked by race; whites are at the top, blacks are at the bottom,
and the European-ness of a mixed-race individual's features determines
how high he or she falls on the racial "staircase" (see Figure 6.1).

At least in terms of perceived racial status, then, Cuba is a "pigmentocracy." Race matters in determining one's status, and the lighter
one's complexion is, the higher one's status is in society. Rather than
eliminate racial hierarchy, miscegenation has only created more steps
on the staircase of racial hierarchy.

Race and Life Chances

While the effects of the revolution are clear in terms of life expectancy
and other opportunities for black Cubans (see de la Fuente 2001),
we had an opportunity to test how race affects the socioeconomic
indicators of income and education. Many concede that whites are
generally doing better than blacks in the dollar economy; it is in the
heavily regulated peso economy where economic parity was most likely
to be found. I tested this hypothesis by asking individuals their income

TABLE 6.2. *Correlations between race, education, and income (one tailed test)*

Correlation between peso, income, and race	$-.202^{**}$
Partial correlation between peso income and race, controlling for level of education	$-.1449^{*}$
Correlation between educational levels and race	$.189^{*}$

TABLE 6.3. *Race and profession*

Race	Professor	Professional	Administrative	Technical	Laborer	Unemployed
White	5.1%	27.8%	13.9%	31.6%	11.4%	10.01%
Mulatto	4.1%	15.5%	9.3%	19.9%	25.8%	15.5%
Black	3.1%	18.5%	13.8%	15.4%	30.8%	18.5%

in pesos and correlating it with their self-described racial identity. It is clear that as one moves down the racial hierarchy, income levels drop (see Table 6.2). When I controlled the results for education, the basic relationship did not change. Even in the socialist peso economy, I found that the racial hierarchy determines economic opportunity.

In Chapter 3, I discussed the opening of educational opportunities for blacks in the post-revolutionary period. Literacy rates have improved rapidly at all levels of Cuban society, and the educational opportunities that are available to all Cubans are lauded as one of the greatest achievements of the revolution. Using a bivariate correlation on the survey results, however, I found that race remains a significant predictor of educational attainment in Cuba; blacks continue to receive less education than whites (see Table 6.2).

The survey also queried individuals as to their profession. Table 6.3 shows a range of professional categories and the percentage of survey respondents who fell into each group.[2] Whites are most frequently found in the professional and technical categories. Blacks reach parity with whites in the administrative category but are more heavily represented among laborers and, even more strikingly, among

---

[2] In order to deal with our small sample size, middle groupings were collapsed into a single category. While this is a strong simplification, it is the only way to make sense of the data given the small sample size and the multiplicity of racial groupings.

the unemployed. In this sample, blacks are unemployed at a rate of 18.5 percent, almost double the 10 percent unemployment rate of whites. Despite more than forty years of revolution, then, there is still employment inequality in Cuba. It is worth noting that those between the poles of white and black are not much better off than blacks. Though in some categories like employment in technical fields mulattos fare better than blacks and have a slightly lower rate of unemployment, blacks are doing better than mulattos in the professional and administrative fields. The sting of economic restructuring that has hit Cuba since the end of Soviet subsidies has been felt most harshly by blacks and mulattos, and while mulattos are perceived to have higher status than blacks in Cuban society, there is no evidence to support the idea that they benefit economically from this status.

Anecdotal reports suggest that dollars are distributed unequally among Cubans. The survey revealed, however, that there is no statistically significant relationship between race and reported income in dollars. While the relationship may in fact not exist, it is also possible that respondents were unwilling to reveal their income in dollars, which until the 1990s were illegal to possess. Because the dollar economy is informal, moreover, they may have inaccurate perceptions of the true level of their income. A companion survey to this one that had more sophisticated tools for measuring dollar income and remittances found that whites have substantially more legal access to dollars than nonwhites do. The study, conducted by Sarah Blue, indicated that both blacks and mulattos are less likely than whites to have relatives living abroad who send remittances (2002).

The survey also provided an opportunity to test racial differences in attitudes about the hybrid capitalist/socialist economy that Cubans now face. The interviews led me to predict that darker Cubans would be less optimistic about the experiments in free enterprise than lighter Cubans. There were no significant racial differences in opinion on the question of whether private enterprise is generally good for the country. When asked specifically about foreign investment, however, whites were significantly more optimistic than blacks (see Table 6.4). When asked about Cuban-owned private enterprise, blacks were more likely than whites to support the proposition that "Some people benefit too much from private business." This demonstrates that – at least in the perceptions of darker Cubans – the pains and gains of the new

TABLE 6.4. *Correlation between race and perceptions of the new Cuban economy (results control for education, income, gender, and age)*

Private enterprise is good for the country	—
Foreign investment is good for the country	.1754*
Some people benefit too much from private enterprise	−.2472**
The economy has improved in the last year	−.1169

economy are being experienced unequally. When asked, "Has the economy improved in the last year?" darker Cubans were more likely than lighter Cubans to agree that it had, though the results fell short of statistical significance. There is some evidence that blacks believed in 2001 and 2002 that the economy was improving. Asked whether the economic position of blacks had improved in the past few years, however, black respondents revealed that they did not feel that blacks were doing better in the new hybrid economy.

Racial Attitudes

Quite clearly, the anecdotal and survey evidence come together to present a picture showing that race strongly influences economic life chances in Cuba. But it is unclear whether this is a result of old-fashioned racism or some other construct. While the interviews discussed in the previous chapter offered anecdotal evidence of palpable racism in the attitudes of many whites toward blacks, it was possible using the survey to test the relationship between race and explicit racism. I conducted partial correlations of a variety of different measures of racism and racial preferences, controlling for age, gender, income, and education. First, a scale of explicit racism was constructed using a variety of measures of racist attitudes toward blacks. Antiblack racism was indexed by use of the following three items: (1) "Dark skinned Cubans are less intelligent than other groups"; (2) "Dark skinned Cubans are lazier than other groups"; and (3) "Dark skinned Cubans are less capable than other groups." Respondents were asked to what degree they agreed or disagreed with each statement. The scale was quite reliable in the sense that there was a high intercorrelation between the measures (Cronbach's Alpha = .82). When the results were analyzed, whites were shown to have significantly higher levels of

TABLE 6.5. *Correlations between race and (1) a composite measure of explicit racism and (2) perceptions of black delinquency (results control for education, income, gender, and age)*

1. Explicit racism (two-tailed test)	$-.210^{**}$
2. Perceptions of black delinquency (one-tailed test)	$.2754^{**}$

TABLE 6.6. *Respondents' attitudes about the decency and intelligence of racial groups (Ramos 1998, 100)*

Skin color of interviewee	Answers regarding the existence of equality or not across groups			
	Values and decency in all racial groups		Intelligence in all racial groups	
	Yes	No	Yes	No
White	31.1%	68.9%	41.7%	58.3%
Black	75%	25%	62.5%	37.5%
Mestizo	37.5%	62.5%	66.7%	33.3%
Total	45.9%	54.1%	54.5%	45.5%

explicitly racist beliefs than blacks and mulattos. When asked whether blacks were more likely than whites to be criminal delinquents, whites agreed with the statement significantly more often than blacks did (see Table 6.5).

These results agree with the work of the Cuban scholar Juan Antonio Alvarado Ramos, who found that whites were significantly less likely than blacks or mestizos to believe that all groups have equal values, levels of decency, and intelligence (1998). The Cuban social scientist Maria del Carmen Caño Secade (1996) argues that racial stereotypes have remained persistent in the Cuban populace despite the revolution. The results of Ramos's study (see Table 6.6) mirror those reported in Table 6.5 and provide strong evidence that racial stereotypes still exist in Cuba.

A third study demonstrated that the mean levels of explicit racism were higher in Cuba than in Puerto Rico, the Dominican Republic, and the United States (see Table 6.7). Thus, contrary to the argument

TABLE 6.7. *Mean and standard deviation of explicit racial prejudice by nation and participant's race (Peña et al. 2004)*

Nation	Whites Mean (std. dev.)	Blacks Mean (std. dev.)
United States	1.41 (1.06)	1.27 (.56)
Cuba	3.29 (1.88)	2.79 (1.59)
Dominican Republic	2.75 (2.47)	2.25 (1.49)
Puerto Rico	1.72 (1.33)	1.70 (1.15)

of Latin American or Marxist exceptionalists, there is actually more explicit racism in Cuba than there is in the United States, and there is comparatively more explicit racism in Cuba than in other societies in the Spanish Caribbean like Puerto Rico and the Dominican Republic. These survey results suggest that there may be a substantial disconnect between Cuban racial attitudes and the progress toward racial equality that has been made in Cuba. The results may reflect the existence of *laissez-faire* racism as a consequence of the earlier period of improvement: Because reforms have not created absolute equality and officially there is no racism in Cuba, whites tend to blame blacks for inequality.

The survey I conducted also collected data on perceptions of physical attractiveness and asked respondents to choose between features associated with whites, such as straight hair, fine noses, thin lips, and light eyes, and features associated with blacks, such as nappy hair, wide noses, wide lips, and dark eyes. Across the board, whites preferred features associated with whites, and blacks preferred features associated with blacks (see Table 6.8). Contrary to the Black Nationalist argument that blacks have assimilated white somatic norms and the Latin American exceptionalist argument that all racial features are valued, there are clear racial differences in preference for features in Cuba. Respondents were similarly divided by race in their response to the question of whether blacks or whites in general were more attractive, though the difference was less significant.

Perceptions of Discrimination

The survey also tested whether blacks perceive there to be discrimination in Cuban society. The interviewers first asked respondents to

TABLE 6.8. *Preferences in terms of phenotype and race (results control for education, income, gender, and age)*

Phenotype preferences in terms of attractiveness	Coefficient
Straight hair versus nappy hair	.4092**
Fine nose versus wide nose	.3382**
Thin lips versus wide lips	.2855**
Light eyes versus dark eyes	.3452**
Whites in general versus blacks in general	.1428*

agree or disagree with the proposition "There is racism in Cuba." On a seven-point scale in which 1 meant "agree" and 7 meant "disagree," the mean answer was 2.27 and the standard deviation was 1.6. Most of the respondents, then, agreed that racism exists in Cuba. When whites' and blacks' responses were compared, the negative result (−.1202) suggested that blacks were more likely to agree with the proposition than whites were, but because of the overwhelming agreement with the proposition, the racial difference in the participants' answers was not statistically significant. There was more disagreement regarding how racism manifests itself in Cuba. We observed racial differences in responses to questions about whether blacks experience racism in certain spheres. When presented with the proposition "In our society all are treated equally by the police regardless of skin color," for instance, those with darker skin were less likely to agree than those with lighter skin. When confronted with the proposition "In our society all receive equal treatment at hotels, discos, and restaurants regardless of race," however, racial differences in response were not significant when age, gender, education, and income had been controlled for. In the bivariate environment without controls, Cubans with darker skin were more likely to disagree with the proposition (see Table 6.9).

In order to explore perceptions of race-based and class-based discrimination, we asked respondents whether black disadvantage can be explained in terms of discrimination based on race or of discrimination based on class. Darker-skinned Cubans were more likely to support a race-based explanation for disadvantage, and lighter-skinned Cubans were more likely to support class-based explanations. Finally, when respondents were asked to agree or disagree with propositions about the representation of blacks in key areas of society, there was less racialized disagreement. Darker-skinned Cubans were more likely

TABLE 6.9. *Perceptions of racial discrimination (results control for education, income, gender, and age)*

There is racism in Cuba	–
In our society, all are treated equally by the police regardless of skin color	.1566*
In our society, all receive equal treatment at hotels, discos, and restaurants regardless of race	.153* (without controls)
Blacks are little represented on Cuban television	−.1679*
Racism needs to be studied and a plan of action adopted to solve the problem	−.2211**

TABLE 6.10. *Of those who claim to have experienced discrimination, where did it happen? (Hernández 1998, 83)*

	Whites		Blacks	
Place	Under 40	Over 40	Under 40	Over 40
Workplace	12%	37%	100%	92%
Street	25%	8%	37%	62%
Public space	4%	12%	29%	12%
Private home	4%	8%	25%	25%

than lighter-skinned Cubans to agree with the proposition that blacks are little represented on Cuban television, but there were no significant differences in responses to the propositions that blacks are little represented in politics and that blacks are well represented in high places in society. Darker-skinned Cubans lend greater support than lighter-skinned Cubans to the proposition that "Racism needs to be studied and a plan of action adopted to solve the problem" (see Table 6.9).

The foregoing results are bolstered by some survey work done by the Cuban scholar Daniela Hernández in Santa Clara, Cuba, which suggests that despite substantial gains made by the revolution, blacks still report widespread experiences of discrimination in the workplace (see Table 6.10).

Race and Civic Involvement

Accounts of life in Cuba emphasize the harmonious nature of inter-racial interactions. The special period and the process of rectification have created openings for interested Cubans to participate in religious

TABLE 6.11. *Race and organizational involvement (results control for education, income, gender, and age)*

I am involved in organizations that are a majority white	–
I am involved in organizations that are a majority black	$-.1936^{**}$
I participate in voluntary labor	$-.1865$
I participate in organizations and groups with my neighbors such as the CDR	$-.1662^{*}$
Whenever possible, blacks should participate in black organizations	$-.2815^{**}$
Blacks should always vote for black candidates	$-.2740^{**}$

organizations or in state voluntary organizations that can improve an individual's "revolutionary merit." Many assume that organizational life in Cuba today is mostly integrated, but the data indicate the opposite. When respondents were asked if they have participated in organizations that are either majority black or majority white, race was not an indicator of whether or not someone had been involved in organizations that were majority white. Blacks were more likely, however, to have been involved in organizations that are primarily black (see Table 6.11).

Since the days of Che Guevara, voluntary labor has been a key symbolic component of the Cuban Revolution, a sign of both nationalism and support for socialism. Through voluntary labor, individuals demonstrate their loyalty to Cuba and the party. Despite their place at the bottom of the party's status hierarchy, it appears that blacks are more "loyal" than whites in this regard. Darker-skinned Cubans participate more frequently in voluntary labor than their lighter-skinned counterparts. Darker-skinned Cubans are also more likely than lighter-skinned Cubans to work and meet with neighbors in neighborhood organizations like the Committee for the Defense of the Revolution (see Table 6.11). There is, however, no difference in participation in local elections based upon race.

When it comes to support for race-based organizations, blacks are more likely than whites to support the idea that blacks should participate in black organizations whenever possible. Blacks are also more likely to support the propositions that blacks should always vote for black candidates and should buy things from stores that are black owned (see Table 6.11). While Dawson, in his work on U.S.

TABLE 6.12. *Race and religious preference*

Race	Catholic	Afro-Cuban	Protestant	Jewish	Atheist
White	46.2%	16.7%	6.4%	1.3%	29.5%
Middle	31.5%	40.2%	2.2%	1.1%	23.9%
Black	22.4%	58.6%	1.7%	–	17.2%

TABLE 6.13. *Correlations relating to Santeria (results control for education, income, gender, and age)*

Correlation between race and feelings about Santeria, positive or negative	−.3054**
Correlation between Santeria and participation in voluntary labor	.1466*

black ideology, associates these propositions with American-style Black Nationalism, they also resonate in Cuba.

But political and economic matters are not the only areas in which there are racial differences; the sacred is also an area of racial difference. Afro-Cuban religions have competed with the Catholic Church for the devotion of Cubans since the times of slavery. The revolution limited the participation of religious believers in the Communist Party – officially, the party is atheist – and it was particularly suspicious of Afro-Cuban religions. It appears, however, that the age-old divide in religious affiliation has survived the Cuban Revolution. While those in the middle groups slightly favor Afro-Cuban religions, there is a stark contrast between blacks and whites. Protestantism seems to be making the greatest inroads among whites, and atheism is significant among all groups, but it is least prevalent among Afro-Cubans, who heavily identify with Afro-Cuban religions (see Table 6.12).

These differences go beyond simple preferences. It appears that not only are whites less likely to practice Afro-Cuban religions than blacks, they also are significantly more likely to speak negatively about Santeria (see Table 6.13). This tendency suggests that there is a palpable amount of animosity among whites toward Afro-Cuban religious practices. If voluntary labor is considered to be a proxy for regime support, however, it is clear that those who practice Santeria are more likely

TABLE 6.14. *Mean and standard deviation of patriotism as a function of race (Sawyer, Peña, and Sidanius 2002)*

Race	Mean (Standard deviation)
Black	6.15 (1.45)
Middle	6.07 (1.34)
White	5.66 (1.52)

to support the regime than members of other religious groups (see Table 6.13). This fact suggests that the regime's negative attitude toward Afro-Cuban religious practices is misplaced.

Race and National Attachment

Patriotism frequently reveals itself to be a troubling construct. Studies in the United States and Israel have revealed an asymmetry in patriotism between dominant and subordinate groups, and patriotism is positively correlated with ethnocentrism, social dominance, and racism for the members of dominant groups. Recent studies in Cuba and other locations in the Spanish Caribbean have shown, however, that this relationship does not exist in these countries. In Puerto Rico and the Dominican Republic, there appear to be no group-based differences in patriotism or in the relationship among patriotism, ethnocentrism, and racism or social dominance (Sawyer, Peña, and Sidanius 2002).

In Cuba, the studies have proven something quite striking. As a result of the rhetoric and policies of the revolution – and in contradiction to the hierarchy observed in Table 6.1 – blacks are significantly more patriotic than other groups (see Table 6.14). Sawyer, Peña, and Sidanius's study demonstrates, however, that patriotism is not a function of the strength of racial identity (see Table 6.15, panel A). Also, as panel B in Table 6.15 indicates, patriotism is not a function of the respondents' feelings about or affect toward other racial groups. Nor is it a function of ethnocentrism or what the respondents feel about other groups subtracted from their feelings toward their own group (see panel C). Patriotism has a powerful and interesting effect in Cuba.

TABLE 6.15. *Patriotism regressed on racial identity, racial affect, ethnocentrism, and group dominance ideologies as a function of race (Participants' self-identified racial group is indicated on the columns; all entries are unstandardized regression coefficients and control for gender, age, and SES) (Sawyer, Peña, and Sidanius 2002)*

Variable	Negro	Mulatto	Blanco	Total
Panel A: Patriotism regressed on racial identity				
Mulattos	0.09	0.08	−0.02	0.01
Panel B: Patriotism regressed on racial affect				
Blancos (Trigueño)	−0.01	−0.03	−0.09	−0.06
Mulatos (Indios)	−0.15	−0.11	−0.04	−0.05
Negros (Indios)	0.08	−0.08	−0.05	−0.01
Panel C: Patriotism regressed on ethnocentrism				
Blancos (Trigueño)	0.07	−0.07	–	0.01
Mulatos (Indios)	0.19	–	−0.04	−0.01
Negros (Indios)	–	0.07	−0.01	−0.02
Panel D: Patriotism regressed on ideologies of group dominance *(Mulattos)*				
SDO	−0.32	−0.01	−0.24	−0.20*
Racism	−0.16	−0.16*	−0.28**	−0.23**

While I have shown that white Cubans are more likely to hold racist beliefs toward black Cubans than the reverse, panel D in Table 6.15 indicates that feelings of both racism and social dominance are attenuated by patriotic sentiments. That is, patriots are less racist and less willing to oppress others than nonpatriots. In this fact, we can observe in these results the success of the Cuban regime in framing national discourse in an antiracist fashion and in forging a civic nationalism despite the existence of an ethnic and racial hierarchy.

The survey conducted in Santa Clara by Daniela Hernández affirms the analysis in Table 6.15. She found that, in general, blacks and mulattos identified themselves as Cuban or Cuban and black more often than they identified themselves as black alone. Especially among younger people, furthermore, blacks and mulattos feel they have more in common with white Cubans than they have with blacks in Africa (see Table 6.16). It is difficult to analyze Hernández's statistics without more information, but the weight of her evidence supports the idea that being black and being Cuban are quite compatible identities. The famed anthropologist Fernando Ortiz wrote a book entitled *Los Negros*

TABLE 6.16. *Questions of identity to blacks and mulattos (Hernández 1998, 82)*

Questions		Under 40	Over 40
What is more important to you?	To be black	8%	–
	To be Cuban	50%	38%
	Both	42%	58%
	Neither	–	4%
Who do you feel closer to?	Black people in Africa	21%	38%
	Whites in Cuba	79%	63%

TABLE 6.17. *Attitudes about black organization (results control for education, income, gender, and age)*

Blacks should organize into a powerful black political force	$-.1364^*$
Blacks should join forces with whites to advance black interests	$-.1488^*$

Curros at the turn of the twenty-first century about black delinquency as an urban Cuban social problem. *Negros curros*, or black male delinquents, were known for their antisocial behavior and their black market activity. Fernandez notes that the modern extension of Ortiz's *Negros curros* are currently called *guapos curros*; they are seen as delinquent, but also patriotic, black tough guys (1996). They are both marked racially and marked as uniquely Cuban.

Black patriotism does not negate the possibility that blacks will form race-based political reform organizations, but it does seem to suggest that such organizations could take a decidedly nonviolent, coalition-building approach to reform. We asked respondents if they agreed with the proposition "Blacks should organize into a powerful black political force." Blacks were more likely than whites to agree with the proposition. Blacks are also more likely than whites to support the idea that blacks need to join forces with whites in order to advance black interests (see Table 6.17). This evidence refutes assertions (often made in the past by the Cuban government) that racial organization by blacks will be divisive and will touch off a race war.

The Case for Comparison

Assessments of racial group position are inherently comparative and transnational in nature; blacks in one country frequently look to the

TABLE 6.18. *Race and international comparison of racial issues (results control for education, income, gender, and age)*

The black struggle is not confined to this country	–
Race relations on the island are better than elsewhere in Latin America	–
Race relations on the island are better than in the United States	–
	(.112* without controls)
General feelings about the United States, positive or negative?	.1613**

position of blacks in other countries and assess their position relative to theirs. Thus Afro-Cubans may perceive racial problems in Cuba while still believing that they are better off with the current regime than they would be if they lived elsewhere. I used the survey to test the degree to which race is a transnational construct in Cuba. When respondents were asked if the black struggle was confined to Cuba, there were no racial differences in response, and there was widespread agreement across racial groups that it was not (mean 1.64 on a 7-point scale, standard deviation 1.40). It seems that Cubans in general have assimilated the regime's attempts to internationalize the struggle against racism. When the respondents were asked to compare race relations on the island with those within other Latin American countries, there was strong agreement that race relations on the island are better than those elsewhere in Latin America. (There are no statistically significant differences given a partial correlation and a bivariate correlation in response, and the mean response was 1.74 on a 7-point scale, with a standard deviation of 1.4.) When comparing race relations in Cuba with those in the United States, there was somewhat less agreement. With controls, there were no statistical differences between racial groups in response to the comparison. In a bivariate correlation, however, darker-skinned Cubans were revealed to be more likely to agree with the proposition that the United States is more racist than Cuba (see Table 6.18). The mean response of 1.76 and standard deviation of 1.4 are not different from the Latin American comparison, but it appears that black Cubans may be somewhat more attentive than white Cubans to propaganda about race relations in the United States. In fact, black Cubans are more likely to feel negatively about the United States in general than white Cubans are (see Table 6.18). The racialized differences in perceptions of the United States suggest that darker Cubans process

TABLE 6.19. *Correlation between race and perceptions of Cuban Americans (results control for education, income, gender, and age)*

General feelings about Cuban migrants to the United States, positive or negative?	.1715*
White Cubans in Miami are more racist than whites on the island	−.110 (−.137* without controls)

information about the United States differently from the way lighter Cubans do.

The Miami exile community is the primary political alternative to the Cuban regime. Even if blacks perceive the regime to be imperfect, it must merely outperform other political alternatives to keep their loyalty. Therefore, it is worth investigating to what extent attitudes toward the Miami exile community vary by race. When asked about their feelings toward Miami Cubans, respondents' replies differed according to race. Darker-skinned Cubans had significantly more negative feelings toward migrants than lighter-skinned Cubans did (see Table 6.19). In order to investigate the genesis of these feelings, we asked specifically if whites who have migrated to the United States are more racist than whites on the island. When the responses were subjected to controls for age, gender, income, and education, there were no clear racial differences, but a bivariate correlation (excluding controls) produced significant results (see Table 6.19). Afro-Cubans' negative feelings toward Miami Cubans are probably not limited to the belief that Cubans in the United States are more racist than those on the island.

Conclusion

The foregoing results give us some additional evidence about Cuba, and the weight of the evidence supports the conclusions reached in the previous chapter: Race is a salient feature of Cuban life, Cuba is a hierarchical society stratified by race, and race structures in important ways the way Cubans view the social political world. Even after years of revolution and miscegenation, Cuban society falls far short of being color-blind: Racial hierarchy has proven to be perfectly compatible with miscegenation and color-blind rhetoric.

Cuban whites still hold racist attitudes toward blacks. They are more likely than darker-skinned Cubans to believe a set of explicitly racist statements and stereotypes about blacks. Whites are also more likely than nonwhites to find physical features associated with whites attractive. It is notable, however, that patriotism, or attachment to the nation, diminishes white racism. This suggests that national symbols are working to combat racism in Cuba, rather than promoting racist attitudes toward blacks, as they do in the United States.

Race is also quite important in determining life chances and organizational involvement in Cuba. Blacks fare worse than whites in the Cuban economy, feel less positive than whites about the new economy, and appear to resent those who are profiting from private business. Also, blacks are more likely than whites to participate in predominantly black organizations, to support traditional means of black empowerment, and to engage in activities that support the state and the regime. The regime's concerns about black organizations and black empowerment, however, seem to be misplaced. Blacks who tend to support black organizing and empowerment are more patriotic than whites, are more likely to support the idea of multiracial reform coalitions, and more frequently support the regime in their behaviors than whites do.

Blacks' disappointment with the regime's failure to eliminate racial hierarchy seems to be offset by their belief that it would be worse to live under an alternative regime. While conscious of the limitations of the current regime and concerned about the "new economy," blacks do not feel positively toward the United States and the predominantly white exile community. Far from being endowed with false consciousness, blacks support the Castro regime out of loyalty to the gains of the past and conviction that their political alternatives are far worse than the current regime.

7

Racial Politics in Miami

Ninety Miles and a World Away

In May 1980, a race riot erupted in Miami following the acquittal of four white Miami police officers for the fatal beating of an African American businessman. The riots broke out in Liberty City, a predominantly black ghetto whose residents had grown weary of police brutality, poverty, and unemployment (Croucher 1997; Dunn 1997; M. C. Garcia 1996). According to the political scientist Sheila Croucher, "Over a three-day period entire neighborhoods were destroyed, fires set, windows broken, and homes and businesses looted" (4). Eighteen people were killed. The riots shocked the nation and resulted in property damage estimated at $200 million. The rioters were primarily African Americans, but they also included Afro-Cubans, Jamaicans, and Haitians (Dunn 1997).

Racial politics in Miami over the past twenty years has often been extremely tense. This tension is a product of divisions based on race, class, ethnicity, country of origin, and era of immigration. The riot highlighted the frustrations of blacks in Miami, who suffered the ongoing effects of an economic recession and watched as a white Cuban elite formed partnerships with a white Anglo elite for control of the city (Garcia 1996; Croucher 1997; Dunn 1997). A new wave of Cuban immigrants continued to arrive in the city, adding to the tension.

The Cuban Revolution is as much a part of the history of Miami as it is a part of Cuban history. While the relationship between Cubans in Miami and those on the island is close, the story of the Cuban exile community is a story of bitterness and tragedy forged on the anvil of the Cuban Revolution of 1959. Members of the white Cuban exile community, ignoring the evidence all around them, have clung doggedly to their conviction that there was never a racial problem in Cuba or among Cubans, and thus that Cubans did not arrive in the United States with unresolved racial conflicts. They have continued to believe that opposing Castro is more important than admitting to racial problems in the United States, acknowledging progress in Cuba, or recognizing the moral authority of friends of the Cuban regime who have fought for racial equality from South Africa to the southern United States (M. C. Garcia 1996). Such admissions would mean granting the enemy a victory and admitting the limitations of both their politics and capitalism.

In this chapter, I will demonstrate that the white leadership of the Miami exile community, because of its myopic view of Cuban history and its single-minded opposition to the Castro regime, has failed to assess racial politics correctly both in Cuba and in Miami. As a result, it is in a poor position to lead the Cuban population, which includes a much larger proportion of educated Afro-Cubans than it did at the time of the revolution. The Cuban exile community has, through its leadership's statements and actions, suggested that it is more likely to move backward on racial issues than to improve upon the policies of the Castro regime. The chapter first examines who the Cuban American exiles are, what their experiences in the United States have been like, and the nature of their ideology and political objectives. It then explores four important political events from recent decades and analyzes public opinion data gathered from Cuban Americans.

Silk Stocking Exodus, 1959–62 and 1965–73

Cuban emigrants have arrived in Miami in four distinct waves. The first wave was made up of officials of the former government, elites, and a large portion of the Cuban middle class. Between January 1959 and October 1962, almost 250,000 Cubans emigrated to the United States (Cortes 1981). Some individuals in this first group had amassed large fortunes that were kept in foreign banks (M. C. Garcia 1996). Some already owned residences in the Miami area. This group was more than 95 percent white. It was also primarily upper-class, and many of its members had participated in racially exclusionary clubs and organizations on the island (Dunn 1997). Thus, the members of this group of exiles had benefited from the racial segregation and political corruption of the Republican era, the very conditions that motivated the Cuban Revolution. Along with emigrants who arrived in the following wave, they would form the core of Cuban American political power and put their ideological stamp on Cuban American political discourse.

The second wave came to the United States during what have been dubbed the "freedom flights" between 1965 and 1973. This group was primarily composed of middle-class Cubans who had quickly grown disillusioned with the regime. A few had supported the revolution, but the vast majority had adopted a wait-and-see attitude. Following the failed Bay of Pigs invasion, many members of the middle class realized that the revolution and Fidel Castro would not be a passing fancy (Gonzalez-Pando 1998). Organizations (some of which included Cuban American emigrants among their members) and embassies worked to facilitate the exit of these dissident middle-class Cubans, and the Castro regime took the opportunity to externalize dissent (Cortes 1981). Hundreds of thousands of Cubans left the island, some after being humiliated and strip-searched by Cuban officials. Forced to leave all their property behind, many of these emigrants arrived in the United States with little more than the shirts on their backs (M. C. Garcia 1996; Croucher 1997). This group would become one of the most successful emigrant groups in American history.

The historian Maria Cristina Garcia describes the factors that explain the triumph of the first and second waves of Cuban exiles in America: "Their middle-class values and entrepreneurial skills, which transferred readily across borders, and the Cuban Refugee Program, which pumped millions of dollars into the economy and facilitated the Cubans' adaptation through vocational and professional retraining programs," both helped these Cubans to assimilate (109). Because of the Cuban exiles' special position in Cold War politics, they received aid from the Eisenhower and Kennedy administrations. Although there was fear and suspicion of the exiles in South Florida, the national media quickly turned them into a cause célèbre. Garcia writes, "Popular magazines such as *Life*, *Newsweek*, and *Fortune* portrayed them as the 'model immigrants,' celebrated their heroism and patriotism, and dubbed them the new Horatio Algers" (110). Thus this primarily white group – which had a connection to the affable white cultural icon Desi Arnaz, who regularly appeared in American living rooms on "I Love Lucy" – was able to gain broad popular acceptance.

It helped their cause that less than 3 percent of the Cuban emigrants were black or mulatto (M. C. Garcia 1996; Croucher 1997; Dunn 1997). The Cuban exile community in Miami was "whitened," moreover, when Afro-Cuban exiles settled in the Northeast and Midwest to avoid southern segregation, integrating themselves into black communities in these areas (Chardy 1993). The popular perception of the Cubans as white was so strong that some of the few black and mulatto exiles were even able to attend school with whites prior to integration. Garcia writes: "Blacks watched in disbelief as Cuban black and mulatto children attended 'white schools.' Prompting one local minister to write, 'the American Negro could solve the school integration problem by teaching his children to speak Spanish'" (1996, 29). The lavish social programs created for Cuban exiles were a slap in the face for African Americans, who were in the midst of the civil rights movement when the emigrants arrived and who had faced generation after generation of neglect and discrimination since Reconstruction (Dunn 1997). In Miami, Cubans received far more federal aid than African Americans did. Dunn explains: "In 1968, for example, Dade County non-Hispanic whites received $3,356,876 in loans from the Small Business Administration (SBA). Hispanics received $1,078,950, and blacks received $82,600. Considering all SBA loans made in Dade County from 1968 to 1980, Hispanics received 46.9 percent of the funds made available ($47,677,660), non-Hispanic whites received 46.6 percent ($47,361,773), and blacks received 6 percent ($6,458,240)" (1997, 34).

Mariel and Beyond, 1980–94

The favored position of the Cuban emigrants lasted only until the next wave of emigration, however; the third wave of emigrants was blacker and poorer than those who had come before. Between April and October 1980, 124,776 Cubans arrived in the United States (Cortes 1981). This wave of emigration set off what can best be described as a moral panic across the country and within the Cuban American community. The exodus, which came to be called the "Mariel Boatlift," was the result of a collision among U.S. interests, the Castro regime, and the Cuban American community. The migration had its origins in 1978 discussions among U.S. officials, the Cuban government, and Cuban Americans who were open to working with the regime (M. C. Garcia 1996). The boatlift was not a product of orderly negotiations, however, but proof that the problems among the United States, Fidel Castro, and the exile community had become intractable.

During the Carter administration, relations between the United States and Cuba were thawing. Preliminary discussions had begun that many felt would result in the release to the United States of thousands of political prisoners held in Cuba. These discussions occurred in secret, however, and they broke down when the Carter administration failed to acknowledge them publicly. In an attempt to make inroads with moderates within the exile community, who he hoped would work to loosen the grip of the U.S. blockade, Castro invited members of the Cuban American community to engage in dialogues (officially called *dialogos*) in order to build a political relationship and to work toward the release of Cuban political prisoners (M. C. Garcia 1996). The gesture quickly divided the exile community. One group saw *dialogos* as an opportunity to bring home political prisoners, while the other saw the talks as an utterly unacceptable validation of the Castro regime. Those involved in the talks (many openly called them communists) became the targets of extremists in the community. Several were victims of terrorist bombings.

As a result of the talks, Castro released nearly 2,400 prisoners and allowed many Cuban exiles to visit their family members in Cuba (M. C. Garcia 1996). Unfortunately, this diplomatic exchange soon degenerated into an embarrassing episode for the Castro regime, the Carter administration, and the Cuban exile community. Emboldened by the visits of their American relatives, 10,000 Cuban dissidents stormed the Peruvian embassy and demanded to be airlifted out of Cuba (M. C. Garcia 1996; Dunn 1997). The standoff lasted more than a week, and it ended when Castro agreed to allow Peru to airlift the dissidents to Costa Rica (M. C. Garcia 1996). The regime then reversed its decision, arguing that the airlift would be used as propaganda against it. Castro demanded that the Cubans be transported directly to the countries where they would eventually reside. An initial plan would have resettled Cubans in several countries, but it quickly unraveled. Inspired by Cuban exiles who had arrived in boats to request the release of dissident relatives, Castro announced that a flotilla would be arranged. Maria Garcia recounts what happened next: "On April 20, the government announced that all Cubans who wished to leave the island would be permitted to do so and urged them to call their relatives in the United States to come pick them up" (60). Cuban exiles rushed to their boats and sailed to the port of Mariel outside of Havana. This was the designated rendezvous point, and camps were set up to process the thousands of Cubans who wanted to leave the island. The flotilla continued to transport Cubans to the United States for almost three months.

The exiles and the United States got more migrants than they had anticipated, however: Castro forced the Cuban exiles who arrived at the port with boats to take on and transport all of the Cubans who were waiting at the docks. Individuals carried their relatives along with scores of other emigrants chosen by the Cuban government (Cortes 1981). More than 3,000 of these refugees had severe and often chronic medical conditions such as mental illness. "Most distressing to U.S. officials, however," Garcia explains, "was the discovery that thousands of the Mariel emigrants – twenty-six thousand by the end of the Boatlift – had criminal records. Estimates varied, but approximately two thousand had committed serious felonies in Cuba" (1996, 64). Word soon got out that Fidel Castro had used the flotilla as a means of ridding his country of "social deviants," including dissidents, homosexuals, the mentally ill, drug addicts, and felons.[1] After this news was released, American public opinion quickly turned against the boatlift emigrants (Cortes 1981; M. C. Garcia 1996; Croucher 1997).

Between 14 and 40 percent of the boatlift Cubans were black (Chardy 1993). In terms of race, class, and culture, they simply did not look like the Cuban emigrants who had arrived in the past. Many refugees were kept in prisonlike structures, and they protested; several riots broke out in refugee camps across the country (M. C. Garcia 1996). Community leaders fought attempts to open refugee camps in their areas. Many of the new emigrants complained that they faced discrimination from their Cuban brothers and sisters (Cortes 1981).

---

[1] Until the early 1990s release of the now-famous film *Strawberries and Chocolate*, gays and lesbians were treated as criminals in Cuba. A cultural transformation followed the AIDS epidemic in Cuba much as it did in the United States, however, and there has been a greater opening in the treatment of Cuban gays and lesbians as AIDS awareness has forced greater openness.

The established Cuban American exile community simply disapproved of the race, ideology, values, and culture of the new exiles, many of whom had grown up with the revolution; and its members took great pains to distinguish themselves from the new emigrants. Having heard reports that Santeria was being practiced by the Mariel emigrants, for example, Miami Cubans from earlier waves of emigration sought to emphasize that Cubans were Catholic and did not believe in Santeria.

Meanwhile, in the rest of America, a moral panic was brewing. In 1983, Brian DePalma remade the film *Scarface*, turning it into an epic about the criminal rise of a Mariel emigrant. The film followed Tony Montana, a dusky-skinned *Marielito* who had a record of violence in Cuba. Upon arriving in the United States, Montana quickly finds a home in the Miami underworld and fights his way to the top of the drug game. This popular movie cemented an enduring association between *Marielitos* and crime, so that the *Marielitos* continue to be associated with crime in the popular mind today. Gordon Baum, for example, leader of the Conservative Citizens Council – a group that received press in 1999 for its racist views and its connections to leaders of the Republican Party – drew sharp distinctions between the waves of Cuban emigrants: "The nation was gulled by the first wave of Cuban immigrants. Then came the Marielitos, the typical ones, the normal ones. We saw what was really there" (quoted in Powell 1999, 112).

The *Marielitos* faced extreme racism in the United States, and many returned to Cuba. Laurence Glasco, who interviewed *Marielitos* for his research, noted that while the *Marielitos* enjoyed the economic opportunities in the United States, they did not miss the racism when they returned to Cuba (1998). The untold numbers of Cubans since Mariel who have either been detained indefinitely or who have returned (or have been returned) to Cuba tell the story of the impact of the Mariel boatlift on U.S. race relations. The Mariel boatlift also affected domestic politics: The combination of the boatlift, the recession, and the hostage crisis in Iran was enough to torpedo Carter's bid for reelection, and the White House went to Ronald Reagan (Croucher 1997; Cortes 1981; M. C. Garcia 1996).

When the special period began in 1993, thousands of Cubans fashioned rafts and attempted to leave the country. The Castro regime took no steps to prevent this exodus, seeing it as another opportunity to externalize dissent. The refugees fled the country primarily for economic rather than for political reasons, and as a result they tend to have more moderate views of the Castro regime and its achievements than the established leaders of the Miami exile community. Like the *Marielitos*, a significant proportion of the emigrants during this fourth wave were black. Many were detained and returned to Cuba (Cortes 1981). Many others died in their attempts to raft to Miami, though some were rescued by Cuban Americans and the U.S. Coast Guard. The Clinton administration eventually negotiated a lottery system with the Castro regime to foster the more orderly immigration of Cubans.

Mobilization from the Right

Many Cuban exiles, even those who have lived in the United States for forty years, see themselves as combatants in an ongoing war against the Castro regime. Some of them suffered abuse and humiliation as a result of the Cuban Revolution (M. C. Garcia 1996). When the U.S.-supported Bay of Pigs invasion failed, the exile community's hope of mounting a successful military operation to end Castro's reign was dashed, though major Cuban American organizations maintained connections with paramilitary groups and continued to make covert attempts to destabilize the Cuban government. Cuban Americans' anger, along with their feeling that they are battling a powerful foe, has shaped exile politics. While opinions in the Cuban exile community are diverse, certain points of view have consistently guided the most powerful Cuban American organizations and, in turn, U.S. policy toward the island of Cuba. Those emigrants with the most conservative and hard-line attitudes toward the Castro regime have been cultivated and financially supported by the U.S. government, especially by the Reagan administration. Thus the most strident and uncompromising Cuban American voices have defined the playing field of Cuban exile politics (M. C. Garcia 1996).

Curiously, insistence on unity and intolerance of dissent have become the hallmarks of both the Castro regime and Cuban exile politics. The power accumulated within Cuban organizations by the first groups of emigrants, their relative homogeneity, and their pre-existing attitudes about race have enabled them to make the unique problems of Afro-Cubans in Miami and on the island invisible. By ignoring racial issues and often using racist or, at best, racially insensitive discourse, the leadership of the Cuban exile community has damaged relations with the African American community in South Florida and across the nation in the name of anticommunism in general and anti-Castroism in particular (Croucher 1997; Dunn 1997).

Afro-Cubans in South Florida tend to be less well off economically than white Cubans and to live in fringe areas wedged between well-off Cuban communities and very poor African American and West Indian communities. A 1991 *Miami Herald* article offered one Afro-Cuban's perspective on the racism of the white Cuban emigrant community: "Migdalia Jimenez is a black Cuban who says black Americans treat her better than white Cubans do. Jimenez was unable to rent an apartment in the Cuban area of Little Havana, while a white counterpart was able to rent the apartment and turn it over to Jimenez. 'Because I am black,' Jimenez said, 'they didn't want to rent to me'" (Goldfarb 1990b).

Race is not the only issue that divides Cuban emigrants, however; it appears that migrants' class at the time of migration and their ideology also play key roles. The vast majority of black Cubans emigrated during the Mariel Boatlift, and their experiences and consequent political opinions make the earlier emigrants uncomfortable. M. C. Garcia explains: "Having lived in a socialist economy for twenty years, they had a different perception of the responsibilities of the state and this tended to favor government intervention. While the older émigrés, for ideological reasons, tended to shut their eyes to the limitations of capitalist democracy, the Cubans of Mariel were more likely to weigh its pros and cons against those of Cuba" (1996, 116). Today, many Afro-Cubans feel caught between two communities, not exactly fitting into either. For instance, Deborah Wilson, a Cuban exile, argued, "White Cubans welcome us because we're Cuban, but with a big 'but' because we're black, and black Americans welcome us because we're black, but with a big 'but' because we're Cuban" (quoted in Chardy 1993, 36). A *New York Times* article discussed two Cuban exiles, one black and one white, who had been neighbors and friends in Cuba. The Afro-Cuban faced racism in Miami, some of it at the hands of white Cubans. Guinier and Torres recount the incident:

The point is driven home to Joel one night when a white Cuban-American policeman stopped and frisked him. Joel had been celebrating Valentine's

Day in a popular Cuban restaurant with his uncle and three women friends. The policeman said to him, "I've been keeping an eye on you for a while. Since you were in the restaurant. I saw you leave and I saw so many blacks in the car, I figured I would check you out." The white Cuban-American police officer disconnected Joel from his national identity and placed him firmly on the black side of America's principal divide, between whiteness and blackness. What Joel's fellow Cubans had already discovered and what was expressed most clearly by this officer's conduct, is that "whiteness" in the United States is a measure not just of the melanin content in one's skin but of one's social distance from blackness. The Cuban-American policeman asserted his own shaky claim to whiteness by harassing Joel for being black. (2002, 224)

The right-leaning Cuban American leadership has failed to come to terms with the racial discrimination that Afro-Cubans suffer; instead, it has continued to portray Cubans either as white, middle-class success stories or as proof that race is not important. Meanwhile, many Cubans live below the poverty line, and in 1990 black Cuban income was short of white Cuban income by almost 40 percent (M. C. Garcia 1996). Maria Garcia notes that it has been ideologically necessary for the early Cuban emigrants to erase the problems of Afro-Cuban emigrants: "The Cuban success story was an essential element in their collective identity. They focused on those who had assimilated economically rather than those who had not. To do otherwise would have been to grant Fidel Castro propaganda to use against them" (111).

The Cuban American leadership's opposition to black leaders who recognize the gains of the revolution and take a moderate position toward the regime has created a series of controversial public conflicts. Some Cuban Americans have criticized black leaders like Nelson Mandela – men who can boast of broad public support and moral authority – because they perceive these leaders to be too friendly toward Castro. The Cuban exile leadership in Miami vigorously attacked Afro-Cuban Mario Leon Baeza, a Clinton nominee to be the State Department's assistant secretary for inter-American affairs, for his moderate views toward the Castro regime. Some Cuban American organizations attacked the vigorously anti-Castro scholar Carlos Moore for arguing that racism existed in Cuba before the revolution and that racial problems also exist within the exile community. These incidents and others provide evidence that the fears of black Cubans on the island about the racial insensitivity of the Cuban American leadership are not unfounded.

Individuals and organizations on the political right have for decades accused those working for racial equality of being communists. These charges have been leveraged largely for rhetorical advantage, but they are also based on a real relationship that exists between the political left and both anticolonial struggles and struggles for racial equality (Robinson 1991; Hutchinson 1995). In the sections that follow, I discuss four highly controversial incidents in which the leadership of the Cuban exile community has drawn fire for its seemingly racist beliefs. These conflicts are about both race and ideology; the perception of the connection between race and communism has created friction that has damaged the credibility of the Cuban American exile community among African Americans and Afro-Cubans alike.

Carlos Moore

Carlos Moore, the Black Nationalist scholar cited frequently throughout this work, became the target of the Cuban American leadership in 1986. Moore was teaching a course at Florida International University (FIU) on Cuban history in which he criticized race relations in Cuba prior to the revolution, and a radio station owned by a Cuban exile, Jorge Rodriguez, vigorously attacked him for his views (Chardy 1990). The exile community objected specifically to Moore's criticism of José Martí and Carlos Manuel de Cespedes for what he deemed their racist beliefs. Ernesto Montaner, a radio commentator, declared on the air, "A few days ago, a young student from Florida International University asked me if it was true that in Cuba there were no patriots, because from Carlos Manuel de Cespedes to José Martí, they were all racists and slave owners who struggled for power to exploit people" (36).

Moore had argued in his course that Afro-Cuban slaves had been manipulated by white Cubans who hoped to garner their support for the struggle against Spain. He asserted that blacks were betrayed by their white fellow revolutionaries, who became concerned about the possibility of black insurgency. This betrayal, in Moore's opinion, paved the way for the collaboration between the Cuban and U.S. governments. As I demonstrated in Chapter 2, much of what Moore asserted was true. Despite his strident criticism of the Castro regime, however, Moore's reassessment of Cuban history did not mesh well with exile ideology: Moore did not cling to the exiles' right-wing philosophy, and he did not believe in Latin American exceptionalism. In the eyes of many members of the Cuban American community, Moore was spreading lies about Cuban history and smearing Cuban heroes.

As the pressure on Florida International University from the exile community grew stronger, Moore was called into the office of Modesto Maidique, the FIU president, along with the historian Marquez Sterling. Moore was asked to explain and account for his views on race and Cuban history. Though FIU ultimately sided with Moore, he felt hurt by the experience and left FIU when his contract expired.

Nelson Mandela

Moore's case represents only one battle in a cultural war that continues to be waged over the issue of race and the Cuban American community. Another battle took place in 1990, when the anti-Castroism of the Cuban American community collided with the most powerful symbol of the battle for racial freedom at the time. The controversy surrounded Nelson Mandela's post-imprisonment tour of the United States, during which he was to speak to the American Federation of State, County, and Municipal Employees. The problem began when Mandela spoke kindly of the support of individuals like Yasir Arafat, Muammar Gadhafi, and Fidel Castro in an interview with Ted Koppel. Arafat, Gadhafi, and Castro had provided needed moral, economic, and military support to the African National Congress (ANC) during its struggle against *apartheid*. Castro's intervention in southern Africa had aided groups that were resisting South Africa's military incursions in Angola, while the Palestinians and other Arab groups had supported the ANC in its opposition to the *apartheid* regime, which had formed close bonds with Israel. This all occurred while most of the West, and in particular the United States, at least tacitly supported the South African government. Within the United States, however, Mandela had won the allegiance of African Americans and individuals on the left who strongly identified with the struggle against *apartheid*, and this support proved invaluable to him. In fact, the ANC and the Pan-African Congress drew heavily on the philosophy of the American civil rights movement.

Mandela's complex web of friendships across national borders inspired racial conflict in Miami. In the mind of the Cuban American leadership, Mandela had stated his support for a regime that they believed represented pure evil. After Mandela's interview with Koppel aired, the mayor of Miami, quick to placate his core constituency, announced, "In view of the statements last night, it would be difficult to give him [Mandela] any kind of recognition or key to the city" (quoted in Croucher 1997, 149). The black community in Miami became angry at the Cuban American community's plan to snub Mandela. Many African Americans had long invested their emotions in the struggle in South Africa as a proxy for their ongoing struggle in the United States. The African Americans whom Mandela had looked to as an inspiration now looked to him as a symbol of racial progress. In response to the city's plan to snub Mandela, H. T. Smith of the Miami Coalition for a Free South Africa wrote, "Miami may go down in infamy as the only city in America that denounced, criticized, castigated and threw its 'welcome mat' in the face of Nelson Mandela" (quoted in Croucher 1997, 148).

Charges of racism were leveled against the Cuban American community, and it did not take long for community leaders to respond. A Cuban lawyer appeared on a black radio station in Miami and stated, "This is not a racial matter. Mr. Mandela is a confessed Communist" (quoted in Goldfarb 1990a). Needless to say, his statement failed to impress the African American community. African Americans would never be convinced by the Cuban American argument that its objection to Mandela was not about race, but about communism. Black radio in Miami continued to castigate the Cuban American community, while Cuban media sources became even more strident and steadfast in their opposition to Mandela (Goldfarb 1990a). Some Jewish groups joined in the criticism of Mandela, and the stage was set for a conflict that lasted for three years.

When Mandela arrived in Miami, he was greeted by thousands of loyal supporters, and he spoke to a friendly crowd, much as he had in all of the other cities he visited. In Miami, however, Mandela was also greeted by protesters from the Cuban American community, and he received no official recognition of his visit. Croucher writes: "According to one estimate approximately three hundred anti-Communists, mostly Cuban Americans, stood on one side of the street waving placards that read, 'Arafat, Gadahfi, and Castro are terrorists,' and 'Mr. Mandela, do you know how many people your friend Castro has killed just for asking for the right to speak as you do here?'" (1997, 142). The black response was equally angry: "Three thousand mostly black supporters stood with placards proclaiming, 'Miami City Council = Pretoria,' and 'Mandela, Welcome to Miami, Home of Apartheid'" (142). These sentiments signaled how deeply an African American community that felt isolated and disenfranchised had been wounded by the controversy surrounding Mandela's visit. Patricia Due, a founding member of CORE, stated: "I feel sick. How dare they do this to us? Mr. Mandela is a symbol. Our link to our motherland. After all the blood, sweat, and tears of black Americans, and people are still trying to tell us who we can hear. To reject Mandela is to reject us. He is our brother. If they say he's not welcome, they're saying we're not welcome too" (quoted in Goldfarb 1990a). The controversy surrounding Mandela's visit involved symbols dear to the people of three diasporas: Mandela stood for the African diaspora's fight for equality, but for Cuban Americans he symbolized opposition to the fight against communism, and for Jews he symbolized opposition to the battle to preserve the state of Israel against Arab threats.

Reacting to the city's failure to welcome Mandela, prominent African American leaders and organizations demanded an apology from the city council. The African American sorority Delta Sigma Theta was holding its convention in Miami during the controversy, and it also officially demanded an apology (Croucher 1997). None came, and the African American community launched a nationwide boycott of conventions and tourism in Miami. The boycott lasted for three years, and it only deepened Cuban Americans' resolve. A Cuban American candidate for the Dade County Commission remarked, "If it's an apology they're waiting for, it will not come" (quoted in Croucher 1997, 152). The demands of the aggrieved African Americans grew more comprehensive over time, as Dunn explains: "To the initial demand for an apology were added demands for the following: an investigation into a recent incident of police brutality against Haitian immigrants, a review of U.S. immigration policy, single-member voting districts, and substantial reforms in Dade's tourism industry to allow increased employment and business opportunities" (1997, 347). These demands reflected longstanding concerns about police brutality, unfairness in immigration policy, and black political and economic isolation.

Insult was added to injury when the black-owned *Miami Times* reported that South African Zulu chief Buthelezi was in Miami and would be received at a private luncheon hosted by the Cuban American president of the *Miami Herald*, Roberto Suarez (Dunn 1997). Buthelezi was widely known to have supported the *apartheid* regime in opposition to the ANC. Buthelezi's political organization, the Inkatha Freedom Party, was famous for its violent attacks in the townships on supporters of the ANC. Facing opposition from the African American community, the *Miami Herald* canceled the luncheon. The Cuban American Foundation, however, stepped in and offered to host the affair (Crockett and Epstein 1990). Buthelezi ultimately canceled his Miami trip, but the actions of the Cuban American Foundation further scarred its credibility on racial issues. Yet a ray of light appeared at the end of the long tunnel. The boycott came to an end in May 1993 after community leaders came to an agreement that included support for an African American–owned, convention-level hotel in Dade County, hotel management scholarships, and increased contracts for black-owned businesses (Dunn 1997).

Mario Leon Baeza

In 1993, the Cuban American leadership would again publicly criticize an Afro-Cuban whom it deemed to be insufficiently anti-Castro. While the leadership denied that race played a role in its attack, the Cuban American community once again appeared racially insensitive in its attempt to fight communism. In early 1993, President Clinton selected a Cuban American attorney from New York for the post of assistant secretary of state for inter-American affairs. Mario Leon Baeza was recommended for the post by the head of Clinton's transition team, Vernon Jordan, as well as by the secretary of commerce, Ron Brown. He was chosen for his skill in international trade policy and, in particular, for his views on privatization in Latin America. Baeza's ties to the staunch anti-Castro groups were weak, however, and the leader of the Cuban American Foundation, Jorge Mas Canosa, quickly went on the offensive against him. Mas Canosa's spokesman stated: "Most of [Baeza's] opinions are antithetical to the Cuban community. Baeza doesn't fit the profile" (quoted in Whitfield and Marquis 1993; Alberola 1993). While Mas Canosa's reference to a "profile" raised questions of racial discrimination, the exile leadership attacked Baeza for political positions he had taken: Baeza had suggested that the Torricelli Bill, which tightened the U.S. embargo on Cuba, might be in violation of international trade agreements (M. C. Garcia 1996). He had also attended a conference in Cancun and Havana at which Cuban officials discussed the Cuban economy and the effects of privatization. During his visit to Havana, Baeza took the opportunity to deliver medicine and other goods to members of his family and to see them for the first time since he was two years old (Baeza 1993). The exile community extrapolated from Baeza's record that he was soft on communism.

Baeza was allowed to write an op-ed piece in the *Miami Herald* confirming his opposition to Castro and his support of human rights, but it failed to stop the attacks on him (1993). When representatives of the Cuban American leadership began claiming that Baeza was not as qualified as the other candidates, Congressman Charles Rangel of New York concluded that the tenor of the conversation involved racial double standards. Rangel wrote a scathing response to the Cuban exile leadership that was published in the *Miami Herald*. In it, he complained, "Despite these high stakes in crafting good economic policy for Latin America and the Caribbean, an extraordinarily gifted nominee is being opposed by right-wing Cuban-American activists because he is not one of them and because he is black." Rangel went on to urge the president not to withdraw Baeza's name for nomination: "I'm a member of the Congressional Black Caucus, and I have a long-standing interest in the region. I am offended by these Cuban Americans' single-issue ideology and racism. I call upon the new President to reject it by advancing Mario Baeza's appointment to the Senate for confirmation." He added, "and make no mistake about it: If he were white, Baeza would not have incurred this firestorm of protest" (1993).

These appeals only hardened Cuban American opposition to Baeza. While it is difficult to pinpoint the exact motives of the Cuban exile leadership, it appears that there is some truth to the claim that the intolerance of Baeza's more moderate stance on Cuba involved both ideology and attitudes toward race. Race, it seems, was used to determine Baeza's qualifications. Baeza was not seen as "representative" of a community that sees itself as white. Like the nominations of many other controversial black Clinton appointees, Baeza's nomination was withdrawn by the president.[2] Ultimately, Alexander Watson, a diplomat from the George H. W. Bush administration, was chosen and confirmed (Marquis 1993). The Baeza episode sent a powerful message to observers of the Cuban exile community that racial and ideological diversity would not be tolerated by Miami's powerful old-guard Cubans.

Andrew Young

The final incident this chapter will discuss involved another famous champion and symbol of the African American struggle, Andrew Young. In 1996, this civil rights leader, mayor of Atlanta, and former U.S. ambassador to the United Nations visited the Miami area in order to promote the Atlanta Olympic games. In 1977, Young had remarked, in his capacity as U.N. ambassador: "Cuban troops have helped to stabilize Angola" (quoted in Tanfani and Pugh 1996a). This nearly twenty-year-old comment inspired the Cuban exile leadership to stigmatize Young. Once again, southern African politics, civil rights, and Cuban exile politics collided to produce an ugly racial incident.

In March, six Dade County commissioners, under pressure from the Cuban exile community, chose to skip the presentation to Young of the key to the county. The snub did not go unnoticed, and Miami's African Americans quickly cried foul. What might have been an explosive situation was quickly defused, however, when Young, hoping to heal the rift, stated that no apology was necessary. Ultimately, five of the six commissioners signed an apology and negotiated a series of dialogues with the African American community over the subject (Tanfani and Pugh 1996b). One commissioner, in an act of contrition, stated: "It was an emotional knee-jerk reaction. I chose not to be present. It doesn't mean it was the right thing to do. That's the last time I let passion get in the way of reason and good judgment" (quoted in Tanfani and Pugh 1996b).

This brief incident, like the controversies surrounding Carlos Moore, Nelson Mandela, and Mario Leon Baeza, demonstrated the inability of the Cuban American community's leaders to understand the complex political relationships between black politics and communism, both in the United States and elsewhere. The anticommunist, anti-Castro litmus test employed by Cuban American

---

[2] Included in this list of Clinton appointees are, notably, Johnetta Cole and Lani Guinier, among others.

political leaders to evaluate black public figures often reveals their racial insensitivity.

Latino National Political Survey, 1989–90

Survey results demonstrate, however, that racially insensitive and even racist attitudes are not limited to the leadership of the Cuban American community but are prevalent in the community at large. Survey data collected on Latinos has rarely been broken down by nationality. The Latino National Political Survey conducted by Rodolfo de la Garza, Angelo Falcon, F. Chris Garcia, and John A. Garcia provides an opportunity to look specifically at Cuban Americans as they compare with Mexicans and Puerto Ricans. The results of this survey have been reproduced in a series of articles and in a book entitled *Latino Voices: Mexican, Puerto Rican, and Cuban Perspectives on American Politics* (1992). The book succeeds in outlining key differences in the communities that are not apparent when one thinks of "Hispanics" as a broad group. "Hispanic" support for the Republican Party, for example, derives from Cuban Americans, not from Hispanic Americans in general.

More interestingly for the purposes of this study, the survey results demonstrate that the vast majority of Cuban Americans identify themselves as white. De la Garza and his colleagues show that within their sample, fewer than 4 percent of Cuban Americans identified as black, while more than 91 percent identified as white. In the 1990 census, 83.8 percent of Cubans identified themselves as white, 3.7 percent as black, and 12 percent as "other." Among Mexicans, on the other hand, 50.6 percent identify as white, 0.9 percent identify as black, and 47.4 percent identify as other. Among Puerto Ricans, 46.4 percent identify as white, 6.5 percent identify as black, and 45.9 percent identify as other. Thus, despite the fact that Cuba is one of the darker islands in the Caribbean, the perception of island Cubans that the Miami population is disproportionately white is accurate.

Two specific measures in the Latino National Political Survey, furthermore, provide strong evidence that the Cuban American community is racially insensitive and feels substantial antipathy toward blacks. The first is a basic feeling thermometer, for which respondents were asked to rank from 0 to 100 (0 indicating negative feeling and 100 indicating positive feeling) their feelings toward blacks. Cuban

TABLE 7.1. *Probability estimates on probit model significant variables*

Cuban	Cubans are 17 percent more likely to think blacks face little or no discrimination
Race	Latinos who identify as white are 10 percent more likely to think blacks face little or no discrimination
Income	Those with higher incomes are 13 percent more likely to think blacks face some or a lot of discrimination
Education	Those with more education are 12 percent more likely to think blacks face some or a lot of discrimination
Age	Older people are 5 percent more likely to think blacks face little or no discrimination
Party ID	Democrats are 6 percent more likely to think blacks face some or a lot of discrimination

TABLE 7.2. *Probit model: Blacks face little or no discrimination*

Number of Observations: 3398
Pseudo R Squared = .01017
LR Chisquare (10) = 391
Log Likelihood = −1726.8

Independent variable	Coefficient	Standard Error	Z
Cuban	.58	.06	9.214
Race	.36	.07	5.23
Income	−.46	.10	−4.07
Education	−.38	.09	7.24
Age	.18	.06	3.09
Gender	.07	.05	1.431
Party ID	−.20	.06	−3.4
Anticommunism	.043	.07	0.6

American feelings toward blacks had a mean of 57 and a median of 50 (standard error 1.0), with a standard deviation of 26. Their feelings toward Anglos had a mean of 77 and a median of 80, with a standard deviation of 24 (standard error 1.1). The difference is startling, and it demonstrates the palpable antipathy that Cuban Americans feel toward blacks as compared with their feelings for whites.

The Latino National Political Survey also produced a few good measures of Cuban American sensitivity to racial problems. Tables 7.1 and 7.2 illustrate Cuban, Puerto Rican, and Mexican opinions about the degree to which African Americans face discrimination. Respondents

TABLE 7.3. *Regression model on feeling thermometer regarding blacks*

Multiple R: .17573
R Square: .03088
Adjusted R Square: .02915
Standard Error: 24.55990

Variable	B (SE B)	
Cuban	−4.03*	(−.06)
Race	−6.57*	(1.09)
Gender	−.033	(.94)
Education	7.81*	(1.70)
Age	−2.15	(1.28)
Party ID (Republican)	−4.22*	(−1.21)
(Constant)	67.56	(1.76)

*P < .05

were asked to choose whether African Americans faced "a lot," "some," "a little," or no discrimination. Fifty-one percent of Cuban American respondents felt that African Americans face little or no discrimination. Of these, 34 percent selected "none." These numbers are startling when compared with the opinions of other Latinos. Only 21 percent of Mexican and Puerto Rican respondents felt that African Americans face little or no discrimination, with only 8 percent selecting "none." In fact, 44 percent of Mexicans and Puerto Ricans felt that African Americans face "a lot" of discrimination, as compared with only 20 percent of Cuban Americans.

These results are tempered when subjected to more sophisticated statistical controls. In a probit model using STATA as the estimator of probability, Cuban heritage produces the largest shift toward the idea that blacks face little or no discrimination (see Tables 7.1 and 7.2). The model does not predict large amounts of variation, however, and the result merely suggests that Cubans are less sensitive to discrimination against blacks than are other Latinos. A regression model using SPSS with the black feeling thermometer reveals that being Cuban and white is a significant, though not overpowering, indicator of negative feelings toward blacks (see Table 7.3).

These survey results suggest that the charges against the Cuban American community of racism and insensitivity toward racial issues are legitimate. Cuban Americans have relatively negative opinions of blacks as compared with their opinions about whites, and they are ambivalent about (or unaware of) discrimination faced by blacks. Thus it appears that the suspicions of Afro-Cubans and African Americans are correct. Cuban American leadership in Cuba would, in all likelihood, represent a step backward for the black population.

Conclusion

The historical record and statistical data demonstrate Cuban Americans' antipathy toward the struggle of blacks against discrimination. Their tendency to see blacks' strategic alliances with communists as support for the Castro regime has fed the discriminatory tendencies of the Cuban exile community, as has its rejection of a diverse image in favor of an image of the community as white, wealthy, and successful. In an attempt to present a unified front against its powerful enemy, the Cuban American community – like the Castro regime – has sought to suppress dissent and diversity in the form of discussions about racial discrimination. This intransigence, when combined with the community's negative view of redistributive policies, its general antipathy toward blacks, and its limited sense of what constitutes Cuban culture, presents a problem for the relationship between Cuban exiles in the United States and Cubans on the island. In Cuba, the Afro-Cuban population rejects the overtures made by the Cuban American leadership, which it deems racist.

The influence of the African diaspora can be felt throughout this chapter. Moments of identification across national borders have motivated important conflicts in the politics of South Florida in which diasporic symbols have played key roles. A triangle of interaction can be drawn among Cuba, Africa, and the United States. This triangle of reference, information, and inspiration is an essential part of contemporary racial politics in South Florida, Cuba, and southern Africa. Alliances and enemies have crossed borders in strange combinations, and if we fail to explore these connections, we will fail to understand important events in racial politics in all three areas.

Conclusion

Race Cycles

The Cuban Revolution followed the race cycles pattern delineated in Chapter 1. When periods of crisis and transnational politics created progress for blacks, subsequent periods of state consolidation institutionalized some of the gains made during the crisis period; these consolidation periods were characterized by stagnant progress for blacks, a resurgence of pre-existing racial ideology, a denial of racism, and assertions that the race problem had been solved. Racial ideology proved to be an extremely powerful variable in Cuba that set limits on progress and justified consolidation. It has defined the limits of racial improvements and state consolidation in Cuba. The adaptability of racial ideologies has defied even revolutionary changes in other realms of society.

The regime of the revolution in 1959 created an opening in Cuban racial politics that had a precedent only in the transition of Cuba from a colony to an independent state. While the independence movement helped to end slavery and to bring formal citizenship rights to Cubans of color, the Cuban Revolution eliminated vestiges of formal segregation that remained within society. It also addressed many private forms of discrimination that had been untouched in the Republican period.

Nevertheless, the intervention of the revolution into racial matters had limits. Following the Bay of Pigs invasion, the Cuban state, concerned about further U.S. intervention but buoyed by the defeat of the United States, began to consolidate around ideals of socialism,

Third World internationalism, and national unity. It turned away from explicit discussions of racial issues and attacked all independent organizations, including black organizations. Castro declared the race problem solved, and the state took little action to solve ongoing racial problems. During the period of consolidation, the ideology of Latin American exceptionalism and a Marxist reductionist point of view about race prevailed in Cuba. These two strong ideological positions conspired to make racial issues invisible and provided a justification for both attacks on black organizations and a generally paternalistic view of blacks. The post-revolutionary consolidation in Cuba created a situation of inclusionary discrimination in which blacks had formal and symbolic inclusion in the state at the same time that a significant racial gap remained between blacks and whites.

As predicted, however, the consolidation period also institutionalized some of the reforms of the transition period. Discrimination remained illegal, and private clubs, schools, and exclusionary unions and professional organizations remained broken up. Blacks benefited from campaigns to expand literacy and from the first round of agrarian reform, which helped the poor, many of whom were black. Similarly, the Cold War offered opportunities and constraints for Afro-Cubans. Cuba's alliance with the Soviet Union brought added resources to the island, and because Cuba's was a socialist society, these resources were shared among the people, aiding the poorest Cubans. Blacks benefited from better health care and education alongside other Cubans. By 1981, as a result of institutionalized reforms, a broad array of social indicators suggested that blacks were reaching parity with whites. The threat of U.S. invasion and the orthodox Marxism that was reinforced by the relationship with the Soviets, however, provided additional justification to crack down on independent organizations and black organizations, preventing the development of an independent black critique and the formation of a black organization within the party.

The Cuban war in Angola, for symbolic and practical reasons related to mobilization, required blacks to be incorporated into the Cuban nation more effectively. The war in Angola produced advances for Cubans of color in terms of both symbolic representation and the incorporation of black culture into Cuban national life. The threat created by the U.S. invasion of Grenada led to reforms that included mass mobilization as part of a new military strategy of civil defense.

It also introduced "the Process of Rectification," which included the first discussion of affirmative action in Cuba. Concerns about unity in the face of a contracting economy, however, made the institution of affirmative action programs impractical.

The collapse of the Soviet Union has demonstrated that economic contractions do not have the opening effect of other crises. The consolidation around the new economic order has brought new challenges that threaten the gains of the revolution. The two most vibrant aspects of the new dual economy – remittances from Miami and tourism – tend to benefit white Cubans more than Afro-Cubans. Without equal access to dollars, Afro-Cubans have turned increasingly to participation in the black market and to other illegal activities to make a living, and these activities reinforce stereotypes about black criminality.

Race in Contemporary Cuba

After forty years of revolution, Cubans still widely believe that there is a racial hierarchy in Cuba. Though racial categorization is multitiered and complex, racial categories are very salient and are highly correlated with skin color. Cuban society appears to be a pigmentocracy, with whites at the top and blacks at the bottom. Whites are still more likely to believe racist stereotypes about blacks and to enjoy higher levels of income, education, and professional attainment than blacks. For whites, however, attachment to the nation reduces racist beliefs; this fact speaks to the symbolic way in which the Castro regime has tied the national project to antiracist projects at home and abroad.

Blacks in Cuba, as in many other countries, have higher rates of unemployment than whites. In many cases, mulattos do not fare much better than blacks, but they are perceived to have higher status. Blacks tend to be more critical of the current racial situation in Cuba than whites but also to be more supportive of the regime. Their support for the regime appears to be bolstered by their dislike of the Miami exile community. Right-wing elements in the Miami exile community, in their hatred of the Castro regime, have frequently conflated black struggles for civil rights worldwide with communism and have condemned popular black leaders, including Afro-Cubans. The community has also failed to deal directly with issues of racism toward Afro-Cubans and African Americans. Taking the Latin American exceptionalist point of view, white Cuban exiles in America have often argued that Castro "invented" racial strife in order to dupe blacks into supporting him. Statements made by blacks on the island, however, along with the concerns they have expressed in public opinion surveys, indicate that they are no dupes, but sophisticated political actors. Things are not perfect on the island for Afro-Cubans, and their situation may be getting worse, but in a comparative assessment, they are probably better off under Castro than they would be under a regime led by members of the current Cuban American community.

Cuba's Racial Future

In the spring of 1999, Disney CEO Michael Eisner stated on "Larry King Live": "One day I envision three-day cruise packages that begin in South Florida and continue on to the Bahamas and finally on to Cuba. We envision Cuba as a key part of the Disney Caribbean vacation in the future." In September 2001, by contrast, at the World Conference on Racism in Durban, South Africa, Fidel Castro commented on the U.S. absence from the conference:

No one has the right to boycott this Conference, which tries to bring some sort of relief to the overwhelming majority of mankind afflicted by unbearable suffering and enormous injustice. . . . Cuba speaks of reparations, and supports this idea as an unavoidable moral duty to the victims of racism, based on a major precedent, that is, the indemnification being paid to the descendants of the Hebrew people which in the very heart of Europe suffered the brutal and loathsome racist holocaust. However, it is not with the intent to undertake an impossible search for the direct descendants or the specific countries of the victim's actions occurred throughout centuries. The irrefutable truth is that tens of millions of Africans were captured, sold like a commodity and sent beyond the Atlantic to work in slavery while 70 million indigenous people in that hemisphere perished as a result of the European conquest and colonization.

Though these two quotations may seem to be unrelated, they present points of view that are critical in understanding the potential future of racial politics in Cuba. Eisner's statement suggests that a flood of capitalist development might bury the effects of the revolution beneath a market economy based upon tourism. The ideological commitment of the current government to managing the economy and continuing economic redistribution is all that is currently preventing the development of even greater inequality. The question seems not to be whether or not Cuba will move toward capitalism, but how. The regime's preferred model of is the Chinese model of economic transition. The Cuban regime hopes to introduce market reforms, joint ventures, and other types of capitalist development while largely maintaining control of the economy. Through government joint ventures with foreign investors, the regime hopes to manage the imposition of markets and tourism while heavily regulating small capitalist enterprises. Through the growth that these policies will foster, the government hopes to reinvigorate the redistribution that has been a major part of the experiment in socialism.

In the wake of the U.S. invasion of Iraq in the spring of 2003 and the threatening posture toward Cuba exhibited by the Bush administration, several members of Congress, including the Cuban American representatives, argued before Congress that Cuba is a rallying point for terrorists and is producing biological and chemical weapons. Such arguments, in the context of the Bush doctrine of pre-emptive war, have become a serious threat to the survival of the Castro regime. In order to challenge the representation of Cuba as a rogue nation, former President Jimmy Carter was invited to visit Cuba in the spring of 2002. The U.S. government, however, continued to take an aggressive posture toward Cuba. When the invasion of Iraq was impending and U.S. sanctions against Cuba were in the process of tightening, Castro again sought to rally the Cuban people to the socialist cause. He made a speech on the topic of education in which he admitted that Cuba had still not done enough to eliminate racial inequality. It is not clear, however, whether any specific policies will emerge from the speech. Castro has proposed few specific racial policies to cope with the racial inequality that has persisted despite the socialist policies of the regime. In his statement to the conference quoted above, Castro expressed solidarity with the idea of reparations but shied away from proposing concrete reparations policies.

The future of Cuba may not be in the hands of an aging Fidel Castro. Though he appears to have nine lives, Castro will not live forever. It is clear today that race will be a significant issue in any upcoming political transition in Cuba, just as it has been in the past. Blacks are a substantial and growing force within the Cuban population. Birth and migration patterns have tended to increase the proportion of

Afro-Cubans on the island; the Cuba of the new millennium is not the Cuba of 1959. Despite the discrimination they face, Afro-Cubans are perhaps the healthiest and best-educated black population in the world. Capitalism that benefits Cubans differentially based on race will not be tolerated for long. Its existence suggests that trouble is on the horizon.

Cuba's Lessons for Understanding Racial Politics

Cuba presents a unique opportunity to understand how racial politics operates in a society following the abolition of *de jure* segregation. When the legal barriers between whites and blacks were erased in Cuba, the nation had a unique opportunity to solve the race problem. Broad efforts at societal redistribution created unprecedented racial equality in Cuba and fused Cubans to an antiracist national project. Yet the social experiment in Cuba also reveals the limits of redistribution policies. Without policies aimed specifically at helping blacks remove structural barriers to equality, and without black organizations that could continue to pressure the regime on racial matters, it became easy for the regime to declare the race problem solved, to allow racial stagnation to creep in. The case of Cuba demonstrates that the capacity to deny the existence of racism is powerful, and that it is even more powerful following the achievement of substantive gains or reforms. The history of racial politics in Cuba also challenges the legitimacy of "color-blind" approaches to solving racial problems. Cuba demonstrates how color-blind approaches invite the argument that no problem exists, and the claim of color-blindness can itself act to halt progress.

Individuals like Ward Connerly who argue that the United States should move toward color-blindness should take note of the lessons that Cuba's history teaches. Railing against affirmative action, Connerly now argues that racial statistics themselves are the problem, and he has crafted a new California initiative called Proposition 54 that would eliminate the collection of racial data, thus making antidiscrimination policies and any exposure of racial inequality through statistics impossible. But racism is neither created nor destroyed by color-blind policies. Color-blindness can act as a justification for racist attitudes and a motivation for halting movements toward racial equality. Race is a coherent social and political construct that structures experiences, opinions, and life chances. Even in Cuba, where the state has taken bold steps to create social equality, race remains a significant predictor of life chances. While a color-blind society may be a laudable end goal, the path toward that goal must be the implementation of a mixture of redistributive policies and race-specific policies. Even when symbolic politics and redistribution effect racial progress, moreover, these gains must be backed up by vigilance and constant pressure on the state, or they are likely to disappear.

Brazil and other countries in South America and the Caribbean should also take note. It is clear that they have done less than Cuba to eliminate racial inequality. Mexico stands out as an interesting case. It is possible, using the race cycles framework, to understand the development of the Mexican mestizo identity in the wake of the Mexican Revolution as well as the resurgence of indigenous movements in the context of the fall of the PRI (Menchaca 2002; Sue 2004). We can view Mexico as a nation that developed a universal nonracial identity by suppressing the specific experiences and inequality experienced by black and indigenous peoples. Racial politics in Cuba teaches us that Latin American denials of the existence of racial inequality are not credible evidence that racism does not exist. Inclusionary discrimination is a common circumstance, and its existence in Cuba suggests that it is important to consider the differential terms of racial inclusion in other national and geopolitical systems. The primary mechanisms by which gains in the area of race relations are erased are the devolution of state power and the imposition of "free markets." In both Cuba and the United States, economic transitions have caused significant gains made in previous eras to be lost. If the case of Cuba teaches us anything, it is that a mix of state activism and grassroots activism is necessary to eliminate racial inequality.

Bibliography

Adams, H. 1999. "Revolution: The Impact of Cuba's Intervention in Angola."
Ph.D. diss., University of North Carolina, Chapel Hill.

Alberola, H. L. 1993. Response to Jorge Mas Canosa on Mario Baeza. *Miami Herald*, February 22.

Anderson, B. 1994. *Imagined Communities: Reflections on the Origin and Spread of Nationalism*. Revised edition. New York. Verso Press.

Arce, L. M. 1984. "The Racist Side of the U.S. Invasion of Grenada." *Granma*, February 26.

Arrechea, C. M. 1998. "*Minerva*: A Magazine for Women (and Men) of Color."

Baeza, M. 1993. "A Response to Accusations: Candidate for Latin America States His Views." *Miami Herald*, January 28.

Bailey, S. 2002. "Brazilian Racial Attitudes: Patterns, Determinants, Consequences." Ph.D. diss., University of California, Los Angeles.

Becker, G. 1971. *The Economics of Discrimination*. Chicago: University of Chicago Press.

Bengelsdorf, C. 1994. *The Problem of Democracy in Cuba: Between Vision and Reality*. New York: Oxford University Press.

Benitez, J. A. 1980. "U.S. Investments and Their Role in South Africa." *Granma*, March 9.

Bentacourt, J. R. 1961. "Castro and the Cuban Negro." *The Crisis* (May): 270–4.

Blue, S. A. 2002. "Remittances in Cuba." Working paper.

Blumer, H. 1985. "Industrialisation and Race Relations." In *Industrialisation and Race Relations: A Symposium*, edited by G. Hunter, 220–53. Westport, Conn.: Greenwood Press.

Bobo, L. 2000. "Race and Beliefs about Affirmative Action: Assessing the Effects of Interest Group Threat, Ideology and Racism." In *Racialized*

Politics, edited by D. Sears, J. Sidanius, and L. Bobo, 137–64. Chicago: University of Chicago Press.

Bourdieu, P., and L. Wacquant. 1999. "On the Cunning of Imperialist Reason." *Theory, Culture and Society* 16:41–58.

Brent, W. L. 1996. *Long Time Gone: A Black Panther's True-Life Story of His Hijacking and Twenty-Five Years in Cuba*. New York: Times Books.

Brock, L. 1998. "Introduction: Between Race and Empire." In *Between Race and Empire: African-Americans and Cubans Before the Revolution*, edited by L. Brock and D. C. Fuertes, 1–32. Philadelphia: Temple University Press.

Bunk, J. M. 1994. *Fidel Castro and the Quest for a Revolutionary Culture in Cuba*. University Park: Pennsylvania State University Press.

Carbado, D. 2002. "(E)Racing the Fourth Amendment." *Michigan Law Review* 35:946–1044.

Carbonell, W. 1961. "Critica cómo surgió la cultura nacional." *Havana Editorial Yaka*.

Casal, L. 1989. "Race Relations in Contemporary Cuba." In *The Cuba Reader*, 471–86. New York: Grove Press.

Castro Speech Database. <<http://lanic.utexas.edu/la/cb/cuba/castro.html>>.

Chardy, A. 1990. "Heresy or History: Teachings on Cuban Racism Still Outrage Exile Community." *Miami Herald*, December 7.

Chardy, A. 1993. " 'Invisible Exiles': Black Cubans in Miami Torn Between Cultures." *Miami Herald*, August 8.

Chaterjee, P. 1993. *The Nation and Its Fragments: Colonial and Postcolonial Histories*. Princeton, N.J.: Princeton University Press.

Chung, E. A. 2002. "Citizenship, Identity, and Racial Politics: A Comparative Study of Korean Communities in the United States and Japan." Paper prepared for delivery at the 2002 annual meeting of the American Political Science Association, Boston, August 29–September 1.

Cleaver, E. 1968. *Soul on Ice*. New York: Ramparts Books.

Cleaver, E. 1969. *Post Prison Writings and Speeches*. New York: Ramparts Books.

Cohen, R. C. 1972. *Black Crusader: A Biography of Robert Franklin Williams*. Secaucus, N.J.: Lyle Stuart.

Comite Estatal de Estadisticas Oficina Nacional del Censo. Publication.

Connor, W. 1984. *The National Question in Marxist-Leninist Theory and Strategy*. Princeton, N.J.: Princeton University Press.

Cortes, C. E. 1981. *Cuban Exiles in the United States*. New York: Ayer Company.

Covarrubia, G. A. 1999. *A Panorama of Afrocuban Culture and History: One Way to Strengthen Nationality*. <<http://www.afrocubawb.comArandia-art.htm>>.

Crockett, K., and G. Epstein. 1990. "South African Leader Cancels Miami Appearances." *Miami Herald*, June 11.

Croucher, S. L. 1997. *Imagining Miami: Ethnic Politics in a Postmodern World.* Charlottesville: University Press of Virginia.

Cruse, H. 1984. *Crisis of the Negro Intellectual.* New York: Quill.

Davis, A. 1974. *Angela Davis: An Autobiography.* New York: Random House.

Dawson, M. 2001. *Black Visions: The Roots of Contemporary African-American Political Ideologies.* Chicago: University of Chicago Press.

de la Fuente, A. 1995. "Race and Inequality in Cuba, 1899–1981." *Journal of Contemporary History* 30:131–68.

de la Fuente, A. 1998. "Race, National Discourse and Politics in Cuba." *Latin American Perspectives* 25(3): 43–70.

de la Fuente, A. 2001. *A Nation for All: Race, Inequality and Politics in Twentieth-Century Cuba.* Chapel Hill: University of North Carolina Press.

De la Garza, R. O., L. DeSipio, F. C. G. J. Garcia, and A. Falcon. 1992. *Latino Voices: Mexican, Puerto Rican, and Cuban Perspectives on American Politics.* Boulder, Colo.: Westview Press.

Degler, C. N. 1971. *Neither Black nor White.* Madison: University of Wisconsin Press.

Dodson, J. E. 1998. "Encounters in the African Atlantic World: The African Methodist Episcopal Church in Cuba." In *Between Race and Empire: African-Americans and Cubans Before the Revolution,* edited by L. Brock and D. C. Fuertes, 85–103. Philadelphia: Temple University Press.

Dominguez, J. I. 1976. "Racial and Ethnic Relations in the Cuban Armed Forces: A Non-Topic." *Armed Forces and Society* 2(2): 273–90.

Dominguez, J. I. 1978. *Cuba: Order and Revolution.* Cambridge, Mass.: Harvard University Press, Belknap Press.

Dudziak, M. L. 2000. *Cold War Civil Rights: Race and the Image of American Democracy.* Princeton, N.J.: Princeton University Press.

Dunn, M. 1997. *Black Miami in the Twentieth Century.* Miami: University of Florida Press.

Eckstein, S. E. 1995. *Back from the Future: Cuba under Castro.* Princeton, N.J.: Princeton University Press.

Elliot, J. M., and M. M. Dymally. 1986. *Fidel Castro: Nothing Can Stop the Course of History.* New York: Pathfinder Press.

Ellis, K. 1998. "Nicolas Guillen and Langston Hughes: Convergences and Divergences." In *Between Race and Empire: African-Americans and Cubans Before the Revolution,* edited by L. Brock and D. C. Fuertes, 129–67. Philadelphia: Temple University Press.

Fanon, F. 1991. *The Wretched of the Earth.* New York: Grove Press.

Fernandez, N. 1996. "Race, Romance, and Revolution: The Cultural Politics of Interracial Encounters in Cuba." Ph.D. diss., University of California, Berkeley.

Fernández, R. T. 1990. *El Negro en Cuba, 1902–1958: Apuntes para la historia de la lucha contra discriminación racial.* Havana: Editorial de Ciencias Sociales.

Ferrer, A. 1999. *Insurgent Cuba: Race, Nation, and Revolution, 1869–1898*. Chapel Hill: University of North Carolina Press.

Fields, B. J. 1982. "Ideology and Race in American History." In *Region, Race, and Reconstruction: Essays in Honor of C. Vann Woodward*, edited by J. M. Kousser and J. M. McPherson, 143–77. New York: Oxford University Press.

Foner, P. S., ed. 1995. *The Black Panthers Speak*. New York: Da Capo Press.

Franco, L. J. 1993. "Mariana and Maceo." In *Afrocuba: An Anthology of Cuban Writing on Race, Politics and Culture*, edited by P. Sarduy and J. Stubbs, 47–54. New York: Ocean Press.

Freyre, G. 1951. *Brazil: An Interpretation*. New York: Alfred Knopf.

Fuertes, D. C. 1998. "Epilogue." In *Between Race and Empire: African-Americans and Cubans Before the Revolution*, edited by L. Brock and D. C. Fuertes, 281–85. Philadelphia: Temple University Press.

Garcia, C. G. 1998. "Cuban Social Poetry and the Struggle against Two Racisms." In *Between Race and Empire: African-Americans and Cubans Before the Revolution*, edited by L. Brock and D. C. Fuertes, 205–48. Philadelphia: Temple University Press.

Garcia, M. C. 1996. *Havana USA: Cuban Exiles and Cuban Americans in South Florida, 1959–1994*. Berkeley and Los Angeles: University of California Press.

Gilroy, P. 1987. *"There Ain't No Black in the Union Jack": The Cultural Politics of Race and Nation*. Chicago: University of Chicago Press.

Gilroy, P. 1994. *The Black Atlantic: Modernity and Double Consciousness*. Cambridge, Mass.: Harvard University Press.

Glasco, L. 1998. "Race in Three Cuban Cities: Havana, Santa Clara, and Santiago de Cuba; Impressions and Observations." *América Negra* 15:67–71.

Gleijeses, P. 2002. *Conflicting Missions: Havana, Washington, and Africa, 1959–1976*. Chapel Hill: University of North Carolina Press.

Goldberg, D. T. 1993. *Racist Culture: Philosophy and the Politics of Meaning*. New York: Blackwell Publishers.

Goldberg, D. T. 2002. *The Racial State*. Malden, Mass.: Blackwell Publishers.

Goldfarb, C. 1990a. "Mandela Backers, Critics Brace for Momentous Visit." *Miami Herald*, June 28.

Goldfarb, C. 1990b. "Prejudice Felt by Latin Blacks." *Miami Herald*, June 28.

Gonzalez-Pando, M. 1998. *The Cuban Americans*. New York: Greenwood Publishing.

Gordon, E. 1998. *Disparate Diaspora: Identity and Politics in an African Nicaraguan Community*. Austin: University of Texas Press.

Gosse, Van. 1998. "The African American Press Greets the Cuban Revolution." In *Between Race and Empire: African-Americans and Cubans Before the Revolution*, edited by L. Brock and D. C. Fuertes, 33–48. Philadelphia: Temple University Press.

Greenberg, S. B. 1980. *Race and State in Capitalist Development*. New Haven, Conn.: Yale University Press.

Guillen, N. 1962. "Racism and Revolution." *Granma*, April 10.

Guinier, L., and G. Torres. 2002. *The Miner's Canary: Enlisting Race, Resisting Power, Transforming Democracy*. Cambridge, Mass.: Harvard University Press.

Gupta, A. 1995. "Blurred Boundaries: The Discourse of Corruption, the Culture of Politics and the Imagined State." *American Ethnologist*, 22(2): 375–402.

Hale, C. R. 1994. *Resistance and Contradiction: Miskitu Indians and the Nicaraguan State, 1894–1987*. Stanford, Calif.: Stanford University Press.

Haley, A. 1991. *The Autobiography of Malcolm X*. New York: Ballantine Books.

Hall, S. 1986. "Gramsci's Relevance for the Study of Race and Ethnicity." *Journal of Communication Inquiry* 10(2): 5–27.

Hanchard, M. G. 1994. *Orpheus and Power: The Movimiento Negro of Rio de Janeiro and São Paulo Brazil, 1945–1988*. Princeton, N.J.: Princeton University Press.

Hanchard, M. G. 1995. "Black Cinderella? Race and Public Sphere in Brazil." In *The Black Public Sphere: A Public Culture Book*, 169–89. Chicago: University of Chicago Press.

Hancock, D. 1990. "Author: Exiles' Plans Out of Touch with Cuba's Blacks." *Miami Herald*, February 22.

Harris, M. 1974. *Patterns of Race in the Americas*. New York: Norton Library

Haskins, J. 1997. *Power to the People: The Rise and Fall of the Black Panther Party*. New York: Simon and Schuster.

Heberer, T. 1989. *China and Its National Minorities: Autonomy and Assimilation?* New York: East Gate Books.

Helg, A. 1990. "Race in Argentina and Cuba, 1880–1930: Theory, Policy and Popular Reaction." In *The Idea of Race in Latin America, 1870–1940*, 37–70. Austin: University of Texas Press.

Helg, A. 1995. *Our Rightful Share: The Afro-Cuban Struggle for Equality, 1886–1912*. Chapel Hill: University of North Carolina Press.

Hellwig, D. J. 1998. "The African-American Press and United States Involvement in Cuba, 1902–1912." In *Between Race and Empire: African-Americans and Cubans Before the Revolution*, edited by L. Brock and D. C. Fuertes. Philadelphia: Temple University Press.

Hernández, D. 1998. "Raza y prejuicio racial en Santa Clara: Un reporte de investigación." *América Negra* 15:75–86.

Higginbotham, E. B. 1992. "African American Women's History and the Metalanguage of Race." *Signs* (Winter).

Holt, T. C. 2000. *The Problem of Race in the Twenty-First Century*. Cambridge, Mass.: Harvard University Press.

Horowitz, D. 2001. *The Deadly Ethnic Riot*. Berkeley and Los Angeles: University of California Press.

Hoston, G. A. 1994. *The State, Identity, and the National Question in China and Japan*. Princeton, N.J.: Princeton University Press.

Hunt, D. M. 1997. *Screening the Los Angeles 'Riots': Race, Seeing, and Resistance*. New York: Cambridge University Press.

Hunter, G. 1985. "Conclusion: Some Historical and Political Factors." In *Industrialisation and Race Relations: A Symposium*, edited by G. Hunter. Westport, Conn.: Greenwood Press.

Hutchinson, E. O. 1995. *Blacks and Reds: Race and Class in Conflict, 1919–1990*. East Lansing: Michigan State University Press.

Ibarra, J. 1998. *Prologue to Revolution: Cuba, 1898–1958*. Boulder, Colo.: Lynne Reiner Publishers.

James, C. L. R. 1984. *At the Rendezvous of Victory*. London: Allison and Busby.

Jimenez, R. D. 1993. "The 19th Century Black Fear." In *Afrocuba: An Anthology of Cuban Writing on Race, Politics and Culture*, edited by P. P. Sarduy and J. Stubbs, 37–46. New York: Ocean Press.

Kelley, R. D. G. 1994. *Race Rebels: Culture, Politics, and the Black Working Class*. New York: Free Press.

Klinkner, P. A., and R. M. Smith. 1999. *The Unsteady March: The Rise and Decline of Racial Equality in America*. Chicago: University of Chicago Press.

Kronus, S., and M. Solaun. 1973. *Discrimination without Violence*. New York: Wiley-Interscience Publishing.

Kryder, D. 2000. *Divided Arsenal: Race and the American State During World War II*. New York: Cambridge University Press.

Kutzinski, V. 1993. *Sugar's Secrets: Race and the Erotics of Cuban Nationalism*. Charlottesville: University of Virginia Press.

Layton, A. S. 1998. *International Politics and Civil Rights Policies in the United States, 1941–1961*. New York: Cambridge University Press.

Lee, T. 2002. *Mobilizing Public Opinion: Black Insurgency and Racial Attitudes in the Civil Rights Era*. Chicago: University of Chicago Press.

Lewis, M. A. 1992. *Ethnicity and Identity in Contemporary Afro-Venezuelan Literature: A Culturalist Approach*. Columbia: University of Missouri Press.

Loveman, M. 1999. "Comment: Is 'Race' Essential?" *American Sociological Review* 64(6): 891–8.

Marquis, C. 1993. "Baeza Bid Is Scrapped; Career Envoy Is Tapped." *Miami Herald*, March 3.

Marx, A. W. 1998. *Making Race and Nation: A Comparison of the United States, South Africa and Brazil*. New York: Cambridge University Press.

McAdam, D. 1999. *Political Process and the Development of Black Insurgency, 1930–1970*. Second edition. Chicago: University of Chicago Press.

McAdam, D., S. Tarrow, and C. Tilly. 2001. *Dynamics of Contention*. New York: Cambridge University Press.

McGarrity, G. 1992. "Race Culture and Social Change in Contemporary Cuba." In *Cuba in Transition*, edited by S. Halebsky and J. Kirk. New York: Westview Press.

McGarrity, G., and O. Cardenas. 1995. "Cuba." In *No Longer Invisible: Afro-Latin Americans Today*, edited by Minority Rights Group. London: Minority Rights Publishing.

Menchaca, M. 2002. *Recovering History, Constructing Race: The Indian, Black, and White Roots of Mexican Americans*. Austin: University of Texas Press.

Michaelowski, R. 1993. "Cuba." In *World Factbook of Criminal Justice Systems*, prepared by the Bureau of Justice Statistics, U.S. Department of Justice. <<http://www.ojp.usdoj.gov/bjs/pub/ascii/wfbcjcub.txt>>.

Mills, C. W. 1997. *The Racial Contract*. Ithaca, N.Y.: Cornell University Press.

Mintz, S. M., and R. Price. 1992. *The Birth of African-American Culture: An Anthropological Perspective*. Boston: Beacon Press.

Montenegro, O. L. 1993. "Despite Cuba's History of Tolerance Castro Is a Calculating Racist – Here's Why." *Miami Herald*, July 30.

Moore, C. 1991. *Castro, The Blacks and Africa*. Third edition. Los Angeles: Center for Afro-American Studies.

Moore, C. 1995. "Afro-Cubans and the Communist Revolution." In *African Presence in the Americas*, edited by C. Moore, T. R. Sanders, and S. Moore. Trenton, N.J.: African World Press.

Moore, R. D. 1997. *Nationalizing Blackness: Afrocubanismo and Artistic Revolution in Havana, 1920–1940*. Pitt Latin American Series. Pittsburgh: University of Pittsburgh Press.

Morris, A. 1986. *The Origins of the Civil Rights Movement: Black Communities Organizing for Change*. New York: Free Press.

Moses, W. J. 1978. *The Golden Age of Black Nationalism, 1850–1925*. New York: Oxford University Press.

Newton, H. P. n.d. Interview at the Havana Libre Hotel. Newton Collection, Stanford University.

Newton, H. P. 1995. *Revolutionary Suicide*. New York: Writers and Readers.

Nobles, M. 2000. *Shades of Citizenship: Race and the Census in Modern Politics*. Stanford: Stanford University Press.

North, J. 1963. "Negro and White in Cuba." *Political Affairs* (July).

Omi, M., and H. Winant. 1994. *Racial Formation in the United States from the 1960s to the 1990s*. Second edition. New York: Routledge.

Parker, C. 2005. *Fighting for Democracy: Race, Service to the State and Insurgency During Jim Crow*. Unpublished manuscript.

Patterson, T. G. 1994. *Contesting Castro: The United States and the Triumph of the Cuban Revolution*. New York: Oxford University Press.

Pearson, H. 1994. *Shadow of the Panther*. Menlo Park, Calif.: Addison and Wesley.

Peña, Y., Sidanius, J., and Sawyer, M. Forthcoming. "'Racial Democracy' in the Americas: A Latin and North American Comparison." *Journal of Cross Cultural Psychology*.

Peralta, L. S. 1998. "Mujer, instruccion, ocupacion y color de la piel: Estructura y relaciones raciales en un barrio popular de La Habana." *América Negra* 15:119–32.

Pérez, L. A. 1999. *On Becoming Cuban: Identity, Nationality and Culture.* Chapel Hill: University of North Carolina Press.

Perez-Stable, M. 1993. *The Cuban Revolution: Origins, Course and Legacy.* New York: Oxford University Press.

Perla, H. Forthcoming. "The Heirs of Sandino: Undermining Reagan's Coercive Policy Against Nicaragua." *Latin American Perspectives.*

Pinderhughes, D. 1987. *Race and Ethnicity in Chicago Politics: A Reexamination of Pluralist Theory.* Urbana: University of Illinois Press.

Planas, J. R. 1993. "The Impact of Soviet Reforms on Cuban Socialism." In *Conflict and Change in Cuba,* edited by E. A. Baloyra and J. A. Morris. Albuquerque: University of New Mexico Press.

Plummer, B. G. 1996. *Rising Wind: Black Americans and U.S. Foreign Policy, 1935–1960.* Chapel Hill: University of North Carolina Press.

Powell, M. 1999. "White Wash: Suddenly, Gordon Baum, Small-Time Race Baiter, Is Big Time News; Let's Hear Him Explain How Incredibly Reasonable He Is." *Washington Post,* January 17.

Ramos, J. A. A. 1998. "Estereotipicos y prejuicios raciales en tres barrios habaneros." *América Negra* 15:89–115.

Rangel, C. 1993. "Don't Let Right-Wing, Racist Pressure Tactics Block Baeza." *Miami Herald,* January 17.

Reitlan, R. 1999. *The Rise and Decline of an Alliance: Cuba and African American Leaders in the 1960s.* East Lansing: Michigan State University.

Robaina, T. F. 1990. *El Negro en Cuba, 1902–1958.* Havana: Editorial de Ciencias Sociales.

Robaina, T. F. 1993. "The 20th Century Black Question." In *Afrocuba: An Anthology of Cuban Writing on Race, Politics and Culture,* edited by P. Sarduy and J. Stubbs. New York: Ocean Press.

Robaina, T. F. 1998. "Marcus Garvey in Cuba: Urrutia, Cubans, and Black Nationalism." In *Between Race and Empire: African-Americans and Cubans Before the Revolution,* edited by L. Brock and D. C. Fuertes, 120–8. Philadelphia: Temple University Press.

Robinson, C. J. 1991. *Black Marxism: The Making of the Black Radical Tradition.* Atlantic Highlands: Zed Books.

Rodney, W. 1995. "Black Power, a Basic Understanding." In *I Am Because We Are: Readings in Black Philisophy,* edited by F. L. Hord and J. S. Lee. Amherst: University of Massachusetts Press.

Rout, L., Jr. 1976. *The African Experience in Spanish America.* New York: Cambridge University Press.

Route, K. 1991. *Eldridge Cleaver.* Boston: Twayne Publishers.

Said, E. 1979. *Orientalism.* New York: Vintage Books.

Sarduy, P. P., and J. Stubbs. 1993. "Introduction: The Rite of Social Communion." In *Afrocuba: An Anthology of Cuban Writing on Race, Politics and Culture*, edited by P. Sarduy and J. Stubbs, 3–26. New York: Ocean Press.

Sawyer, M. 2003. "What We Can Learn from Cuba: Comparative Perspectives on the African American Experience." *Souls* 2(5): 63–80.

Sawyer, M., Y. Peña, and J. Sidanius. 2004. "Cuban Exceptionalism: Group Based Hierarchy and the Dynamics of Patriotism in Puerto Rico, the Dominican Republic and Cuba." *The Dubois Review* 1(1):93–114.

Scott, J. C. 1990. *Domination and the Arts of Resistance: Hidden Transcripts.* New Haven, Conn.: Yale University Press.

Secade, M. C. C. 1996. "Relaciones raciales, proceso de ajuste y political social." *Temas* 7(July–September): 58–65.

Segal, R. 1995. *The Black Diaspora.* New York: Giroux Press.

Serviat, P. 1985. "El problema negro en Cuba y su solucion definitiva." *Editoria Política Havana.* As "Solutions to the Black Problem," appears in *Afrocuba: An Anthology of Cuban Writing on Race, Politics, and Culture*, edited by P. P. Sarduy and J. Stubbs, 77–90.

Sewell, W. 1996. "Historical Events as Transformations of Structures: Inventing Revolution at the Bastille." *Theory and Society* 25:841–81.

Shakur, A. 1987. *Assata.* Westport, Conn.: Lawrence Holland Company.

Sidanius, J., S. Feshbach, S. Levin, and F. Pratto. 1997. "The Interface Between Ethnic and National Attachment: Ethnic Pluralism or Ethnic Dominance?" *Public Opinion Quarterly* 61:103–33.

Sidanius, J., Y. Peña, and M. Sawyer. 2001. "Inclusionary Discrimination: Pigmentocracy and Patriotism in the Dominican Republic." *Journal of Political Psychology* 22(4): 827–51.

Skidmore, T. 1993. *Black into White: Race and Nationality in Brazilian Thought.* Durham, N.C.: Duke University Press.

Smith, L. M., and A. Padula. 1996. *Sex and Revolution: Women in Socialist Cuba.* New York: Oxford University Press.

Stein, J. 1986. *The World of Marcus Garvey.* Baton Rouge: Louisiana State University Press.

Stepan, N. L. 1991. *The Hour of Eugenics: Race, Gender, and Nation in Latin America.* Ithaca, N.Y.: Cornell University Press.

Stoler, A. L. 1997. "Racial Histories and Their Regimes of Truth." *Political Power and Social Theory* 11:183–206.

Sue, C. 2004. "Race and National Ideology in Mexico: An Ethnographic Study of *Mestizaje*, Color and Blackness in Veracruz." Unpublished manuscript.

Tanfani, J., and T. Pugh. 1996a. "Blacklash: Black Response to Walkout on Andrew Young." *Miami Herald*, March 7.

Tanfani, J., and T. Pugh. 1996b. "An Apology from Metro." *Miami Herald*, March 8.

Telles, E. 2004. *Race in Another America: Race Mixture, Exclusion and the State in Brazil.* Princeton, N.J.: Princeton University Press.

Thomas, H. 1998. *Cuba, or, the Pursuit of Freedom*. New York: Da Capo Press.

Tilly, C. 1999. *Durable Inequality*. Berkeley and Los Angeles: University of California Press.

Tyson, T. B. 1999. *Radio Free Dixie: Robert F. Williams and the Roots of Black Power*. Chapel Hill: University of North Carolina Press.

Wade, P. 1997. *Race and Ethnicity in Latin America*. London: Pluto Press.

West, C. 1988. "Marxist Theory and the Specificity of Afro-American Oppression." In *Marxism and the Interpretation of Culture*, edited by C. Nelson and L. Grossberg, 17–29. Urbana: University of Illinois Press.

Whitfield, M., and C. Marquis. 1993. "Lawyer's Bid for Latin Job in Trouble." *Mimai Herald*, January 20.

Wright, W. 1990. *Cafe Con Leche*. Austin: University of Texas Press.

Young, I. M. 1990. *Justice and the Politics of Difference*. Princeton, N.J.: Princeton University Press.

Zaller, J. R. 1993. *The Nature and Origins of Mass Opinion*. Cambridge: Cambridge University Press.

Zeitlin, M. 1967. *Revolutionary Politics and the Cuban Working Class*. Princeton, N.J.: Princeton University Press.

Index

Made in the USA
San Bernardino, CA
04 October 2016